THE
WESTERN ALLIANCE
AFTER INF

THE
WESTERN ALLIANCE
AFTER INF

Redefining U.S. Policy
Toward Europe and the Soviet Union

Michael R. Lucas

Lynne Rienner Publishers • Boulder & London

Published in the United States of America in 1990 by
Lynne Rienner Publishers, Inc.
1800 30th Street, Boulder, Colorado 80301

and in the United Kingdom by
Lynne Rienner Publishers, Inc.
3 Henrietta Street, Covent Garden, London WC2E 8LU

Library of Congress Cataloging-in-Publication Data
Lucas, Michael R.
  The Western Alliance after INF : redefining U.S. policy
  toward Europe and the Soviet Union / by Michael R. Lucas.
  Includes bibliographical references.
  ISBN 1–55587–159–3 (alk. paper)
  1. United States—Military policy. 2. United States—Military
relations—Europe. 3. Europe—Military relations—United States.
4. North Atlantic Treaty Organization. I. Title.
UA23.L83 1990
355'.031'091821—dc20   89-38359
                                                           CIP

British Cataloguing in Publication Data
A Cataloguing in Publication record for this book
is available from the British Library.

Printed and bound in the United States of America

The paper used in this publication meets the requirements of
the American National Standard for Permanence of Paper for
Printed Library Materials Z39.48–1984.

Contents

Acknowledgments

During the writing of this book it was of considerable help to use the facilities of a number of research institutes in West Germany. I am grateful for the assistance of the Berghof Stiftung für Konfliktforschung, the Otto Suhr Institute of the Free University in West Berlin, and the Peace Research Institute Frankfurt. My deepest thanks go to the World Policy Institute in New York. Many of the ideas for this book were developed in the course of my work as an institute fellow and in conversations with Sherle Schwenninger, Archibald Gilles, and other members of the staff. I would also like to express my gratitude to the following individuals for critical comments on sections of the manuscript or other types of support: Ulrich Albrecht, Lothar Brock, Richard Kaplan, Adrienne Edgar, Helmut Köster, Ekkehart Krippendorff, Lynne Rienner, Hildegard von Meier, Saul Mendlovitz, Norbert Ropers, Kathy Falk, Rubin Falk, Bruno Schoch, Peter Schlotter, Manfred Stennis, Brigitte Thinz, Jutta Tiedtke, and Heinrich Vogel. I also want to express special thanks to my mother and my brother Peter. I alone am responsible for any shortcomings in this book.

Michael R. Lucas

Introduction

Throughout the postwar era, the arms race on the European continent has been justified in East and West as the necessary and indispensable guarantee of security. This dismal fact of life of the East-West conflict has been put into question by the Intermediate-Range Nuclear Forces (INF) Treaty, the waning Soviet military threat, the reform movements throughout the communist world, and the dramatic achievements of European détente. The world is experiencing a paradox: East-West forms of cooperation that only a few years ago would have been considered a breach and weakening of military security are now finding acceptance as a higher form of security. The United States and the Soviet Union compete in disarmament, carry out on-site monitoring of each other's nuclear tests, and even inspect each other's weapons factories and military bases. Such inspections of these secret, inner sanctums of postwar security are now mutually recognized as a form of confidence building, a way to ease military and political tensions, and a contribution to greater East-West and global security.

Examples of this historic reversal in security thinking have dramatically increased during the late 1980s and range from East-West cooperation in settling regional conflicts, for example in Angola and Namibia, to exports of formerly restricted advanced technology to Eastern countries. Certainly, such cooperation remains highly controversial. Critics, operating with the status quo assumptions that have governed international relations since the end of World War II, correctly argue that it violates the postwar rules of the game on which Western defense is based. Yet, to supporters, the range of potential benefits provides the justification for the new East-West interaction. The West German–Soviet nuclear partnership is a case in point. The Federal Republic is contracted to overhaul the safety systems of Soviet nuclear power stations, which will allow both countries to acquire detailed knowledge of each other's nuclear power facilities. A short time ago this cooperation would have been hard to imagine, given the military importance and sensitivity of nuclear facilities. Today, it is being hailed as the opening of a new dimension of East-West security that straddles the areas of military security, nuclear safety, energy production, and environmental protection.

How has this new approach to security evolved to challenge the postwar verities of the East-West conflict? What has been the role of Western and Eastern Europe and the Soviet Union in intensifying East-West interaction and breaking the bipolar mold of the postwar era? What are the political and economic implications of this process for East-West and West-West relations in the coming years?

This book is an attempt to answer these questions. I argue that the model, or paradigm, of East-West security is shifting and that the Western Alliance has reached a historical watershed in which the military, political, and economic foundations of the postwar policy consensus are being challenged by powerful political and economic forces. I suggest that European détente became in the 1980s a driving force and the most important arena of the structural reformation of East-West and U.S.-Soviet relations.

Confronted by a breathtaking pace of change during the second half of the 1980s, the study of international relations and policy research are being challenged to catch up conceptually with the political developments that have rendered intellectually inadequate the postwar notions of security. With the decline of U.S. and Soviet military and economic power, two diametrically opposed models of security are now competing against each other in both East and West. The postwar model is linked to retaining the status quo notions of security based on traditional arms competition; this viewpoint is being countered by a post-containment model that proponents outspokenly claim offers a higher and more effective form of security. The theoretical framework of this book is based on these two models of security and is designed to explain their role in international relations during the 1980s.

Throughout the book, the term *paradigm* will refer to (a) the economic, political, and military-technological premises of security policy and (b) the relationship of a security policy to its overall international political-economic environment. A key criterion for evaluating (b) is that of consistency. In order to function and maintain its legitimacy, a particular military doctrine or strategy must be consistent with the economic and political realities of its domestic and international environment. Only then can it be sustained.

During the postwar era, security policy has been linked to the following:

1. The East-West political-military conflict, characterized by an increasing accumulation of nuclear and conventional weapons and technological-military competition
2. The economic-political division of East and West, in which economic and other forms of cooperation between the two systems have been relatively closed out
3. The unilateral formulation of security policymaking, in which

security has been defined predominantly in military terms and pursued by both sides with the help of complex systems of secrecy

4. An adversarial political culture based on the systematic building out and global extension of Western "anticommunism" and Eastern "anti-imperialism"

These four characteristics form the main components of what will be referred to throughout this book as the *postwar model of security*. I will argue that postwar security policy based on the East-West adversarial framework is no longer consistent with the changing political, economic, and military realities of East-West relations. The advanced erosion of postwar status quo structures has made "business as usual" in defense policy increasingly untenable. As a result, major policy adjustment has become unavoidable.

The *post-containment model of security* can be understood as a gradually emerging structure of *common security*[1] in which both East and West

1. Take account of each other's security needs in formulating their security policy
2. Undertake significant reductions in military spending as a result of economic pressures
3. Compete in the international political arena in pursuing active policies of confidence building, arms control, and disarmament
4. Implement demilitarizing forms of cooperation and create new forms of East-West interdependence that delegitimize and tend to displace postwar iron curtains—a process through which East and West are able to promote their respective and mutual economic, political, and ecological welfare and create a new environment for North-South relations

The interplay of the postwar and post-containment models of security will be explored in the three parts of this book. Part 1 examines the Western political-military policy debate preceding and immediately following the INF Treaty on eliminating intermediate-range missiles. Chapter 1 describes how the U.S. administration focused on NATO interests that viewed the accord as a weakening of Western defenses, whereas pro-détente and pro–arms control forces, most notably in Europe, viewed the treaty as a confirmation of the waning of the Soviet military threat and the beginning of a second wave of détente. A result of this polarization, I suggest, is that the treaty could have uncertain results because it could lead to further steps in the direction of demilitarization and deepened détente or to a new arms race. Chapters 2 and 3 discuss the danger of a high-tech U.S. and West European arms buildup and several military programs pushing the Western Alliance in this direction. Chapter 4 deals with the disparity between U.S. calls for larger West

European defense outlays ("burden sharing") and the economic, demographic, and political constraints that make clear why West European governments did not meet U.S. demands nor are likely to do so in the future. In fact, U.S. efforts here demonstrate just how out of touch with West European realities the United States had become. Chapter 5, also focusing on Western Europe, examines three models of NATO's future and shows how disarmament, common security, and extended détente appear to offer the more promising road for resolving NATO's increasing policy dilemmas.

Part 2 deals with economic and technological development trends and how they reflect the uneven shift from the postwar to the post-containment model of security. This process is examined in the context of the competition of these two models as policy alternatives within the Western economies. Chapter 6 analyzes the attempt during the Reagan era to use over $2 trillion in military spending to reinforce the postwar model of security, spur economic growth, and achieve technological renewal. Despite this effort, the U.S. economy further weakened during the 1980s, a deterioration that reflects the decline of military spending as an instrument of macroeconomic management. Chapter 7 takes up the debate on the direction of technological development and the interplay between the military and civilian dimensions of West European research and development (R&D) programs. The technological watershed that has emerged pits a potential high-tech arms race fueled by military R&D against competing and overlapping nonmilitary R&D programs designed to restructure and technologically upgrade West European economies. Chapter 8 examines how the competition between the postwar and post-containment models of security as policy alternatives is also reflected in the intensifying West-West debate on security restrictions on high-technology exports to the East. I argue that as a result of its export control practices, the United States now faces a serious economic-security dilemma. On the one hand, it must expand its high-tech exports to overcome its trade deficit and restore international confidence in the U.S. economy. On the other hand, export restrictions foreclose new outlets for U.S. high-value products even as U.S. partners are expanding their commerce with the East. I suggest that by isolating U.S. exporters from emerging East-West markets and by alienating U.S. trading partners in Europe and Asia, U.S. restrictions have become a major bottleneck in U.S. policy adjustment.

Part 3 focuses on the Soviet Union, European economic-political trends, and the emerging East-West forms of détente that I argue form the nonmilitary cutting edge of an emerging new European security order. In this shifting constellation of forces, the United States has found itself playing a secondary, recalcitrant role—resisting change yet repeatedly springing into action to try to catch up with the more confidently advancing West and East European powers and the Soviet Union in their push for policy adjustment. Chapter 9 attempts to show how the decline of the postwar order is reflected in the diminishing Soviet military threat and in Soviet reforms linked to perestroika, glasnost, and democratization. I also argue that the long-term aims of the Soviet reform leadership approximate the central assumptions of the post-containment model of security based on disarmament, common security, and deepened détente. Chapter 10 discusses how the reform trends in Eastern Europe and East-West détente illustrate the political-economic dimension of the transition to a post-containment order. The example of Poland is used to show that the cooperative involvement of East and West, including the United States, has been essential in bringing about the historic Polish reforms of 1989. The chapter then shows how European economic détente appears to be creating long-term and irreversible forms of nonmilitary East-West interaction. The 1988 treaty between the European Community (EC) and the Council for Mutual Economic Assistance (COMECON) to normalize economic relations, the rapidly evolving West German economic-political partnership with the Soviet Union, Franco-Soviet economic and technological collaboration, and Soviet-Western joint ventures provide empirical examples of this trend. Chapter 11 examines the Conference on Security and Cooperation in Europe (CSCE) and its role as a crucible of the post-containment security order and new forms of East-West interaction based on the peaceful resolution of conflicts and non-military forms of security. The concluding chapter offers several recommendations for adjusting U.S. policy to changing international realities.

The concept of "security paradigm" was chosen as the overarching conceptual framework of this analysis because it is broad enough to circumscribe and provide a unitary framework to understand the disparate sets of phenomena linked to the currently changing conditions of security policymaking.[2] This framework expands the accepted notion of common security and enables the analyst to use it as a more powerful instrument to examine the consistency and sustainability of specific security-related policies. Underpinning this usage is the assumption that the current policy watershed in East and West cannot be understood without going beyond the limits characteristic of more specialized approaches to the study of security and foreign policy. Because the foundations of defense policy are historically shifting, an investigation of security must map that broader, still largely unfamiliar terrain of international relations on which economic, political, ecological, technological, and military factors are now interacting in novel ways and creating a qualitatively changed pattern of givens to challenge the policymaker and the student of international relations. This book is intended as a contribution to this emerging field of scholarly and policy research.

Notes

1. An important component of the conceptual framework of this book is the notion of *common security*, a still-maturing theory first developed

by the Palme Commission during the early 1980s. Its basic principles are:

• Unlike the doctrine of nuclear deterrence, common security requires taking the potential adversary's security needs into consideration in formulating one's own security policy. Each side takes seriously the threat perceptions of the other side and acknowledges the legitimacy of its demand for security guarantees.

• In a security and international political environment based on unilateral security policymaking, there is a strong propensity to worst-case thinking: Each side tends to suppose that of all possible assumptions concerning the potential opponent's future behavior, the most threatening should be the basis of one's own action. Common security, in contrast, is based on developing increased mutual transparency and confidence in order to overcome worst-case thinking and the arms-racing consequences that follow from it.

• In the postwar East-West conflict, it has been customary to think of security according to the principle that the opponent's security is inversely proportional to one's own—that is, an increase of security on one side is a reduction for the other. Security tends to be equated less with stability, war prevention, and reducing imbalances than with strength, superiority, or matching the opponent's military capabilities. In this framework, confidence-building measures, arms control, and disarmament play at best a secondary role in order to mitigate the danger of the arms race getting out of control of both protagonists. In a common security environment, in contrast, these cooperative security factors play a primary role. One side increases its own security by making the potential opponent feel more secure; the other side simultaneously does the same. In this environment, both sides tend to become "security partners." See in this context Margaret Johannsen, "Beyond Deterrence Through Common Security," (Paper presented at the International Conference "Rethinking European Security," Forum per i Problemi della Pasce e della Guerra, September 23–24, 1988); The Independent Commission on Security and Disarmament Issues, *Common Security: A Blueprint for Survival* (London: Pan Books, 1982).

2. Throughout this book, the notions of the postwar and the post-containment security paradigms will be applied in three different ways: (1) to specify two antagonistic lines of development in international relations; (2) to distinguish roughly between two historical periods—from the end of World War II approximately to the mid-1980s and from the mid-1980s on; and (3) to refer to the sets of normative principles and values that form the guiding frameworks for the two paradigms.

PART 1

The Political and Military Context of the INF Treaty

CHAPTER 1

Divergent U.S.-European Responses to the INF Treaty

The INF Treaty eliminated all U.S. and Soviet intermediate-range and shorter-range land-based nuclear and conventional missiles from Europe.[1] Although the December 1987 Reagan-Gorbachev summit held to sign the treaty provoked speculation about the beginning of a new détente between the United States and the Soviet Union, the thrust of U.S. policy was to focus on the anxieties the agreement was said to engender in West European allies. In the months before the treaty's signing, much was made of West German "hesitations," British "worries," and French "alarm."[2] The accord, it was said, threatened to create a momentum for denuclearization that would eventually leave Western Europe vulnerable to the Soviet Union's superior conventional strength.

Moreover, in this U.S. view, West European allies could not help but see the INF agreement as a downgrading of U.S. commitment to defend Western Europe. Their concern was that withdrawal of U.S. missiles might lead not only to subsequent missile reductions but also to a possible pullout of the 350,000 U.S. troops based in Europe.[3] Given U.S. financial and budgetary problems, it would be just a matter of time before the United States would bring its troops home. Diminished U.S. presence would in turn leave Western Europe more susceptible to Gorbachev's adept diplomacy. Thus, as more than one NATO analyst argued, in order to prevent the INF Treaty from setting Western Europe adrift, the United States needed to take measures, including the deployment of new weapons systems, to reassure the West Europeans of its security commitment—a position the Reagan administration adopted.[4]

Even after the NATO defense ministers gave their blessing to the treaty at their November 2 meeting in Monterey, California, and even after the alliance summit and many West European statements supporting the treaty's ratification, these U.S. readings of Western Europe's mood persisted. In highlighting the doubts and hesitations that the accord precipitated, the United States presented a highly misleading picture of the treaty's reception and the political environment in Western Europe. The anxieties were greatly exaggerated and misunderstood, and Western Europe was of more than one mind on the treaty and its security future. Some government officials in Britain and West Germany expressed concern about the INF agreement, but opinion polls showed the public's response to the accord to be overwhelmingly positive in both countries.[5] And although some NATO defense ministers worried about the impact of the removal of the cruise and Pershing II missiles on NATO's strategy of flexible response and about the prospect of further denuclearization, other government officials confidently began to move ahead with new political and economic agreements with Moscow and declare a second phase of East-West détente that could at last end forty years of confrontation.

Western Europe's Road to the INF Treaty and its Aftermath

When the basic principles of the INF Treaty were first announced in October 1987, the most outspoken opposition came not from the mainstream Atlanticists but from a few distinct groups: the conservative steel-helmet wing of West Germany's Christian Democratic Union/Christian Socialist Union (CDU-CSU), a faction known for hawkish and often cold war views; defense ministers; and officials close to military-industrial interests in France, West Germany, and Britain. These groupings in Britain and France were concerned that the agreement would create pressure for arms control that might impinge on their countries' own nuclear arsenals and modernization plans.[6]

The treaty's double-zero solution, to eliminate all intermediate and shorter range nuclear missiles, was initially proposed by Washington with little expectation that it would meet with Moscow's approval. A widespread view is that the proposal was made for tactical reasons because the demand for a double-zero solution was not negotiable with the Soviets at the time it was proposed.[7] The expectation was that it would embarrass Moscow and reinforce the image of the Soviet Union as basically uninterested in arms control except to achieve military advantage. This tactic on the part of the NATO leadership and Western governments reflected a serious misreading of Western public opinion, which had shifted to impatience for more resolute action to achieve arms reduction. When Gorbachev agreed to conclude a separate INF agreement in February 1987 and subsequently welcomed the double-zero solution, it threw NATO governments into disarray and at the same time generated even greater political pressure to move forward on the proposals without unnecessary delay. The ambiguity of the reactions of West European governments to the Soviet moves also led to a decline in the credibility of their commitment to arms control.

West European acceptance of the deployment of Pershing II and cruise missiles on European soil was based on the NATO double-track decision of 1979, according to which the U.S. missiles would not be deployed if the Soviets removed their SS-20 intermediate range nuclear missiles. The steel-helmet wing, including Defense Minister Manfred Wörner, spearheaded the opposition to the pending agreement in West Germany. Its strident protest was perceived by large segments of the West German electorate as an unacceptable backtracking from the government's official position in favor of arms control. Events quickly mushroomed into a government crisis as Chancellor Helmut Kohl, well known for his indecisiveness on polarizing issues, was unable to restrain the members of the steel-helmet group from publicly lambasting the reduction proposals as detrimental to West German security. Their tortuous public statements, supported by a chorus of NATO officials, proved to be politically embarrassing for the hard-liners and other political lobbies close to the defense industry.

In direct opposition to the conservative campaign against the double-zero proposal, West German Foreign Minister Hans-Dietrich Genscher, representing the Free Democratic Party (FDP) within the government coalition, announced his unambiguous support for the proposals. The polarization within the cabinet also extended deep into the conservative CDU-CSU camp. The political isolation of the steel-helmet position (notwithstanding possible unofficial support from like-minded interests in Washington and Paris) materialized in the state elections in May 1987 in Rheinland Palatinate and Hamburg with the strong electoral comeback of the Free Democrats. The defeat of the CDU-CSU was unanimously attributed by postelection analysts to the rejection by West German voters of Kohl's equivocation on double zero and to public approval of Genscher's unflinching and tenacious opposition to the steel-helmet group's position. The electoral slap in the face to Chancellor Kohl's party was also an unmistakable popular rejection of any policy shrifts by Bonn that would risk isolating the Federal Republic from Washington, which by then had reasserted its approval for the double-zero solution.[8]

The political crisis the steel-helmet wing ignited can be attributed in part to the ongoing support for this minority by similar pro-defense elements in other NATO capitals and in the United States. Among these voices were Secretary of Defense Caspar Weinberger and high-ranking Democratic experts on security policy such as Senator Sam Nunn and Representative Les Aspin. In retrospect, it became clear that Washington and Bonn had been trading incorrect political signals, which in turn had resulted in policies that, although based on long-term NATO planning, could no longer be politically sustained. The United States received the false signal that West Germany wanted additional U.S. support in the form of new weapons systems instead of political solutions in the form of arms control and disarmament; West Germany received the highly divisive message that it must increase its arms budget if it wanted continued U.S. friendship. These misreadings reinforced each other and bolstered the confidence of the steel-helmet group and other defense-minded minorities on both sides of the Atlantic. They saw themselves as defenders of long-standing NATO traditions based on strengthening deterrence and flexible response and on fostering transatlantic friendship. Yet by resisting the tide of change, this transatlantic coalition set itself adrift from the political mainstream and failed to anticipate the importance that arms control and disarmament would assume for the future of East-West relations. Furthermore, these pro-defense forces were supported by formidable U.S. and European military-industrial groupings whose influence grew as a result of the large military buildup of the Reagan administration.

France's initial reaction to President Reagan's support for an INF agreement with Moscow was one of shock and rejection. As the "small world power" of Western Europe—its strategic nuclear forces equal only 2 percent those of the United States or the Soviet Union—the French government opposed the agreement that it said risked "denuclearizing" Western Europe and thereby placing it at the mercy of superior Soviet conventional and chemical weapons.[9] Minister of Defense André Giraud, reflecting the interests of the French armed forces and the military-industrial establishment, perceived the INF double-zero proposal as a threat to the French nuclear deterrent and the modernization of its prestrategic (tactical) nuclear and conventional systems. He announced his grave concern that the West was "falling into a trap."[10] His Socialist predecessor, Paul Quilés, branded the Soviet proposals for a double-zero accord a hoax, while prominent Gaullists accused President Reagan of "dealing a terrible blow to the Western Alliance."[11] Raymond Barre, the leading light of moderate conservative parties of the UDF (Union pour la Démocratie Française) warned of the zero option decoupling the security of Western Europe from the United States.[12] While Giraud is said to have termed the U.S. president's announcement for double zero a "European Munich," Jacques Baumel, the neo-Gaullist deputy and vice president of the defense committee of the National Assembly, branded double zero "an American Munich."[13] Both officials thus recalled the 1938 meeting in which the French and British prime ministers, Edouard Daladier and Neville Chamberlain, bowed before Hitler.

Despite this storm of outrage, President François Mitterrand, after holding hard discussions within his cabinet, announced he would not oppose the treaty. He was concerned that France not be the sole country in Europe in opposition to the Gorbachev and Reagan proposals. Mitterrand also wanted to avoid projecting the image of France as an opponent of arms control, especially after having supported the arms control clause of the double-track decision of 1979. Finally, Mitterrand made it clear that the potential first-strike capability of Pershing IIs and cruise missiles, if fired at the Soviet Union from West German territory, was not in the interests of France.[14]

This response to the INF Treaty can be explained in part by economic pressures. France, even more so than West Germany, faced a fiscal crisis in its military budget. It had to adjust long-standing, expensive plans for modernization of its armed forces to changing fiscal and political realities.[15] This spurred interest in lowering military spending and pursuing a more active policy of détente. Mitterrand resisted the conservative, pro-defense elements in his government during the INF debate and sought to establish closer economic and political links with Eastern Europe and the Soviet Union.[16] France, like Great Britain, made its strategic nuclear deterrent the single most important pillar of its military-political claim to be a major European power. But because of the cost, neither nation can afford strategic modernization without making significant trade-offs in conventional preparedness and R&D programs.[17]

Both England and France generally followed the Reagan lead in the period from 1980 to 1987 preceding the signing of the INF Treaty. Under pressure from Defense Secretary Weinberger during the early 1980s, they continued to delay fiscal adjustment and therefore came under greater pressure to cut their defense spending.[18] While making clear gestures to encourage détente, they were more reserved than the Federal Republic concerning the second wave of détente and resistant to Soviet offers on far-reaching arms reductions. This attitude was reflected in the British and French emphasis on nuclear deterrence and plans for developing new weapons systems.

France's reluctance to change course was linked to the fact that its long-term modernization plans were formerly based on the expectation that the deployment in Western Europe of intermediate-range and shorter range missiles would dovetail with the ambitious strategic and prestrategic nuclear buildup of French forces.[19] Despite traditional misgivings of too much West European reliance on the United States in matters of security, the U.S. military buildup that began in 1979 and reached unprecedented heights for peacetime under Reagan helped to legitimize French programs. Similarly, though France is not militarily integrated in NATO and is critical of the aims of the Strategic Defense Initiative (SDI), France's commitment to modernizing its conventional and nuclear forces earned the country a great deal of favor in Washington. Mitterrand's help in rallying support in Western Europe for the Pershing II and cruise deployments is an example of the mutual warming of French and U.S. policy during the heyday of the Reagan arms buildup. Franco-U.S. military relations broke new ground when important SDI and other military contracts were awarded to French high-tech firms.[20] Socialist France demonstrated its "model behavior" as a U.S. ally not only by meeting U.S. and NATO quotas for hikes in military spending but also by being strongly supportive during Mitterrand's first term of the U.S. administration's tough ideological line vis-à-vis the Soviet Union.

West European doubts about the INF agreement thus can be attributed to the fear that it not only would erode the U.S. security guarantee but would also disrupt the well-laid plans of West European military interests for new, high-tech modernization programs—joint undertakings worked out with the

Pentagon as well as projects designed specifically to give West European firms a stronger competitive position in the international arms market. Even if an INF agreement did not directly affect those programs, it was feared that a post-INF disarmament process might. At the very least, it would make it difficult for military interests in Britain, France, and West Germany to justify maintaining their expensive modernization plans during a time of fiscal restraint and East-West détente. This also explains why the INF accord was initially seen as a significant defeat for hard-line elements within both the Reagan administration and West European governments.

Western Europe's soul-searching regarding NATO's future cannot be attributed solely to the INF agreement or to the prospect of future arms control agreements. Broader considerations were involved.[21] U.S. preoccupation with the Pacific and other parts of the world, its intensifying financial crisis that pressured the defense budget, the SDI's troubling implications for NATO's defense, and Reagan's cavalier attitude at Reykjavik toward trading away NATO's nuclear deterrent were also factors that contributed to uneasiness about the future on the part of conservative as well as center forces in Western Europe. These developments helped to generate a feeling across the political spectrum that Washington had become rudderless, moving in several directions at once—reaffirming NATO's traditional doctrine of nuclear deterrence and flexible response, then promoting abolition of nuclear weapons and fanciful notions of strategic defense, arguing one day that the U.S. commitment to Western Europe was unshakable while the next day stressing the increasing burden of the Pentagon's military obligations.

Partly in response to the uncertainty concerning future U.S. commitment to Western Europe, President Mitterrand and Chancellor Kohl took the occasion of the highly publicized Franco–West German joint military maneuver "Bold Sparrow" in September 1987 to launch an initiative for the creation of a European Defense Council.[22] Its aim was to "coordinate decisions and harmonize analyses in the areas of security, research, defense, armaments and the deployment of joint units."[23]

In a separate initiative in October, the seven-nation Western European Union (WEU) formally adopted a "defense policy platform," which British Foreign Secretary Sir Geoffrey Howe described as "a set of principles that will serve to guide the future development of the WEU."[24] The new platform stated that the WEU member states intended to develop a more "cohesive defense identity."[25] Participating foreign ministers took pains to emphasize that their aim was to strengthen the West European pillar of the Atlantic Alliance, not to put into question Western Europe's enduring security partnership with the United States.

Strengthening the European pillar reflects the aspirations of a growing portion of Western Europe's establishment for a Western Europe relatively more independent of the United States in security as well as economic and foreign policy.[26] According to this perspective, military dependence on

Washington narrows Western Europe's options and tends to hinder its political and economic flexibility vis-à-vis Washington, Eastern Europe, and the Soviet Union.[27]

The New West European–Soviet Détente

After the unsuccessful opposition of West German conservative elements to the INF Treaty, the West German government had little choice but to adopt a more resolute arms control and détente policy. At the same time, some archconservatives who had built their careers on anti-Sovietism—including the since-deceased legendary leader of the Christian Socialist Union (CSU), Franz-Josef Strauss—joined the ranks of détente enthusiasts. After his visit to Moscow in 1987, Strauss declared that the postwar period was over and that the West need no longer fear that the Soviets have "offensive, aggressive intentions."[28] In a relatively short period of time, deepened détente with the Soviet Union gained a consensus among the majority of West German conservatives, Free Democrats, Social Democrats, and Greens, a shift that reflected not only West Germany's special interest in a less confrontational East-West environment but also the public's view that the Soviet threat was dramatically diminishing under Mikhail Gorbachev. Opinion polls in the 1986–1988 period consistently showed that most West Germans believed Gorbachev was more interested in peace than was Ronald Reagan. According to a poll by the West German Allensbach Institute in early 1988, only 24 percent of West Germans viewed the Soviet Union as a military threat, as opposed to 55 percent five years before, while 50 percent of West Germans favored unilateral disarmament, as compared with 35 percent five years before.[29]

The tidal change in public perception also reflected the fact that West Germany and other countries of Western Europe during the 1970s had opened a new phase of detente with the Soviet Union. European détente successfully weathered the cold war winds of the early 1980s and became the basis for the new wave of cooperation of the late 1980s.

Détente in the late 1970s and early 1980s remained a defensive venture— an effort by its European proponents to shield countries on both sides of the iron curtain from increased superpower confrontation and to maintain an expanded level of political and economic relations. In the end, this did not fundamentally affect NATO's security policy or the division of Europe. But with the emergence of Gorbachev and his perestroika, democratization, and glasnost policies, European détente developed into a more active mix of economic cooperation, political liberalization, cultural exchange, and confidence building—a development that began to challenge the structures of the postwar division of Europe.

The 1985–1989 period, in particular, saw the flowering of East-West consultations, joint declarations, high-level meetings, and an ongoing boom in economic, cultural, and environmental East-West agreements. Notwithstanding the Reagan-Gorbachev summits, the United States was slow to appreciate the implications that Gorbachev's reform efforts would have for East-West relations. Yet in Western Europe, his reform program had been the subject of intense discussion. In a February 1987 speech at Davos, Switzerland, West German Foreign Minister Genscher urged the West to recognize the importance of the transformation taking place in the Soviet Union and to help Gorbachev succeed. Genscher offered a three-part program for a new phase of détente involving a process of cooperation designed to help the Soviet Union modernize, and he proposed increased political engagement intended to ensure respect for human rights and to overcome the barriers separating those who live in the East from those in the West.[30]

The visit of West Germany's Richard von Weizsäcker in 1987 to the Soviet Union was the first visit of a West German president to Moscow in the postwar era and was interpreted as the beginning of a new chapter in Soviet–West German relations. In part to emphasize the significance of the event, the first West German–Soviet agreement for a joint venture project (the machine tool company Homatec) was formally signed.[31] The historic visit of Erich Honecker as first party secretary of the German Democratic Republic (GDR) to the Federal Republic in September 1987 marked a milestone in relations not only between the two Germanies but also between the two blocs[32] and set the stage for France's official reception of Honecker in January 1988, also a first in postwar history. As Franz-Josef Strauss remarked after his 1987 visit to Moscow, East-West relations had entered "a new era which will be ruled not by Mars, the god of war, but by Mercury, the god of trade and business."[33]

The response of officials in other West European capitals to improving East-West economic and political relations was more muted but no less real: British, French, and Italian companies have all concluded new joint ventures with the Soviet Union. Italy joined West Germany in welcoming Gorbachev's many disarmament moves and in seeing the possibilities for ending the military confrontation in Europe. France and Britain initially were more cautious, adopting what might be called a bifurcated approach. On the one hand, they cautioned Bonn about letting down its defense guard, warning that Gorbachev was trying to lure West Germany out of NATO, and argued for the need to pursue their own military programs. On the other hand, they became active in supporting Gorbachev's initiatives and reforms through cooperation agreements and lines of credit.[34]

Key in this shift were the Soviet disarmament initiatives and the fact that the Moscow leadership adopted the West European language of common, or "mutual," security based on the notion that one nation cannot achieve security at the expense of another. It also put forward ideas very similar to those advocated by leading West European security experts—notions like "nonoffensive defense,"[35] "reasonable sufficiency," the withdrawal of offensive forces from forward areas, on-site and challenge inspections, and nuclear-free zones.[36] For this reason, Moscow's proposals for conventional reductions, for a combination of disarmament and development on a regional scale, and for discussion of each side's military doctrine received serious attention in Western Europe.[37] Gorbachev's admission that certain asymmetries exist in conventional arms and his commitment to significant unilateral reductions of troops, tanks, combat aircraft, and artillery, along with the military implications of his ambitious plans for economic restructuring, convinced the majority of European elites and publics that progress on ending the conventional as well as the nuclear confrontation can be made. Taken together, these developments raised for many the possibility that a framework of common security and détente, entailing greatly reduced and reconfigured forces on each side, could one day replace the current strategy of nuclear deterrence.

The Search for a New Security Order

Both the INF Treaty and the dramatic developments in East-West relations that dominated the world political stage after its signing left no doubt that NATO and transatlantic relations were in a state of radical transition. Proposals on the future of Western Europe's security from this period can be simplified for the purpose of analysis into three general and partly overlapping groupings: (1) traditional Atlanticist, (2) Europeanist, and (3) those based on common security and deepened détente.

The Traditional Atlanticist Approach

Traditional Atlanticists are concerned about U.S. commitment to Western Europe and the erosion of flexible response. They share with Europeanists an emphasis on increasing Western Europe's role as the second pillar of NATO and of improving NATO forces. These objectives would mean additional military deployments, including new high-tech weapons systems that would tend to alter the traditional strategy of NATO from a near-the-border forward defense to a more "war-fighting" across-the-border offensive strategy.[38] Traditional Atlanticist proposals are characterized by a strong attachment to the military and political traditions of NATO, to Western Europe's postwar links to the U.S. security umbrella, and to North America in a broader economic and cultural sense. Atlanticists are thus genuinely concerned about the risk of a U.S. "abandonment" of Western Europe.[39]

The Europeanist Approach

Europeanists place greater emphasis on making Western Europe relatively more independent of the United States. For them, the INF Treaty is good reason not merely to seek traditional security assurances from Washington but also to continue to call for strengthening the European pillar of NATO. The Europeanists want to increase Western Europe's military and foreign policy autonomy, both within the alliance and in organizations and suballiances that would be parallel or overlapping with NATO.[40] This concept has been underpinned by the increasing role of the Eurogroup in NATO, the upgrading of the WEU, Franco–West German military cooperation, and the increased foreign policy activity of the European Political Cooperation (EPC) of the European Community.[41] The new assertiveness of Europeanist interests reflects a number of different geopolitical and economic factors, including the intensifying transatlantic competition in military production and, as a result, competitive shifting of military procurement patterns. Symptomatic of this development was the policy speech of French Defense Minister Jean-Pierre Chevènement in November 1988 in which he declared that the European pillar for Western security must have a broader foundation in defense industries in Western Europe. In this context, he called for a "European preference" in military procurement.[42] The statement must be read as a direct challenge to the large U.S. share of the NATO procurement market and also reflects the drive to expand West European high-tech industrial conglomerates. Firms such as Thompson and Matra in France and Daimler Benz in the Federal Republic launched merger strategies that combine high-tech military with civilian production in an effort to increase their own and West European competitiveness vis-à-vis the United States and Japan and prepare the way to the unification of the European Common Market in 1992.

With the U.S. nuclear umbrella in question—the result of the 1986 Reykjavik summit,[43] reduced public support of the doctrine of nuclear deterrence, the INF Treaty, and declining West European confidence in U.S. economic and political leadership—many of Western Europe's military-industrial lobbies are taking a less Atlanticist view of their own interests than formerly. They are using the specter of U.S abandonment to cautiously promote more independent military-political policies and military research and procurement programs.

Both Europeanist and Atlanticist proponents of a stronger European pillar have maintained that a more cohesive and relatively more autonomous Western Europe, although still ultimately dependent on the U.S. strategic arsenal, would be more effective in dealing with the growing number of transatlantic political-economic rifts and potential differences on security questions. These issues are becoming more salient and tending to polarize traditional Atlanticists and Europeanists on the question of whether or not additional West European military-political input into the East-West equation should be developed within or outside of NATO.

Common Security and Pro-Détente Forces

The third approach in the debate on Western Europe's future, based on common security, links minimal deterrence and radical arms reductions with deepened détente and steps in the direction of nonmilitary forms of security. The long-term aim of this approach is to create a new European security order that would gradually tend to replace the current system of deterrence and arms racing.[44] This new view corresponds to the post-containment model of security discussed in the introduction to this book.

While the initial West European response to the proposal for the INF accord polarized the public from NATO officialdom, the prospect of eliminating two entire categories of nuclear weapons from Europe significantly strengthened pro-détente forces. As a result of the progress made during the late 1980s in European East-West relations, the INF accord was seen by many proponents of détente less as a climactic breakthrough than as an overdue first step in removing military-political structures viewed as dangerous sources of tension in East-West and West-West relations. These observers felt that the post-INF NATO arms buildup—the plans for which were drawn up prior to the treaty—threatened to block the cooperation agreements and disarmament proposals on the agenda of most West and East European countries. In this view, East-West rapprochement, which has accelerated since 1985–1986 in a manner unprecedented in the postwar era, put into greater relief the anachronism of existing security arrangements.

The flowering of Eastern and Western proposals for reorganizing European security included both official and unofficial proposals for confidence building, arms control, and disarmament, as well as initiatives for creating new organs and expanding the competence of existing institutions that deal with defense and disarmament policymaking.[45] These included the protocols of the Social Democratic Party (SPD) of the Federal Republic and the Socialist Unity Party (SED) of the German Democratic Republic on the creation of nuclear- and chemical-free zones in the two Germanies; the SPD-Polish proposals on structural nonoffensive defense; the Greek government's proposals for a nuclear-free Balkans;[46] the initiative for a nuclear-free Nordic zone;[47] the numerous Soviet proposals for far-reaching nuclear and conventional reductions from the Urals to the Atlantic; the Jaruzelski Plan for nuclear and conventional cuts; and the Polish–West German SPD proposal for the creation of a European Council for Confidence Building.[48]

The Jaruzelski Plan. The Jaruzelsi Plan was first announced by Poland in May 1987.[49] An important example of the multisided approach to disarmament for East and West, the plan called for the following:

- Phased reduction of tactical nuclear weapons and their total elimination in Europe from the Atlantic to the Urals
- Mutual reductions of conventional weapons
- A fundamental review of military doctrines
- A package of accompanying confidence-building measures[50]

The plan proposed the division of the Atlantic-to-Urals area into at least two zones. The first-priority area for reduction was to cover central Europe, with the Federal Republic and the Benelux countries on the western side and on the east the German Democratic Republic, Czechoslovakia, Poland, and part of Denmark and Hungary. The second zone was to include the rest of the Atlantic-to-Urals area, which could be divided into subzones that could cover the northern and southern NATO flanks.[51]

An important element in the Polish scheme was its recommendation that arms control negotiations begin not with a quantitative comparison of overall forces but with the particular weapons systems each side considered particularly threatening to its security because they could be used for a surprise attack.[52] Negotiations would aim at a phased withdrawal of such systems. Complementing its emphasis on structural nonoffensive defense, the proposal also called for negotiations on altering military doctrines in order to move away from nuclear deterrence.[53] Unprecedented was the plan's recognition of the Warsaw Pact's conventional superiority in specific weapons categories and its acceptance of the principle that reductions must be sought that are acceptable to both sides.[54] These innovations anticipated Gorbachev's later statement in 1987 that existing asymmetries must be removed by reductions undertaken by the side that enjoys the advantage.[55] The Jaruzelski Plan also anticipated Moscow's opening positions at the Negotiations on the Conventional Armed Forces in Europe and at the Conference on Confidence- and Security-Building Measures in Europe, both of which opened in Vienna in March 1989.

Like the Warsaw Pact proposals that have followed it, the Jaruzelski Plan reflected the comprehensive thrust of the East's ideas for confidence building and disarmament. Their aim is not merely quantitative reductions of armaments to achieve a new military balance in Europe but alteration of the fundamentals of East-West military confrontation through the proposed acceptance by both sides of moving in the direction of a nonconfrontational European security order. These qualitative proposals have surpassed expectations of many in the West, but their far-reaching character must be read also as a response to traditional Western objections to the existence of the Soviet military threat and a result of ongoing dialogue between Eastern and Western security researchers, policy experts, and policymakers.

The Jaruzelski Plan pointed the way to subsequent proposals by the Soviet Union, including the dramatic measures announced by President

Gorbachev at the United Nations in December 1988.[56] These included the following unilateral measures to be carried out within two years: withdrawal of 500,000 Soviet troops from Eastern Europe and removal of 10,000 tanks, 8,500 artillery pieces, 800 combat aircraft, and all forward-based assault equipment. The Soviet leader's speech was also noteworthy because it included references to global economic and ecological concerns.[57] The link between military and nonmilitary dimensions of East-West relations reflected a broader conception of disarmament.

A culture of intersystem peaceful competition and cooperation. The growing mesh of East-West cooperative relations in Europe challenged traditional notions that Western democratic nations and state-controlled Eastern communist regimes cannot work together. A vital dimension of such collaboration was initiatives to codify the past experience and lessons of European détente and its political and normative meaning for the future of international relations.[58]

"Conflicting Ideologies and Common Security," a declaration of the ruling Socialist Unity Party (SED) of the GDR and the West German Social Democratic Party (SPD), was an example. The document was based on the overriding principle that "war must no longer be a means of politics in the nuclear age" and that the concepts of common security and détente must replace the notion that security can be achieved by "continually adding new means of mass destruction to the existing stockpiles."[59] The authors outlined what they consider to be the foundations of a new politics of East-West relations as follows:

> The relations between the two systems are not only characterized by a common, parallel or convergent interest but also and above all by contradictory interests. The coexistence of, and controversy between, qualitatively differing and opposed socio-economic and political systems are fundamental characteristics of international relations.
>
> But the debate about which is the better social system can only be conducted if peace is assured and history continues. . . .
>
> Equitable cooperation between East and West to their mutual benefit encourages the necessary change in international relations to be made and serves détente in Europe. This has been proved not least by the experience gained during the . . . seventies. . . . Progress made in détente provides greater opportunities for cooperation amongst states in the political, economic, scientific, technological, cultural and humanitarian sphere.
>
> Both social systems need such cooperation, because the intertwining of the world economy is progressing, the development of the productive forces goes beyond national boundaries and the global problems are coming to a head.
>
> Hence, cooperation between the systems and states becomes a

prerequisite for the development of national economics and the world economy as a whole, for the gradual resolution of the global problems facing mankind, for the elimination of poverty and underdevelopment throughout the world, for exchanges in the field of culture and information, in short, for the development of human civilization.[60]

The statement stresses a comprehensive notion of peace,[61] in which security is linked to nonmilitary areas and the cooperative resolution of problems of both social systems is placed in a global context. The authors maintain that the competition between the two social systems can be progressively demilitarized through the adoption of a common security approach to military policy combined with deepening East-West economic-political and cultural interpenetration. Arms control and disarmament are linked to creating new avenues of intersystem cooperation and competition.

Yet the authors do not submerge East-West differences. On the contrary, they call for a new "culture of political debate" and argue that "open discussion concerning the competition of the two systems, their successes and failures, advantages and disadvantages, must be possible in both systems."[62] The authors suggest that it is through such debate that differences can be reduced and an intense interactionary form of coexistence achieved.

Détente as a social force of reform.   The call for restructuring East-West relations in the late 1980s also reflected the changing political and cultural aspirations of East European polities. Political elites in Eastern Europe and the Soviet Union were under increasing pressure from domestic populations no longer satisfied with the status quo, resting as it did on an outmoded political culture of isolation. Within elites and publics, there was a desire for greater freedom to travel, to express individual political views, and to participate more actively in constructing a more open domestic—and global—society.

The new social climate that emerged in the late 1980s was itself a product of almost two decades of European détente. During this period East Europeans were increasingly exposed through mass media, tourism, and the accelerating integration of the international economy to the higher living standards, more varied lifestyles, and greater political and intellectual freedoms of the West. West Europeans, particularly those living in areas adjacent to Eastern Europe, on the other hand, became more conversant with the East and realized they had a fundamental stake in the progress of Eastern reforms. This was particularly evident in East and West Germany.

Internal East German reform and détente.   The SED-SPD declaration is an important example of the GDR's opening to the West. The commitment in principle to a politics of greater domestic and external glasnost would have been almost inconceivable for an East European socialist state to make just a few years earlier. The new trend reflected the powerful external and domestic forces that had left the somewhat reluctant East German leadership little choice but to open the regime's economic, political, and ideological borders to a potentially far-reaching internal liberalization and Western penetration in the coming decades. This loosening was considered necessary and beneficial, despite the internal political adjustments and risks that it would entail for an entire postwar generation of East German leaders, administrators, and economic managers socialized under the shadow of a cold-war, Stalinist political culture.

The declaration must also be viewed as an uneasy political bargain between East and West Germany because it further legitimated socialist popular protest by opening the door to internal reform reinforced by external détente and criticism. The increasing number of political incidents in the GDR, which involved arrests and the forced exile of scores of civil-rights and ecological protesters to West Germany, reflected the dynamic contradiction embodied in the GDR's approach to internal change.[63] Its policy could not but encourage the expansion of protest and reform movements, which appeared to be hastening the end of East Germany's one-party system. But they also helped to move the leadership in a direction that was progressive and innovative by East European standards, notwithstanding that the trend is still insufficient to solve basic economic and political problems facing the country.

Domestic protest activity in the GDR inevitably tends to flow over the boundaries of official toleration, but it has nevertheless been endured out of a politically volatile compound of conscious political choice and the fact that the leadership is paradoxically locked into an inescapable reform course. In this process, the West, particularly the Federal Republic, has become a critical partner—"critical" both in the sense of offering generous economic and humanitarian cooperation and providing noncoercive encouragement, but at the same time objecting promptly and audibly to violations of basic human and political rights when they occur. The opening to the West also has placed the East German government under the intense spotlight of Western media, which has the effect of limiting state repression because the leadership would be at risk and could easily jeopardize its deepening relations with the Federal Republic were it to resort to unrestrained violent reprisals.

Conclusions

This chapter analyzed the watershed context of the INF Treaty and its meaning for the debate on NATO's future. Despite the acceptance of the INF Treaty by Western powers, it did not generate a consensus on NATO policy.

On the contrary, it polarized the West on the policy alternatives of modernization or a more resolute policy of disarmament.

The West European and transatlantic debate preceding and following the INF Treaty illustrates the interplay between the postwar model of security based on a military-technological arms race and at the same time the shift away from this model in the direction of disarmament, common security, and qualitatively intensified forms of East-West détente. The controversy that evolved around the INF Treaty reflects the competitive antagonism between two positions: On the one hand, the treaty was viewed as a weakening of Western security and therefore had to be followed by compensatory measures. On the other hand, many of the treaty's supporters considered it not a weakening but a strengthening of Western security precisely because the treaty was a step in the direction of the post-containment model of security based on demilitarization, détente, and cooperation. The proliferation of East-West disarmament proposals and cooperation projects discussed in this chapter, which will be taken up again in Part 3, tends to support this interpretation.

The uneven, polarizing character of the paradigm shift from the postwar to the post-containment model of security is also evident in the changing positions of governments, parties, and interest groups in the debate before the treaty and in the discussion after it on the future of European and East-West security. Many of the opponents of the INF Treaty, particularly in Western Europe, became supporters of it. Moreover, in the course of the debate, traditional NATO positions were put into question. The Atlantic Alliance became polarized not merely on the question of intermediate missiles but, more fundamentally, on the nature of security policy and whether Western Europe should continue in the traditional postwar groove of producing and deploying more sophisticated weapons systems or instead should pursue a cooperative, demilitarizing approach to the Soviet Union and Eastern Europe.

The SED-SPD declaration is an example of the efforts being made within the two Germanies to move beyond the passive acceptance of the status-quo, a divided Europe, in the direction of the post-containment model of East-West relations. The authors of the statement justify the need for such a reorientation with propositions based on the changing political, economic, technological, and ecological conditions that mandate a shift to disarmament, common security, and East-West cooperation as a prerequisite to future European and global development.

Although the competition between the postwar and post-containment notions of security is most pronounced in the West in the debate within the Atlantic Alliance on security policy, the collision of these two policy approaches is evident in Eastern Europe and the Soviet Union in the polarization around the pace and goals of glasnost, perestroika, and democratization. In the GDR, the example given in this chapter, the party leadership finds itself pursuing an incremental reform process in which cooperation with the West is viewed as indispensable to the further development of socialism. This assumes far-reaching disarmament by both military alliances. Nevertheless, the question for the relatively conservative GDR leadership of how far-reaching the nonmilitary reforms should be remains highly controversial.

The broader reform context of the security debate in the East is reflected in the agreements, official proposals, and informal initiatives pertaining to East-West disarmament, common security, and détente that have emerged in the late 1980s. Some of these were briefly discussed in this chapter. Taken as a whole, they are concerned with the following three areas:

- Existing security-political structures that have formed the foundations of the postwar security order, such as the doctrine of nuclear deterrence and the production and deployment of nuclear and conventional weapons
- Current plans for a new military buildup, including the NATO modernization program
- Economic, political, and ecological consequences of existing security structures, including their effects (present and future) on the domestic and international economy, on East-West cooperation and competition, and on efforts to solve regional and global problems (such as the ecological crisis, poverty, and hunger)

An important characteristic of the wide range of pro-détente and disarmament initiatives thus is their tendency to be comprehensive—to view security policy not only in the strict military sense but also in relation to nonmilitary aspects of the East-West conflict.[64] This general characteristic reflects the view of pro-détente forces that a significant alteration of security arrangements in East and West cannot be implemented and would fall short of its purpose without changes in nonmilitary areas of policy. The converse is also generally held to be true: Meaningful economic, political, or ecological reforms in their domestic, regional, interalliance, and global contexts are no longer possible without the removal of existing East-West military barriers.

The far-reaching perspectives of the pro-détente forces also suggest why many pro-defense interests view the process of disarmament as a threat not merely to specific military programs they support but also to the postwar security order as such. Notwithstanding the possible justification for such apprehensions on the part of Atlanticists and Europeanists, it is by no means clear what the outcome of the post-INF debate will be. In this context, the remaining chapters of Part 1 will analyze in more detail the following three areas: (a) the danger of a post-INF arms buildup; (b) the improbability that the United States will be able to implement its version of NATO modernization and greater West European burden sharing; and (c) the possible consequences of U.S. policy in relationship to the Atlanticist, Europeanist, and pro-détente models of NATO's future.

Notes

1. Treaty Between the United States of America and the Union of Soviet Socialist Republics on the Elimination of Their Intermediate- and Shorter Range Missiles, December 1987, reprinted in "Summary of the INF Treaty and Protocols," (INF Supplement, pp. 1–16), *Arms Control Today*, Vol. 18, No. 1, January/February 1988. See also George Shultz, "The INF Treaty: Strengthening U.S. Security," *Current Policy* (U.S. Department of State, Bureau of Public Affairs), No. 1038. The treaty defines intermediate-range missiles as land-based systems having ranges between 1,000 and 5,500 kilometers and shorter range missiles as land-based systems with a range between 500 and 1,000 kilometers. The treaty requires both signatories to eliminate their shorter range missiles within 19 months. Also contained in the agreement is a memorandum of understanding giving the locations, numbers, and characteristics of each side's missile stocks and a detailed protocol on procedures to eliminate the missiles and their support systems. The treaty was interpreted by Western and Eastern experts as a historic breakthrough. According to one Soviet writer:

> It may prove a turning point in Soviet-American relations and East-West relations in general, and in a broader sense, in the evolution of world politics as a whole. The treaty not only signals the end of a complicated and highly tense stage of international political development in the late 1970s and the first half of the 1980s. . . . What is also important is that the world has gained its first practical experience in implementing a fundamentally new approach to security whereby political means prevail over military ones, and joint actions in the search for solutions to security problems enjoy unconditional priority over unilateral actions.

Vladamir Baranowsky, "The Treaty on the Elimination of Intermediate-Range and Shorter-Range Missiles," in Institute of World Economy and International Relations (hereafter Institute of World Economy), USSR Academy of Sciences, *Disarmament and Security: 1987 Yearbook* (Moscow: Novosti Press Agency Publishing House, 1988), p. 58.

2. See in this context R. Jeffrey Smith, "NATO Defense Ministers Endorse INF Accord," *Washington Post*, December 11, 1987; John Fialka, "Europe Debates Missile Pact's Aftermath," *Wall Street Journal*, December 7, 1987; D. Bruce Marshall, "France and the INF Negotiations: An 'American Munich'?" *Strategic Review*, Vol. 15, No. 3, Summer 1987, pp. 20–30.

3. See in this context Michael Howard, "A European Perspective on the Reagan Years," *Foreign Affairs*, Vol. 66, No. 3 (*America and the World 1987–88*), pp. 478–493; D. Bruce Marshall, ibid. On the broader question of U.S. troops in Europe see Pascal Boniface and François Heisbourg, *Les puces, les hommes et la bombe: L'Europe face aux nouveaux défis technologiques et militaires* (Paris: Hachette, 1986), pp. 96–118.

4. Daniel Charles, "NATO Looks for Arms Control Loopholes," *Bulletin of Atomic Scientists*, Vol. 43, No. 7, September 1987, pp. 7–12.

5. Andrew Nagorski, "A New Page in Relations Betweeen the East and Bonn," *Newsweek*, January 25, 1988; U.S. Information Agency, "Foreign Media Reaction," November 7, 1987, November 21, 1987, December 9, 1987;

U.S. Department of State, unclassified media reaction, November 11, 25, 27, 1987. For a discussion of this material, see Hugh de Santis, "After INF: The Political-Military Landscape of Europe," *Washington Quarterly*, Vol. 11, No. 3, Summer 1988, pp. 29–44.

6. See in this context "Die Angst vor der Null-Lösung," *Der Spiegel*, Vol. 41, No. 12, April 6, 1987; Charles, op. cit; Jonathan Dean, "The INF Agreement: Pluses and Minuses for Western Security," *Arms Control Today*, Vol. 17, No. 6, July/August 1987, pp. 3–10.

7. On the INF negotiations process in general, see Strobe Talbot, *Deadly Gambits* (New York: Knopf, 1984).

8. *Der Spiegel*, "Die Angst," op. cit.; Charles, op. cit. This aspect of electoral behavior in West Germany was highly significant because it was an important indicator that rising West German anti-Americanism should not be viewed as an irreversible public attitude but rather as the result of particular U.S. policies, especially those favoring military buildups leading to new weapons deployments on West German soil. Similarly, the electoral results also suggested that U.S. policies that are congruent with the West German majority consensus for arms reduction could be a solid post-INF basis for U.S.–West German relations. See in this context Harald Müller and Thomas Risse-Kappen, "Origins of Estrangement," *International Security*, Vol. 12, No. 1, Summer 1987, pp. 52–88.

9. See the communiqué of the Foreign Ministry reprinted in *Politique Étrangère*, Vol. 52, No. 2, 1987, p. 462; Marshall, op. cit.

10. Marshall, ibid. Many of the most important advisers to Giraud were lobbyists of the French defense industry; for most of his career, Giraud himself worked for arms firms. See Jolyon Howorth, "Die französische Verteidigungspolitik im Widerstreit zwischen Abrüstung und Abschreckung," *Europa-Archiv*, Vol. 43, No. 12, pp. 331–348.

11. Roger de Weck, "Angst vor einem europäischen München," *Die Zeit*, Vol. 42, No. 12, March 12–13, 1987.

12. Marshall, op. cit. See also Jacques Amalric, "L'affaire des euromissiles devise la majorité," *Le Monde*, March 6, 1987.

13. Marshall, ibid.

14. Mitterrand clarified his position at his news conference March 10, 1987. Jean-Pierre Chevènement, the influential Socialist who would become defense minister during Mitterrand's second term, supported Mitterrand's decision, but in his comment on the proposal, he emphasized the changing nature of the U.S. security commitment to Western Europe, implying that France would have to draw the consequences for the future of European security. See Marshall, ibid.

15. François Heisbourg, "Conventional Defense: Europe's Constraints and Opportunities," in Andrew Pierre, ed., *The Conventional Defense of Europe: New Technologies and New Strategies* (New York: Council on Foreign Relations, 1986), pp. 71–111. Howorth, op. cit.

16. Christoph Bertram, "Zwischen Vision und Versuchung," *Die Zeit*, Vol. 43, No. 48, November 25, 1988.

17. Heisbourg, op. cit.; Roger de Weck, "Muss eine Schlacht verloren gehen," *Die Zeit*, Vol. 42, No. 40, September 25, 1987.

18. Heisbourg, op. cit. Mimicking the fiscally unrealistic Reagan policy on defense spending, both the UDF and the neo-Gaullist Rassemblement pour la République (RPR) had strongly criticized the Socialists for not spending enough on defense. See Marshall, op. cit.

19. On nuclear proliferation see William Arkin et al., "Nuclear Weapons"

28   The Political and Military Context of the INF Treaty

in *SIPRI Yearbook 1988* (Oxford: Oxford University Press, 1988), pp. 23–64.

20. See in this context Michael Lucas, "SDI and Europe," *World Policy Journal*, Vol. 3, No. 2, Spring 1986, pp. 219–249.

21. Howard, op. cit.

22. On the "Bold Sparrow" exercise, see Walter Schütze, "Der 'Erbfeind' als Ersatzfreund," *Blätter für deutsche und internationale Politik*, Vol. 33, No. 1, January 1988, pp. 25–36. On Franco–West German military cooperation, see Helmut Schmidt, "Deutsch-französische Zusammenarbeit in der Sicherheitspolitik," *Europa-Archiv*, Vol. 42, No. 11, 1987, pp. 303–312; Boniface and Heisbourg, op. cit., pp. 236–270; Karl Kaiser and Pierre Lellouche, eds., *Deutsch-französische Sicherheitspolitik. Auf dem Wege zur Gemeinsamkeit* (Bonn: Europa Union Verlag, 1986); James Markham, "Paris, Bonn Propose Military Council," *International Herald Tribune*, September 25, 1987.

23. Markham, ibid.

24. David Buchan, "WEU Ministers to Set Out Charter on East-West Security," *Financial Times*, October 26, 1987.

25. Ibid.

26. See in this context Helmut Schmidt, *A Grand Strategy for the West* (New Haven: Yale University Press, 1985), particularly Chapter 2; see also Schmidt 1987, op. cit.; Boniface and Heisbourg, op. cit. pp. 78–116; Ian Davidson, "Mitterrand Spells out Programme for Elysee Race," *Financial Times*, April 7, 1988.

27. Schmidt 1985, ibid.

28. Robert McCartney, "West Germany Feels the Impact of New Detente," *Washington Post*, January 17, 1988.

29. Nagorski, op. cit. Public opinion concerning nuclear disarmament in Europe has been even more striking. According to another Allensbach poll, 79 percent of the West German population want all nuclear weapons removed from Europe. Similarly, 51 percent of the poll's respondents rejected the premise that nuclear deterrence has been responsible for assuring peace in Europe for the past forty years. See Elisabeth Noelle-Neumann, "Wenn das Gefühl der Bedrohung schwindet," *Frankfurter Allgemeine Zeitung*, July 22, 1988.

30. Hans-Dietrich Genscher, "Taking Gorbachev at His Word," Speech of Hans-Dietrich Genscher, Minister of Foreign Affairs of the Federal Republic of Germany, at the World Economic Forum, Davos, Switzerland, February 1, 1987, published in *Statements and Speeches* (New York: German Information Center), Vol. 10, No. 3, February 7, 1987.

31. Niklaus Piper, "Glasnost in St. Georgen," *Die Zeit*, Vol. 42, No. 34, August 14, 1987; "Erste Joint Ventures mit der Sowjetunion," *Frankfurter Allgemeine Zeitung*, July 11, 1987; Christian Schmidt-Häuer, "Ihre Schwäche ist auch unsere Schwäche," *Die Zeit*, Vol. 42, No. 30, July 10, 1987.

32. Serge Schmemann, "Leaders of 2 Germanies Agree to Disagree," *New York Times*, September 9, 1987; Diana Johnstone, "Honecker's Visit Marks New Era for the Two Germany's Relations," *In These Times*, September 23–29, 1987.

33. See "Wir werden niemals das Schwert erheben," *Der Spiegel*, Vol. 42, No. 1, January 4, 1988.

34. On the détente dimension of British foreign policy, see Geoffrey Howe, "East-West Relations: The British Role," *International Affairs*, Vol. 63, No. 4, Autumn 1987, pp. 555–562. On the British insistence on NATO modernization, see British Information Services, "The NATO Summit: The

British View" (*Policy Statement*), March 4, 1988. On the warming of French foreign policy toward Moscow, see Bertram, op. cit.

35. In the space of approximately three years, the notion of nonoffensive defense (NOD) has developed from an idea largely unknown (except in such specialized circles as peace research groups) into an internationally accepted notion that is challenging current East-West military doctrines. Similar to, and often used synonymously with, the concepts of "structurally nonoffensive defense" and "nonprovocative defense," NOD has become an important building block of a new security thinking. As the Danish expert Björn Möller notes:

> First of all, a number of established (albeit oppositional) parties have included the demand for non-offensive military strategies and postures in their party platforms: the SPD [Social Democratic Party] in the FRG, the Labour Party in the UK, the Social Democrats, Liberal Centre Party and the Socialist People's Party in Denmark, the New Democrats in Canada, etc. Secondly, concepts and terms originating in the NOD theory are gradually finding their way into policy statements along the entire political spectrum (in statements of Hans-Dietrich Genscher, Alfred Dregger, and Les Aspin, just to mention a few examples). Thirdly, even official NATO documents and negotiation guidelines have begun to define the problems in ways compatible with NOD thinking. Finally, the very policy goal of NOD has been adopted by the USSR as one component of its 'new political thinking.'

"Status of the NOD Debate," Non-Offensive Defence NOD, International Research Newsletter, No. 10, August 1988.

36. See in this context Mikhail Gorbachev, *Perestroika* (New York: Harper and Row, 1987) Chapter 7, pp. 210–245. A good reference source on Soviet disarmament proposals with a discussion of Western positions is Institute of World Economy, op. cit.

37. See also "Speech by Mikhail Gorbachev at a Formal Meeting in Murmansk on October 1, 1987," in *Reprints from the Soviet Press*, Vol. 45, No. 9, November 15, 1987, pp. 5–35.

38. On the changes in NATO strategy and operational tactics, see Josef Joffe, *The Limited Partnership* (Boston: Ballinger, 1987), pp. 156f. Cf. Alfred Mechtersheimer, *Zeitbombe NATO, Auswirkungen der neuen Strategien* (Cologne: Eugen Diederichs Verlag, 1984), pp. 32–55.

39. For a defense of the traditional Atlanticist viewpoint with emphasis on the strategy of flexible response and the U.S. nuclear strategic umbrella, see Joffe, op. cit.

40. The calls for a Western Europe more autonomous militarily go back to the founding of the NATO alliance and have continued to play an important role in transatlantic debates throughout the postwar era. For a discussion of this dimension of NATO history, see the concluding chapter in Joffe, ibid., pp. 173–214.

41. On the European discussion of the need for new security arrangements, see Werner Weidenfeld, "Neuorganisation der Sicherheit Westeuropas," *Europa-Archiv*, Vol. 42, No. 9, 1987, pp. 259–268; Boniface and Heisbourg, op. cit., pp. 78–156; Joffe, ibid.; Calleo, op. cit. Part 3. See

also John Baylis, "Nato Strategy: The Case for a New Strategic Concept," *International Affairs*, Vol. 64, No. 1, Winter 1987/88, pp. 43–60.

42. Joseph Fitchett, "National Security Gives Protectionists a Weapon," *International Herald Tribune*, December 16, 1988.

43. In a discussion of U.S disarmament proposals, David Yost comments on the corrosive effects of the exchange of accusations between the United States and Western Europe in the wake of the Reykjavík summit as follows:

> The charge that the United States has not recognized the dangers in far-reaching arms-control proposals is related to concerns about the long-term implications for Alliance policy. The essence of this vein of criticism is that the LRINF zero option, the zero ballistic missile proposal, and the ultimate goal of abolishing nuclear weapons all have the de facto effect of stimulating a process in which the Western force posture is delegitimized in public perceptions. . . . Some West Europeans find it all the more disconcerting that the U.S. Reykjavík proposals seem part of a pattern evident over the past decade. Since the late 1970s antinuclear movements and slogans have burgeoned in the United States across the political spectrum—from the freeze and no-first-use movements to the Catholic bishops to SDI and the LRINF zero option. To critical West European analysts there appears to be a general trend in the United States toward nuclear disengagement. . . . Some critics hypothesize that the United States "feels free to sacrifice fundamental European security interests in order to salvage its own"— that the United States is suspected of trying to reduce the nuclear and ballistic missile threat to the U.S. homeland at the price of security in Europe.

David Yost, "The Reykjavík Summit and European Security," *SAIS Review*, Vol. 7, No. 2, Summer 1987, pp. 1–22.

44. For a West German critique of deterrence by a high-ranking navy officer, see Admiral Elmar Schmäling, "German Security Beyond American Hegemony," *World Policy Journal*, Vol. 6, No. 2, Spring 1989, pp. 371–384.

45. There is an extensive literature in East and West on proposals for confidence building, arms control, and disarmament. For a good introductory overview of recent proposals and literature in this area, see Stanley Sloan and Mikaela Sawtelle, *Confidence-Building Measures and Force Constraints for Stabilizing East-West Military Relations in Europe*, Congressional Research Service, Washington, D.C., August 30, 1988. Appendix B (pp. 41–65) contains both a listing of agreed measures as well as unofficial proposals by Western and Eastern experts. See also in this context Institute of World Economy, op. cit. For a useful European treatment of confidence-building measures, see Rolf Berg and Adam-Daniel Rotfeld, *Building Security in Europe: Confidence-Building Measures and the CSCE* (New York: Institute for East-West Security Studies, 1986).

46. Berthold Meyer, *Atomwaffenfreie Zonen und Vertrauensbildung in Europa* (Frankfurt: Campus, 1985). For an overview of efforts to establish nuclear-free zones throughout the world, see Alexander Kalyadin, "Non-Proliferation of Nuclear Weapons: Nuclear-Free Zones," in Institute of World Economy, op. cit., Chapter 28, pp. 511–524. Bulgaria and Romania have

played a major part in the proposals for a nuclear- and chemical-free zone in the Balkans, which the Soviet Union supports. According to one Soviet source: "The agenda of multilateral talks on this issue has been expanded to include the broad questions of ridding the Balkan Peninsula of any foreign troops and military bases, developing a stable healthy atmosphere in the Balkans and turning that region into a zone of peace and cooperation." Ibid., p. 521.

47. Ibid., p. 516f. The plan was drawn up in 1987 by parlamentarians of the Nordic countries. The zone would embrace Denmark, Norway, Finland, Iceland, and Sweden, as well as Greenland, the Faroe Islands, and Finland's Aland Islands. The document includes clauses prohibiting the training of military personnel in the methods of using nuclear weapons; the deployment, testing, or production of nuclear weapons; or their transport through territories of the signatories. The plan also contains the proposal that monitoring of the implementation of the plan would be coordinated by a special commission in cooperation with international organizations.

48. The Social Democratic Party of the Federal Republic of Germany and the Polish United Workers' Party, "European Council for Confidence Building" (mimeo), Mragowo, Poland, May 27, 1987.

49. Jim Hoagland and Jackson Diehl, "Warsaw Pact Makes a New Arms Offer," *International Herald Tribune*, November 12, 1987; Institute of World Economy, op. cit., p. 392f.

50. The Western unofficial expert discussion and proposals were similar in their emphasis and general thrust to the Polish and Warsaw Pact proposals. See in this context the discussion of Eastern and Western positions on conventional force reductions, military doctrine, and NATO–Warsaw Pact asymmetries in Robert D. Blackwill, "Conventional Stability Talks: Specific Approaches to Conventional Arms Control in Europe," *Survival*, Vol. 30, No. 5, September/October, pp. 429–447; Jack Snyder, "Limiting Offensive Conventional Forces: Soviet Proposals and Western Options," *International Security*, Vol. 12, No. 4, Spring 1988, pp. 48–77. Also interesting in this context was the Soviet discussion of Western positions; see Institute of World Economy, ibid., pp. 393–395ff.

51. Institute of World Economy, ibid., p. 393.

52. "Polen präzisiert den Jaruzelski-Plan," *Frankfurter Allgemeine Zeitung*, July 2, 1987; Institute of World Economy, ibid., p. 251.

53. This plan anticipated the Warsaw Pact's subsequent proposals on in-depth discussion of military doctrines. In its May 1987 statement, the Warsaw Pact proposed

consultations to compare the military doctrines of the two alliances, analyse their nature, and jointly discuss the patterns of their future development so as to reduce the mutual suspicion and distrust that has accumulated over the years, to ensure better perception of each other's intentions and to guarantee that the military concepts and doctrines of the two military blocs and their members are based on defensive principles.

Session of the Political Consultative Committee of the Warsaw Treaty States, *Documents* (Berlin: 28–29 May 1987) as cited in Blackwill, op. cit.

54. Institute of World Economy, op. cit., p. 396.

55. For a discussion of this point, see Blackwill, op. cit.

56. Quentin Peel, "Gorbachev Plans Sweeping Unilateral Arms Reductions," *Financial Times*, December 8, 1988.

57. Ibid.

58. See in this context the discussion of the CSCE in Chapter 11.

59. The Academy for Social Sciences attached to the Central Committee of the Socialist Unity Party of the German Democratic Republic and the Basic Values Commission of the Social Democratic Party of the Federal Republic of Germany, "Conflicting Ideologies and Common Security" (mimeo), Berlin/Bonn, 1987. The original German text, "Der Streit der Ideologien und die gemeinsame Sicherheit," can be found in *Politik Informationsdienst der SPD*, No. 3, August 1987.

60. Ibid.

61. See in this context Max Schmidt and Wolfgang Schwarz, "Das gemeinsame Haus Europa—Realitäten, Herausforderungen, Perspektiven," *IPW-Berichte*, Vol. 17, No. 9, pp. 1–10 and No. 10, pp. 1–11, 1988.

62. "Conflicting Ideologies," op. cit. It should be noted in this context that as détente evolved in the 1980s, the ideological anomalies of current system competition increased and tended to become unmanageable in both East and West. This has produced a legitimation crisis, particularly in the more Westernized East European societies, in which Western values were both lauded as modernizing and progressive and simultaneously damned as capitalist and imperialist. An ideological "cognitive dissonance" related to system cooperation and competition became manifest throughout the West and East. This condition stems from the fact that the repertory of postwar enemy images and ideologies of "anticommunism" and "anti-capitalism" no longer corresponded to changing East-West realities, not to mention popular or elitist aspirations. Several interesting examples of such cognitive dissonance in the case of Hungary are discussed in Lászlo Kiss, *Die Rolle Ungarns im europäischen Sicherheitssystem*, PRIF Research Report, Frankfurt, 1987. See also Daniel Frei, *Perceived Images* (Totowa, N.J.: Rowman and Allanheld, 1986).

63. For an overview of the new wave of protest in the GDR, see Helga Hirsch, Marlies Menge, Joachim Nowrocki, and Gerhard Spörl, "Mit Glasnost gegen die alte Garde," *Die Zeit*, No. 6, February 5, 1988. On changes in the foreign and security policy of the GDR, see Hans-Joachim Spanger, "Die Aussen- and Sicherheitspolitik der DDR auf neuen Wegen," *Friedensforschung Aktuell*, No. 18, Fall 1987, pp. 1–8; Marion Gräfin Dönhoff, "Ob endlich die Zukunft beginnt?" *Die Zeit*, Vol. 42, No. 38, September 4, 1987; Christiane Rix, "Ansätze für eine neue Sicherheitspolitik der DDR," *Hamburger Beiträge*, Heft 10, December 1986, pp. 1–76.

64. See in this context Max Schmidt, "Neue Wege zur Sicherheit in den internationalen Beziehungen," *Aus Politik and Zeitgeschichte*, No. 10, March 4, 1988, pp. 3–10.

CHAPTER 2

The Danger of a Gray-Area Arms Race

Three days after the INF accord was signed, President Reagan announced U.S. plans to strengthen conventional forces and modernize nuclear and chemical weapons before reaching any further arms agreements with Moscow. The administration used the INF Treaty as an occasion to press for strengthening NATO and thus demonstrate continuing commitment to it. Similarly, Secretary of State George Shultz argued that the allies must increase spending on conventional arms and that the only way to reduce conventional forces in the future would be to strengthen them now.[1] This position, which became a familiar administration argument, was formalized (in softer terms) in the NATO communiqué issued at the March summit in Brussels.[2]

Except for the Strategic Arms Reduction Talks (START) on strategic offensive weapons, the Reagan administration's approach to arms control was to delay and go slow. It insisted that the process of nuclear disarmament in Europe be suspended for a time because going further at that point could lead to Western Europe's denuclearization. In particular, the administration opposed talks on cutting or eliminating tactical nuclear weapons with ranges of less than 500 kilometers until progress could be made on reducing conventional arms. But the administration also did not feel the alliance could immediately respond to Moscow's offers on conventional forces (negotiations were planned with the Soviets in Vienna) because the Soviets would not have sufficient incentive to reduce the offensive threat posed by their conventional forces until NATO made a sustained effort to strengthen its conventional capabilities.

Even before the INF Treaty was finally negotiated, U.S. and NATO circles had decided that the alliance would have to strengthen its conventional forces and deploy new nuclear weapons systems to compensate for the withdrawal of ground-launched cruise missiles and Pershing IIs. As one NATO official put it, "Everyone agrees that if we accept the zero option we need compensating measures."[3] At the ministerial meeting of the Defense Planning Committee in May 1987, NATO officials had recommended improvements of both nuclear and conventional forces. The ministers reaffirmed NATO's goal of 3 percent real growth in defense spending and declared that the momentum of NATO's conventional defense initiative, adopted in May 1985, must be maintained. The committee also called for proceeding with the 1983 decision of the Nuclear Planning Group to modernize and upgrade NATO's tactical nuclear force.[4]

These goals were reiterated at the November 1987 meeting of NATO ministers in Monterey, California.[5] The ministers discussed plans that included options for deploying new fighter aircraft, adding air-launched cruise missiles to B-52 and F-111 bombers, equipping NATO's nuclear capable fighter-bombers with the nuclear standoff weapon, the Tactical Air to Surface Missile (TASM), modernizing NATO's ground-launched tactical missiles with ranges less than 500 kilometers and deploying cruise missiles on surface and submarine vessels.[6] Although NATO officials assiduously tried to avoid the impression that they intended to install substitutions for the INF forces that were withdrawn, the program in essence replaced with one hand what the other gave up when Washington accepted the double-zero option. Together, the broad array of measures considered suggested a NATO arms buildup in the gray areas not covered by the INF Treaty: air- and sea-launched cruise missiles, short-range tactical nuclear missiles, medium-range tactical aircraft and bombers, high-tech nuclear missiles, high-tech deep-strike conventional weaponry, and if one considers unofficial NATO encouragement, additional French and British nuclear forces. This proposed build-up suggested that the INF agreement could become for the 1980s what the Strategic Arms Limitation Talks (SALT) were for the 1970s: a prelude to an arms race legitimated by arms control discussion.

NATO Modernization

The tensions and conflicts within NATO in the post-INF period have surrounded its plans for tactical battlefield modernization—plans that call for the replacement of the 70-kilometer-range Lance missiles in West Germany with a 480-kilometer-range nuclear missile. There are 88 Lance launchers with 1200–2000 missiles in Europe, most of which are on West German territory.[7] 600–700 of their warheads are nuclear, the remainder conventional. Prior to the INF Treaty the follow-on to the Lance nuclear missile was to have a range of 250 kilometers. Following the conclusion of the accord, it was decided to increase the range to 450–480 kilometers, placing the Lance's proposed replacement just below the intermediate-range missiles eliminated by the INF Treaty. The United States and Britain viewed the Lance modernization as critical to preserving the credibility of flexible response and to stopping any movement toward denuclearization.[8] They also saw it as necessary to cement West Germany's commitment to NATO. Some NATO officials worried at that time that the West Germans would see Gorbachev as an excuse to "opt out" of the East-West conflict, as one former U.S. official put it.[9] West Germans had a different perspective: They saw their country as being singled out for nuclear destruction because the replacement missiles would explode on German territory. "The shorter the range the deader the Germans," West Germans on both the right and the left were saying.[10] Even prominent conservatives, including Alfred Dregger and Volker Rühe, while rejecting the complete removal of short-range nuclear missiles, supported their reduction to a minimum through the disarmament process. Their position contrasted with that of the West German defense department and the CSU which came out in support of a Lance follow-on. The West German public, however, overwhelmingly rejected any new short-range nuclear missiles and, even more worrisome to NATO officials, favored a triple-zero option that would remove all land-based nuclear missiles below the 500-kilometer range. This would supplement the INF accord's elimination of intermediate-range missiles.

Conflict was averted temporarily with the agreement reached between President Reagan and Chancellor Kohl to delay a decision on Lance modernization.[11] While Kohl reiterated that he opposed the triple-zero option and only favored *reductions* in the numbers of short-range missiles, the Reagan administration, in an unusual spirit of compromise, embraced the West German argument that the alliance must have an overall concept for arms control and arms reduction before it could move forward with Lance modernization. This compromise, however, did not in any way resolve the underlying conflict or, for that matter, Kohl's dilemma in West Germany, where government approval for Lance modernization could spell defeat for his CDU-CSU party in the national elections in 1990. It was clear that any decision deploying new Lance missiles would be opposed by the majority of the population. Yet Britain's Prime Minister Margaret Thatcher remained adamant about Lance modernization, as did many U.S. defense officials.

West German opposition to nuclear weapons and flexible response had grown dramatically following NATO's deployment of cruise and Pershing II missiles in 1983. Over 50 percent of the West German public favored unilateral disarmament.[12] This growing opposition extended to a wide spectrum of the German body politic—even former chancellor Helmut Schmidt, once a staunch NATOist. When Schmidt declared that the first nuclear weapons to explode on German soil would result in the surrender of West Germany's armed forces,[13] he struck another blow to the legitimacy of flexible response by publicly stating what had been long accepted in private in West German establishment circles. The position against flexible response and nuclear modernization had been made all the more compelling by Gorbachev's willingness to respond to West German security concerns and to accept asymmetrical reductions of Soviet forces. As one Bonn diplomat described the political climate in West Germany:

The feeling is that we are not under immediate threat of a Soviet invasion. We have to give Mr. Gorbachev the chance to show that he means it when he talks of conventional reductions and restructuring Soviet forces to take on a more defensive role. In such a climate it would be politically impossible to launch into a massive spending spree on modernizing our nuclear conventional weapons.[14]

Many West Germans obviously wondered why they should go forward with the deployment of new Lance missiles when the Soviet Union was offering to eliminate a much large number of its own short-range nuclear missiles. The Soviets offered to remove 1,400 launchers and 6,000 missiles in comparison to NATO's smaller number of launchers and missiles.[15] If implemented, this proposal would create a nuclear-missile-free zone that would greatly reduce the risk of nuclear war.

The proposals for conventional force improvements and greater burden-sharing assumed that Western Europe would increase its defense efforts by cooperating with the United States in the development of high-tech weapons while doing more for basic readiness and manpower. Yet, as more than one West European observer pointed out, the economic, political, and demographic trends in Western Europe pointed dramatically in the other direction—toward significant reductions. The waning fear of a Soviet military threat, the widespread perception that Gorbachev would carry out his program of arms reductions, and the increasing emphasis on investment in nonmilitary technological development was creating a political environment highly unfavorable to Washington's plans.

Despite differences within the alliance, agreement was reached among U.S. and European NATO officials at the Brussels summit on the general need for some NATO modernization.[16] In part, this consensus reflected their awareness that the INF accord threatened both individual and joint military programs. Prime Minister Thatcher declared that it was necessary to create a "firebreak" of modernization programs in order to protect the alliance.[17]

On the basis of official statements, NATO's compensatory programs were viewed in part as an instrument to break the political momentum of denuclearization encouraged by the INF Treaty and by Gorbachev and thus also to hold at bay the pro-détente forces, including European peace movements. This momentum was feared as a threat to more ambitious high-tech military programs—the further development of conventional weapons systems, NATO's Conventional Defense Initiative, and SDI—all of which the Reagan administration saw as essential elements of future Western defense. At the same time, the administration, increasingly aware of the limits on the U.S. military budget, used the occasion of the treaty and the adoption of compensatory measures to press the case for burden sharing. In his December 14 speech to the Center for Strategic and International Studies in Washington, Reagan argued that the nations of Europe must become more equal partners in the NATO alliance.[18] Secretary of Defense Frank Carlucci, while recognizing the budgetary constraints on most NATO members, argued that those countries with relatively strong economies—by implication West Germany—may need to do more for common defense.[19] In particular, Washington asked the West Europeans to spend more to increase their own reserve forces, expand stockpiles of ammunitions, improve infrastructure for receiving quick reinforcements, and contribute to high-tech weapons programs.[20] Moreover, in contrast to their critical position several years before, U.S. officials began to encourage recent West European efforts to strengthen the alliance's European pillar. General John Galvin, Allied Supreme Commander, gave his blessing to bilateral Franco–West German military cooperation, and the administration dropped its earlier objections to the revival of the WEU.[21]

The most authoritative statement of the U.S. position under the Reagan administration is found in Carlucci's report to Congress about support of NATO in the 1990s.[22] Prepared partly to reassure potential critics of the INF Treaty that NATO could maintain its strategy of flexible response without Pershing IIs and cruise missiles, the report detailed the weapons systems that the United States was pursuing under NATO's modernization program. In addition, it highlighted the Pentagon's emphasis on deep-strike, highly accurate conventional weaponry and on "competitive strategies" whereby NATO would seek to exploit Warsaw Pact weaknesses through its own strengths in technology and tactics. In this regard, the report reaffirmed that the "achievement of a modern Follow-on Forces Attack (FOFA) capability complemented by vital offensive and defensive counter-air forces, as well as command and control, and active and passive measures for dealing with the combined air-and-missile threat must remain priority objectives.[23] Although the report also mentioned more traditional defensive measures, such as tank barriers and combat readiness, its overall emphasis on advanced conventional munitions capable of striking Warsaw Pact territory would give the alliance a distinctly more offensive military posture.[24] The development of air and ballistic missile defense systems at the theater and strategic levels would add to that offensive character, because they would act as a shield for NATO's deep-strike nuclear and conventional capability.

The report also argued that "reductions can help improve stability but cannot in themselves achieve stability."[25] It made clear that NATO's planned conventional and nuclear modernization is not contingent upon or subject to the process of arms control or arms reduction. Moreover, the report reinforced the Reagan administration's negotiating posture on conventional arms—that NATO resolve in maintaining its conventional strength is a prerequisite for successful arms control and that "any Warsaw Pact reductions should be large and highly asymmetrical."[26] "Small reductions, or less asymmetrical ones," the report argued, "would simply make the conventional force balance worse and more unstable."[27] Despite some controversial elements, such as its recommendations for deploying chemical weapons, there was general bipartisan support during the 1988 presidential election campaign for the main features of the Carlucci plan.[28]

The program of Senator Sam Nunn shared many of the assumptions of the Pentagon plan: the inviolability of flexible response, the need for nuclear modernization and conventional force improvements, the stress on high-tech weaponry and competitive strategies (or what Nunn called "technological leapfrogging"), and the necessity of greater burden-sharing and cooperative weapons development.[29] Nunn placed more emphasis on "bold and innovative" conventional arms control proposals and criticized the Reagan administration for its delay in developing a conventional arms control program, but he favored the dual-track approach of force improvements and negotiations.[30] Nunn also advocated a third track of public education, designed partly to help Americans and Europeans get over what he considered their nuclear allergy and growing trust of the Soviets. Although Nunn's proposals for thinning out combat units in Western Europe were innovative by U.S. standards and dovetailed with some West European ideas, his commitment to nuclear modernization and deep-strike weaponry differed significantly from the thinking of many European advocates of reductions and common security. The ultimate goal of the Nunn plan was not disarmament or common security but merely a reduction of NATO and Warsaw Pact forces to make the military situation more stable and favorable to the United States. Similar programs were put forth by avowedly bipartisan study groups.[31]

U.S.–West European Arms Competition

As already noted, the INF agreement increased anxieties in Western Europe's defense establishments about the region's security,[32] a reaction linked to the apprehension that Washington was moving in several directions simultaneously.[33] But uncertainties also were linked to the fact that Western Europe's defense establishments and pro-military interests have their own high-tech agendas that could propel them into a gray-area offensive-defensive arms race with the United States. West Europeans sought reassurances from Washington, but were at the same time discussing moves to increase West European autonomy.[34]

The U.S. emphasis on compensatory measures was also intended to demonstrate U.S. political will to continue to support a variety of complex and expensive military programs, which have come under increasing political and fiscal pressure independent of the INF agreement. Some of these projects involve U.S.–West European contracts and memorandums of understanding and would require for their realization West European R&D and procurement support. In many cases this became problematic (or threatened in the future to become so) not only because of Western Europe's cuts in defense outlays[35] but also because of its increasing reluctance to purchase U.S. equipment rather than supporting its own high-tech arms firms. Spain's insistence in 1987 that the U.S. reduce its tactical aircraft based on Spanish territory and for a phased withdrawal of these forces is a case in point. This conflict was not merely about security but also concerned Spain's stake in the development of the West European fighter aircraft that will compete against its U.S. counterpart.[36] Such conflicts have led to greater joint efforts to reduce tension between the U.S. and West European arms firms, but here too domestic political, special-interest, and fiscal limits on both sides of the Atlantic have hampered collaboration.[37] The following brief discussion of several weapons systems illustrates this point.

Weapons and Procurement

The Patriot missile. Favored by the United States for both European antiaircraft and tactical missile defense, the U.S. Patriot missile is a multipurpose system for the Federal Republic and the subject of the U.S.–West German Patriot-Roland Missile Treaty approved by the Bundestag in January 1985.[38] By the early 1990s, the U.S. Army, the West German Bundeswehr, and the Dutch air force are supposed to acquire 82 Patriot batteries. Over 5,112 Patriot missiles are scheduled to be deployed in the Federal Republic alone, with approximately half controlled by the Bundeswehr and the other half by the United States.[39] The full complement of Patriots on West German soil will then number five times as many missiles in the Nike systems the Patriot is to replace.

The Patriots have advantages over the Nike system: They are extremely mobile, have a non-nuclear warhead, and reach a speed of Mach 6; although they lack an antitactical ballistic missile (ATBM) capability, they can eliminate cruise missiles. The Patriot also can be upgraded with an additional booster, a feature discussed prior to the INF Treaty as a potential counterweapon effective in a point defense mode against Soviet intermediate- and short-range missiles. In 1985 U.S. General Wagner pointed out: "The Patriot self-defense program is designed to give it a capability against SS-21s and SS-22s . . . Preliminary studies show that with extensive modification they can be upgraded and given a capability against SS-22s and the Advanced Cruise Missile threat."[40] Prior to the INF Treaty, a two-phase upgrade program was planned to turn the Patriot into an ATBM.[41] The first upgraded version was tested as an ATBM by the United States in September 1986 at the White Sands Missile Range. A Patriot rocket, under highly artificial conditions, successfully intercepted a Lance rocket considered roughly equivalent to a Soviet SS-21. The phase-two upgraded Patriot is to be available in the early 1990s.[42]

The Hawk missile. An example of intra-NATO military-industrial cooperation and competition, the Hawk missile is scheduled for a number of upgrades in the coming years by its U.S. manufacturer, Raytheon. If upgraded to an ATBM capability, the Hawk could be integrated into a larger battle control system that would include SDI-related terminal image radars and surveillance aircraft. The technology includes the airborne early warning (AEW) system and the airborne optical adjunct (AOA) system. The AOA is being developed within the framework of SDI. The West German high-tech firm MBB is participating in the AOA's development.

West European Procurement

The Independent European Program Group (IEPG), which was set up to encourage greater West European defense cooperation, came to the conclusion that even the planned improvements would leave the Hawk unable to counter what West European defense ministers, prior to the INF Treaty, predicted would be the Soviet threat at the end of the 1990s. Required, according to the IEPG's view, would be a surface-to-air missile system effective against "very fast and flexible aircraft, cruise missiles traveling at Mach-plus speeds, a variety of advanced stand-off weapons and tactical ballistic missiles."[43] This expected gap in West European force structures led the IEPG to recommend the development of a West European surface-to-air missile (SAM) that could replace the Hawk by the late 1990s. This proposal competed with the U.S. suggestion to replace the Hawks in Western Europe in the late 1990s with a further upgraded version of the Patriot. The IEPG rejected this solution because of its high costs, which were viewed as prohibitive, given the large number of missiles assumed to be necessary for this extended air defense role.[44]

The IEPG's decision is an example of its efforts to "Europeanize" military R&D and procurement. The evolving discussion over the West European alternative to the upgraded Patriot could develop into a more serious transatlantic controversy because the U.S. Defense Department and the Strategic Defense Initiative Organization (SDIO) have plans to make upgraded versions of the Patriot and Hawk into a multifunctional "family of weapons" designed to serve a variety of different missions. These would include traditional air defense; extended air defense against cruise missiles; an ATBM capability against tactical ballistic missiles; and an offensive counter-air (OCA) role for "deep strikes" in the framework of FOFA. This agenda was summed up by the U.S. Defense Department in 1984: "In the long term we will be able to counter the entire range of tactical threats through active and passive counter-measures and counter-strikes."[45] Although the INF Treaty has constrained a number of the missiles' potential functions originally envisioned by the Pentagon, it is likely that the planned Patriot and Hawk upgrade programs will be modified in order not to violate the accord.

The British officially endorsed the NATO Defense Planning Committee's decision in May 1986 to study ways of upgrading NATO air defense, including defenses against tactical missiles, as part of the larger NATO program of improving conventional defenses. As a member of the IEPG, Britain was involved in the group's deliberations on the replacement of the Hawk surface-to-air missile and plans for acquisition of anticruise and ATBM systems.[46] Like France and West Germany, Britain was considering various cooperation schemes, but it had less commitment to developing ATBM systems prior to the INF Treaty because of constraints on its defense budget.[47] The government thus decided in May 1987 to block a planned increase in military R&D outlays. Nevertheless, British companies have received SDI research contracts,[48] including for participation in programs for West European missile defense, although these have in part been put into question by the INF Treaty.

In the Federal Republic, a consortium of weapons firms headed by MBB is developing the MFS 2000 air defense system, which the manufacturers maintain would be more advanced than the upgraded Hawk.[49] The system, according to its West German proponents, will not only outstrip the Hawk in air defense performance but will cost considerably less per unit,[50] which will allow for the procurement of far greater numbers of missile batteries than would be possible with the considerably more expensive Patriot. The MFS was designed to be deployed together with Patriots having an ATBM capability. The MBB development of the MFS is closely linked to the larger plans of the West German military-industrial establishment. In the words of one analyst, "The development of a MFS . . . could place German industry in the international technological forefront in a number of different fields (ultra high-speed projectiles, modern radar systems and high-speed calculators)."[51]

Conclusions

The INF Treaty marked a historic break in the pattern of postwar arms racing, but its effect on the future of the arms race remains ambiguous. On the one hand, the treaty covers only two classes of intermediate-range missiles in a large, expanding inventory of emerging military systems, a few of which were described in this chapter. On the other hand, the treaty has raised fundamental questions concerning the future of French, British, and U.S. military R&D and procurement programs. The post-INF arms race reflects in this sense the competitive antagonism between the two models of security: the postwar, status quo based on arms racing and military technological competition versus the uneven movement in the direction of disarmament and growing East-West cooperation.

The INF Treaty removes some of the justification for the development of ATBM and other related systems. The thought of removing ATBM programs from the Western European-U.S. arms agenda also raises questions concerning the wisdom of retaining advanced types of missiles for air defense, since these are technologically closely related to ATBMs. Just as the development of ATBM systems implies extended air defense, so too the arms control elimination of one suggests, or even makes imperative, the elimination of the other, if a fully effective verification and an anti-breakout regime is to be established. The logic of the INF Treaty in this context consisted of extending the "single zero option" to eliminate intermediate-range missiles with a 1000–5500 kilometer range to the "double zero option" of eliminating shorter range missiles with a 500–1000 kilometer range as well. The next step would be a third zero that would constrain short-range systems below the 500 kilometer range.

This chapter showed that Western European R&D programs for extended air defense and other related military systems are being pursued in competition and ambiguous concert with the United States. Such "cooperative competition" and "competitive cooperation" has become a driving force of Western conventional and strategic military programs. The arms programs discussed in this chapter suggest that the plans for missile upgrades and new systems and the efforts of the major Western European suppliers to achieve or maintain a forefront position could very well intensify competition among Western defense establishments in the coming years. If not constrained, the result could be additional, costly programs pursued by the United States, Britain, France and West Germany.

The new circumstances are producing political fragmentation and erosion of the postwar pattern of arms racing. Increasing competition in defense production among Western partners may also paradoxically increase as a result of the diminishing Soviet threat. The diminution of this threat is already having centrifugal effects on NATO unity, as discussed in Chapter 1, and giving NATO states more options: They can pursue military-industrial strategies with less heed paid to the will of the United States and under less of the pressure to stand unified that flowed from traditional perceptions of a Soviet threat and the enemy image of communism. The resulting competition could lead to greater fragmentation in arms production among NATO powers—or it could lead in the direction of more far-reaching arms agreements precisely to avoid a more anarchic arms race with unpredictable effects on East-West détente.

Notes

1. Elaine Sciolino, "Shultz Asks NATO to Raise Defense Spending on Non-Atom Arms," *New York Times*, December 12, 1987.
2. John Fialka and Gerald Seib, "NATO Leaders Finish Summit in Unified Stand," *Wall Street Journal*, March 4, 1988.
3. Dan Charles, "NATO Looks for Arms Control Loopholes," *Bulletin of Atomic Scientists*, Vol. 43, No. 7, September 1987, pp. 7–10.

4. Ibid.

5. R. Jeffrey Smith, "NATO Evaluates Its Nuclear Strength After Medium-Range Arms Are Gone," *Washington Post*, November 3, 1987.

6. Charles, op. cit.; Richard Halloran, "U.S. General Proposes Modifying B-52's to Take Conventional Arms," *International Herald Tribune*, September 19-20, 1987; Robert Mauthner, "NATO Stresses Urgent Need for Build-up in Conventional Forces," *Financial Times*, May 22, 1987; David Buchan, "Respinning the Arms Web," *Financial Times*, November 3, 1987.

7. Mathias Dembinsky, et al., *No End to Modernization?* PRIF Reports 6–7 Frankfurt: Peace Research Institute Frankfurt, 1989, p. 5–6. The U.S. Army Tactical Missile (ATACM) is considered a likely candidate for the Lance replacement. In 1988 the Department of Defense selected the Multiple Launch Rocket System (MLRS) as the launcher. Although Congress rejected a request by the Army to develop a new nuclear warhead for the ATACM, it approved preliminary studies. See William Arkin et al., "Nuclear Weapons" in *SIPRI Yearbook 1988* (Oxford: Oxford University Press, 1989), pp. 3–48.

8. See in this context François Heisbourg, "Nach dem INF-Abkommen von Washington: Fur eine Weiterentwicklung der Grundlagen des Atlantischen Bündnisses," *Europa-Archiv*, Vol. 43, No. 5, 1988, pp. 119–128. On British as well as European positions on modernization and denuclearization, see House of Commons, Foreign Affairs Committee, *The Political Impact of the Process of Arms Control and Disarmament* (July 20, 1988).

9. Andrew Nagorski, "A New Page in Relations Between the East and West," *Newsweek*, January 25, 1988.

10. See in this context Erich Hauser, "Brussels NATO Summit: Outlook Overcast," *German Tribune*, March 6, 1988 (reprinted from *General Anzeiger*, February 24, 1988). For a comprehensive overview of the positions on Lance modernizations of West German political parties, see PRIF Reports 6–7, op. cit., pp. 9–18.

11. Julie Johnson, "Unity Stressed at NATO Summit But Tough Issues Are Unsolved," *New York Times*, March 4, 1988.

12. Nagorski, op. cit.; see also Elisabeth Noelle-Neumann, "Wenn das Gefühl der Bedrohung schwindet," *Frankfurter Allgemeine Zeitung*, July 22, 1988.

13. See in this context Robert Keatley, "Schmidt Would Disband NATO, Establish a Franco-German Force," *Wall Street Journal*, June 16, 1987.

14. Michael Evans, "Europe Cool on Pentagon High-tech Arms Report," *The London Times*, January 13, 1988. See also in this context Noelle-Neumann, op. cit.

15. Dennis Gormley, "'Triple Zero' and Soviet Military Strategy," *Arms Control Today*, Vol. 18, No. 1, January/February 1988, pp. 17–20.

16. Fialka and Seib, op. cit.

17. Christoph Bertram, "NATO Can Afford to Take Its Time over Next Move in East-West Ties," *German Tribune*, February 21, 1988.

18. "Reagan Hails INF Accord, Praises CSIS," *CSIS News*, January/February 1988, p. 1.

19. *Support of NATO Strategy in the 1990s* (Washington, D.C.: Department of Defense, 1988). Hereafter "Carlucci Report."

20. Ibid.; David Abshire, "NATO's Conventional Improvement Effort: An Ongoing Imperative," *Washington Quarterly*, Vol. 10, No. 2, Spring 1987, pp. 49–59.

21. "NATO Chief Backs Paris-Bonn Accord," *Financial Times*, February 11, 1988.

22. "Carlucci Report," op. cit.
23. Ibid., p. xii. In January the Commission on Integrated Long-Term Strategy set up by the Reagan administration also emphasized a FOFA approach for U.S. military policy in its report *Discriminate Deterrence* (Washington, D.C.: 1988). The report also lays stress on the role of using new technologies for combining nuclear and conventional, offensive and defensive, strategic and substrategic systems for counteroffensive operations deep into enemy territory and capabilities for "discriminate nuclear strikes."
24. "Carlucci Report," op. cit., p. xii.
25. Ibid.
26. Ibid., p. III-7.
27. Ibid., p. x.
28. See in this context Gerald Seib, "Candidates' Call for Allies to Share Defense Costs Raise Complex Questions About World Role," *Wall Street Journal*, March 2, 1988; Morton Kondracke, "Make 'Em Pay," *New Republic*, October 12, 1988.
29. Senator Sam Nunn, "The American-Soviet Disarmament Negotiations and Their Consequences for NATO" (Speech to the Wehrkunde Conference), February 7, 1988; see also Sam Nunn, "NATO Challenges and Opportunities: A Three-Track Approach," *NATO Review*, Vol. 35, No. 3, June 1987, pp. 1–7; Abshire, op. cit.
30. Nunn, ibid., 1988.
31. See in this context The Aspen Strategy Study Group and the European Strategy Group, *After the INF Agreement: Conventional Forces and Arms Control in European Security* (Lanham, Md.: University Press of America, 1988).
32. See in this context Jonathan Dean, "The INF Agreement: Pluses and Minuses for Western Security," *Arms Control Today*, Vol. 17, No. 6, July/August 1987, pp. 3–10; Werner Weidenfeld, "Neuorganization der Sicherheit Westeuropas," *Europa-Archiv*, Vol. 42, No. 9, 1987, pp. 259–268.
33. Weidenfeld, ibid; Hans Günter Brauch, "From SDI to EDI—Elements of a European Defence Architecture," in Hans Günter Brauch, ed., *Star Wars and European Defence* (New York: St. Martin's Press, 1987), pp. 436–499. See also in this context Ernst-Otto Czempiel, "SDI and NATO: The Case of the Federal Republic of Germany," in Sanford Lakoff and Randy Willoughby, eds., *Strategic Defense and the Western Alliance* (Lexington, Mass.: Lexington Books, 1987), p. 155. Pierre Lellouche has pointed to SDI's impact on the defense consensus in France and Britain:

> France and Britain have invested the most effort during the past twenty-five to thirty years in nuclear deterrence as the basis for their security policy, and they were the primary beneficiaries of the Anti-Ballistic Missile Treaty. The reintroduction of defence, particularly on the massive scale contemplated in the SDI programme, directly threatens the very lifeline of their defense policy as well as the existing defense consensus at home (particularly in France).

Pierre Lellouche, "SDI and the Atlantic Alliance," *SAIS Review*, Vol. 6, No. 3, Summer-Fall 1985, pp. 67–80, cited in Brauch, ibid. For a critique of nuclear deterrence, see Elmar Schmähling, "Damit kündigen die USA faktisch ihre atomare Schutzgarantie auf," *Frankfurter Rundschau*, March 10, 1988.
34. Weidenfeld, op. cit.; Michael Howard, "A European Perspective on the

Reagan Years," *Foreign Affairs*, Vol. 55, No. 3 (*America and the World 1987–1988*), pp. 478–493; John Baylis, "NATO Strategy: The Case for a New Strategic Concept," *International Affairs*, Vol. 64, No. 1, Winter 1987/88, pp. 43–63; See also in this context Pascal Boniface and François Heisbourg, *La Puce, les hommes et la Bombe* (Paris: Hachette, 1986), pp. 78–116.

35. François Heisbourg, "Conventional Defense: Europe's Constraints and Opportunities," in Andrew Pierre, ed., *The Conventional Defense of Europe: New Technologies and New Strategies* (New York: Council on Foreign Relations, 1986), pp. 71–111.

36. David Buchan, "A Dog Fight Between Good Friends," *Financial Times*, November 6, 1987; cf. Peter Bruce, "Bonn May Order Tornadoes," *Financial Times*, November 8, 1987.

37. On West European defense cooperation, see Trevor Taylor, *Defence, Technology and International Integration* (London: Frances Pinter, 1982); Karl Kaiser and Pierre Lellouche, eds., *Deutsch-französische Sicherheitspolitik. Auf dem Wege zur Gemeinsamkeit* (Bonn: Europa Union Verlag, 1986). Michael Lucas, "Zur Dialektik von transatlantischer Konkurrenz und Kooperation in der Rüstungsproduktion und Militärforschung," in Die Grünen, ed., *Euromilitarismus* (Bonn: Die Grünen, 1985), pp. 120–150.

38. Wolfgang Bartels, *Eine Rakete, die uns teur zu stehen kommt* (Bonn; Die Friedensliste, 1986); Wolfram von Raven, "Das Patriot-Roland-Abkommen, Drei Fliegen mit einer Klappe," *Europäische Wehrkunde*, No. 8, 1984, pp. 460–466; see also "Patriot Air Defense for the 1980s and Beyond," prospectus published by the Patriot manufacturer, Raytheon Corporation.

39. Bartels, ibid.; Thomas Enders, Raketenabwehr als Teil einer erweiterten NATO-Luftverteidigung, Interne Studien, No. 2, mimeo, Konrad Adenauer-Stiftung, 1986, p. 76.

40. Cited in Erwin Horn, "Es ist nur ein europäischer Ableger des SDI-Projektes," *Frankfurter Rundschau*, April 5, 1986 (this and subsequent translations of passages from Horn back into English by M.L.). See also in this context Brauch, op. cit., pp. 455, 469–470.

41. Bartels, op. cit.

42. Enders, op. cit., p. 80; Horn, ibid.

43. Enders, ibid.

44. Enders, op. cit.

45. Horn, op. cit. On the linkages between FOFA and OCA, see also Heinrich Buch, "The Debate in Germany: A Political View," Chapter 9 in Marlies ter Borg and Wim Smit, ed., *Tactical Missile Defense in Europe* (Amsterdam: Free University Press, 1987), pp. 48–63.

46. Sheena Phillips, "Britain, France and the Future of ATBM," Chapter 7 in Borg, Smit, ibid., pp. 94–112.

47. Ibid.

48. Ibid.; *Financial Times*, June 25, 1986; see also "SDI Contractor Study," *F.A.S. Public Interest Report*, Vol. 40, No. 4, April 1987.

49. Enders, op. cit., p. 81.

50. Ibid.

51. Ibid., p. 82.

CHAPTER 3

SDI and
NATO Modernization

U.S. proponents of a military buildup to compensate for the impact of the INF accord also urged that certain of the Strategic Defense Initiative R&D programs be integrated into West European defense efforts. These U.S. suggestions predated the INF accord and complemented the proposals by former West German Defense Minister Manfred Wörner made in 1986 for a West European extended air and tactical missile defense.[1]

Senator Pete Wilson, for example, argued that near-term deployment of SDI systems in Western Europe would be an important contribution to the region's defense. He went even further: "If the United States is seen as nurturing defense technologies that could be applied to the problem of Europe's defense but are withheld because of obscure political theories, then our allies will legitimately question not only SDI and its implications for them, but the larger issue of the U.S. commitment to NATO."[2] Arguing from the point of view of the benefits for the United States of applying SDI to West European missile and air defense, Wilson also maintained that the near-term European option would be an effective gradualist tactic for improving the domestic political prospects of SDI: "Once allies and Congressional skeptics can be convinced of the near-term and tangible contribution by SDI to urgent U.S. and allied security interests, they will have less cause to withhold political support or resources to the implementation of the larger design of a strategic defense."[3]

The SDI-related systems proposed as possible near-term options for a West European ATBM system include the 2500-mile-range exoatmospheric reentry vehicle interceptor subsystem (ERIS); the 15- to 45-kilometer-range high endoatmospheric interceptor (HEDI); and the very short 6-kilometer-range low endoatmospheric interceptor (LEDI).[4]

The technological continuity between strategic missile defense and tactical missile and air defense forms the technological bridge between SDI and current West European and transatlantic efforts to develop and eventually deploy tactical missile and advanced air defense systems. Air and tactical missile defense systems and subsystems can serve as a testbed for the ground-based segments of SDI.[5] That the Pentagon has intended to develop missile defenses in tandem in the United States and Western Europe is suggested by numerous official statements. According to one study, "Currently available radars, air defense missiles and control systems could provide the basis for a near-term theater anti-tactical ballistic missile system that eventually would become part of an overall Western strategic defense system."[6]

The Pentagon has viewed transatlantic collaboration on tactical missile defense and related systems for Western Europe as the preferred path for West European companies to participate in SDI.[7] The countries that have signed SDI memorandums of understanding are collaborating with the United States on tactical missile defense R&D programs.[8]

Strategic Defense and NATO Substrategic Weapons Systems

U.S. SDI efforts are also linked to the NATO strategy of follow-on forces attack (FOFA) based on "deep-strike" interdiction behind enemy lines.[9] Its aim is to halt second echelon forces either preemptively or in the early stages of a conflict, with emphasis on conventional rather than nuclear weapons.[10] Conceived partly as a framework for applying and further developing advances in modern electronics, information technologies, computer sciences, and new types of non-nuclear explosives, FOFA has been offically adopted by NATO as a long-term goal. Since 1980 the Pentagon has underlined the need to meet the increasing Soviet conventional threat by improving NATO's air defense capabilities in the context of the FOFA doctrine. Extensive work on offensive counter-air (OCA) strategy was carried out in the United States in order to integrate it operationally with tactical point defense against aircraft and missiles.[11] The 1986 policy guideline, "Aerospace Application Study-20," emphasized in this context the need for active defenses against Soviet short-range missiles. Passive, active, and offensive counter-air are viewed as three levels in a defensive-offensive architecture of deterrence and flexible response.[12] On the upper levels, strikes would be launched against the enemy's short-range missiles. The joint surveillance and target attack radar system (JSTARS) and the joint tactical missile system (JTACMS) are systems designed to contribute to West European defense by increasing the range and accuracy of tactical missiles and forming part of OCA capabilities. These would be supported by antitactical missile defenses.

Offensive air strikes would require—or certainly greatly benefit from—space-based sensors and communications systems of the type that would functionally overlap with SDI-related battle management systems. These would back up and enhance the effectiveness of the counter-air or antitactical missile defenses by increasing NATO's capabilities in communications, surveillance, and tracking.[13]

The concept that emerges from these different programs is that of an escalation ladder with no missing rungs that ascends from the ground level of conventional warfare to the extraterrestrial reaches of SDI. Defensive and offensive, tactical and strategic, conventional and nuclear systems would be interlinked in a single all-purpose shield-and-sword. Each level of defense and offense, according to this model, would serve as an escalator to the next higher rung in the ladder and at the same time function as a backup to the levels below.

This military and technological vision suggests why NATO defense establishments were initially resistant to the prospect of an INF accord. By removing intermediate-range missiles, the double-zero agreement removes what Pentagon experts call the "mid-level escalatory potential" in the chain of escalation envisioned for West European defense.[14] NATO ministers agreed that the INF Treaty would necessitate compensatory measures to fill in the scrapped rungs in the escalation ladder as well as to prevent political and military support for the military buildup as a whole from further unraveling.[15]

The SDI Agreements

The United States has signed SDI agreements with Britain, the Federal Republic of Germany, Italy, Israel, and Japan. Prior to these accords, the SDIO promised billions of dollars worth of contracts, but West European governments and large corporations had more or less accepted that the United States was not ready to share substantial amounts of technological know-how or budgetary resources with West European allies. Barriers to extensive SDI contracts with foreign firms, universities, and government agencies include the ABM Treaty, restrictive contracting regulations and practices of the Pentagon, competition with U.S. firms, and national security considera-tions.[16] After two years of negotiations, foreign contracts accounted for less than 1 percent of the SDI program. The authors of a study on allied participation, carried out by the Federation of American Scientists, describe three phases of West European participation in SDI and explain why foreign collaboration has been meager:

> So far only seventeen foreign entities have been involved with SDI
> projects. These include foreign government agencies, foreign
> universities, as well as foreign corporations. . . . The participation of
> non-U.S. firms in the SDI program has gone through a complex
> evolution, with three distinct periods. In the first phase, the Reagan
> Administration tried to sell the Allies on the vision of a perfect
> defense. When this failed, the second phase attempted to buy support
> from Allied contractors. But the lack of significant industrial base in
> Europe effectively precluded significant alliance participation in the
> SDI. Thus the third phase of alliance management has focused on

anti-tactical ballistic missile defense, and work on these technologies is perhaps within reach of Allied companies.[17]

Although contracts with U.S. allies continued to represent a small percentage of SDI spending, individual West European corporations and research institutes (including leading electronics and military-industrial firms in Britain, the Federal Republic, Italy, and France) received contracts and vied for additional work from the SDIO. West German firms and research laboratories participating in SDI, for example, received $47 million worth of contracts. Contracts let in Britain amounted to $34 million, in Israel $6.2 million, in France $5.2 million, and in Italy $1.5 million.[18]

Although the agreements were secret, important details of the British memorandum were aired and the text of the West German–U.S. agreement was leaked to a Cologne newspaper.[19] The document's publication was an embarrassment to the Bonn government—not only because of the breach of security but also because the terms of the agreement were sharply criticized as compromising West German economic and military-industrial interests.

An important purpose of the SDI agreements was to lay down general ground rules of transatlantic cooperation in areas of common military-industrial concern within NATO and the Western Alliance. These include SDI-related military R&D, technology transfer, the civilian application of military, scientific, technological, and engineering data, and the protection of patents.

The U.S.-British memorandum of understanding on SDI replaced a 1975 memorandum that governed defense trade between the two countries.[20] The West German defense magazine *Wehrtechnik* considered the U.S.–West German agreement in a similar light—as an instrument for placing traditional export-import technology transfer and other forms of U.S.–West European defense cooperation on a firmer juridical and political-economic basis.[21]

An important motive for West European firms to participate in SDI was their expectation that such involvement would further their efforts in the development of new technologies for conventional warfare. SDI was viewed as a larger framework for weapons development—less for "Star Wars" than for what was designated as the evolving "battlefield of the future."

Here it is possible to separate different factors that played a role in West European interest in SDI. Though aware of the reluctance of U.S. firms, the Pentagon, and political constituencies in the United States to allow large amounts of U.S. military know-how to be transferred to U.S. allies, leading high-tech West European firms (such as MBB in West Germany and Matra in France) expected a sufficient quid pro quo in technology transfer, coproduction, and access to U.S. markets to take the calculated risk of entering into SDI contracts. Many of the West European SDI partners have long-standing relationships with U.S. firms; SDI-related contracts thus represented a continuation of commercial ties that foreign firms considered politically and economically in their interest to maintain, even if the returns on cooperation were not to meet their initial expectations. These companies also felt they had developed sufficient expertise in advanced technology to hold their own with the United States in certain key areas and therefore insisted on what they considered a fair deal with the SDIO and individual U.S. companies.[22] Moreover, the West Europeans' experience of technology transfer and coproduction with the United States made them more skillful in their dealings with the Pentagon and U.S. corporations. They were also in a better position to proceed independently in R&D projects (if necessary to avoid the risks of technological dependence or unfavorable contracts) than they had been at any other time during the postwar era. These factors provided certain West European firms with an important set of bargaining chips to achieve close and equitable cooperation in selected areas.

In contrast to the large and highly prestigious West European high-tech firms, middle- and small-sized companies did significantly less well in gaining access to SDI contracts. Nor were the prospects favorable that this would change, given Pentagon contracting regulations and practices, the U.S. preference for U.S. firms, and growing protectionism.

SDI and Conventional Weapons Development

In the U.S.–West German SDI memorandum of understanding, apart from direct SDI-related cooperation concerning strategic missile defense, special attention was given to the development of conventional weapons. Both powers agreed "to exchange know-how in those mutually agreed areas of SDI research and those considered useful for improving conventional defense, in particular, air defense."[23] An article in *Wehrtechnik* explained it this way:

> In all the projects which will be developed in the framework of the SDI research agenda we can expect military spin-off. In particular, this will be the case in the development of sensors, information technology and lasers. Taken together, the military benefits from the SDI research program will advance conventional military technologies in such a way that new, revolutionary weapon systems will result.[24]

The author went on to list the following dual-use (civilian and military) technologies in which West German participation in SDI research programs could, in his view, revolutionize the conventional and dual-capable (nuclear and conventional) weapons systems of NATO and the Bundeswehr:

> Sensor technology with integrated signal processing will create new standards in optronics and produce a new quality in munitions and submunitions.
> New computer hard- and soft-ware with components characterized

by very large-scale integration and very high-speed integrated circuits, complex circuit architectures, artificial intelligence, expert systems and new programing languages will make possible new forms of command, control and communication (C3).

The technologies of high-speed missiles and electro-magnetic rail-guns will endow air-defense with an ATM/ATBM capability.

High-energy laser technology will have application for weapon systems for defense against aircraft, helicopters and guided missiles.[25]

A Post-INF Conventional Buildup and SDI

The links between SDI and substrategic conventional weapons programs for Western Europe raised a number of sticky questions concerning the position of Democratic and Republican defense experts who were critical of SDI but who continued to support the current conventional buildup in Western Europe as an alternative to SDI. Senator Sam Nunn called for "revolutionary conventional force improvements" and "leapfrogging" the Soviet Union by waging an economic-technological war in which high-tech military breakthroughs would force the Soviets to devote more resources to its military competition with the West.[26] U.S. programs such as the Balanced Technology Initiative and the Conventional Defense Initiative were designed to promote closer military R&D cooperation between the United States and its West European allies. Senator Nunn's ambiguous position was reflected in his changing position on SDI. In January 1988 he called for a "small" SDI in the form of "a limited system for protecting against accidental and unauthorized missile launches."[27]

An important U.S. goal of cooperation, particularly evident in the period prior to the INF Treaty, was to apply SDI systems and components to European NATO conventional improvement programs and thus implement FOFA more effectively and expeditiously. The ambiguity in Senator Nunn's pre-1988 position that emphasized a conventional military buildup partly as an alternative to SDI was that the technological and military-operational intersection of SDI and FOFA formed a gray area—a fertile ground for a destablizing strategic-substrategic arms race. Conventional improvements in the framework of FOFA, particularly in the area of air defense, would, according to proponents, tend to encourage and in important respects overlap with work on SDI. Conversely, advances in SDI-related R&D would in many areas be applicable to and thus also could politically fuel the conventional weapons programs that leading anti-SDI defense experts on Capitol Hill were staunchly defending. Lack of arms control constraints in the one area would tend to become a gray-area window for the other.

In sum, many of the planned conventional force improvements were hardly a clear alternative to SDI because they could facilitate the further development of a number of important SDI programs. Senator Nunn's call for a "small" SDI was therefore consistent with his support for a conventional buildup.

Given European NATO and separate national R&D programs in advanced air defense and antitactical missile technologies, there were a number of advantages from the official U.S. point of view in the use of transatlantic cooperation to promote SDI. Although the Federal Republic, for example, did not support the strategic aims of SDI, Manfred Wörner had called for developing a West European air defense and antitactical missile defense system that would complement SDI.[28] Wörner's initiative seemed at the time—before the INF Treaty—to dovetail with military interests of other West European NATO powers and France, which were calling for greater "Europeanization" of military high technology and using the framework of cooperation with the United States on SDI and conventional improvement programs for achieving this end.

Notes

1. Manfred Wörner, "A Missile Defense for NATO Europe," *Strategic Review*, Vol. 14, No. 1, Winter 1986, pp. 13–18.
2. Pete Wilson, "A Missile Defense for NATO: We Must Respond to the Challenge," *Strategic Review*, Vol. 14, No. 2, Spring 1986, pp. 9–15. Cf. Hans Günter Brauch, "From SDI to EDI—Elements of a European Defense Architecture," in Hans Günter Brauch, ed., *Star Wars and European Defence* (New York: St. Martin's Press, 1987), pp. 436–499.
3. Wilson, ibid.
4. Manfred Hamm and Kim Holmes, "A European Ballistic Missile System: Deterrence and the Conventional Defense of NATO," *Washington Quarterly*, Vol. 10, No. 2, Spring 1987, pp. 61–78.
5. Jürgen Scheffran, "Die Europäische Verteidigungsinitiative-Testfall für SDI," in Dieter Engels, Jürgen Scheffran, and Ekkehard Sieker, eds., *SDI—Falle für Europa* (Cologne: Pahl-Rugenstein, 1987), pp. 271–337; Brauch, op. cit., p. 437ff.
6. "12 Teams of U.S., European Contractors Submit Bids for Missile Defense Study," *Aviation Week and Space Technology* (hereafter *AW & ST*), September 29, 1986.
7. Brendan Greeley, Jr., "Army Missile Intercept Success Spurs SDI Theater Defense Study," *AW & ST*, September 29, 1986.
8. Ibid.; Brauch, op. cit.
9. For a detailed study of FOFA, see Office of Technology Assessment, *New Technologies for NATO, Implementing Follow-On Forces Attack* (hereafter, *OTA Study*) (Washington, D.C.: Government Printing Office, 1987); Günther Baechler and Albert Statz, "EDI, European Defence Initiative: Implications of Missile Defense in Europe for West German Security Policy," *Hamburger Beiträge zur Friedensforschung und Sicherheitspolitik*, Heft 12, December 1986, Chapter 3; Jonathan Dean, *Watershed in Europe* (Lexington, Mass.: Lexington Books, 1987).
10. On the deep-strike strategy, see *OTA Study*, ibid.; Dean, ibid.; Sutton Boyd, John Landry, Malcolm Armstrong, et al., "Deep Attack in Central

Europe," *Survival*, Vol. 24, No. 2, March/April 1984, pp. 50–69. For a critique of FOFA from an Atlanticist viewpoint, see Josef Joffe, *The Limited Partnership* (Cambridge, Mass.: Ballinger, 1987), pp. 156–165. For a Soviet discussion of deep-strike concepts and their relationship to U.S. strategies of global conventional and nuclear war, see "'Conventional War': Strategic Concepts," in Institute of World Economy and International Relations, *1987 Yearbook Disarmament and Security* (Moscow: Novosti Press Agency Publishing House, 1988), pp. 347–368.

11. Baechler and Statz, op. cit., pp. 40–43; Department of the Army, U.S. Army Combined Arms Combat Development Activity, Fort Leavenworth, JATM.SSG: JATM Action Plan, April 30, 1985 (this and other U.S. defense studies are cited in ibid., p. 99).

12. See in this context Michael Feazel, "German Study Encourages Development of Antitactical Ballistic Missiles," *AW & ST*, July 7, 1986. The article gives a brief summary of Thomas Enders, Raketenabwehr als Teil einer erweiterten NATO-Luftverteidigung, Interne Studien No. 2 (mimeo) 1986, Konrad Adenauer-Stiftung, 1986; Brauch, op. cit., pp. 455–459.

13. Hamm and Holmes, op. cit.: Enders, ibid., p. 73. In *Discriminate Deterrence* (Washington, D.C.: 1988), written by the Commission on Long-Term Strategy set up by the Reagan administration, there is a similar emphasis on qualitatively refining the connecting links between different levels of escalation and thereby making possible more "discriminate" application of nuclear and conventional weapons with the help of emerging technology. For a discussion of this aspect of the report, see Marek Thee, "Science and Technology for War and Peace," *Bulletin of Peace Proposals*, Vol. 19, No. 3-4, 1988, pp. 261–292.

14. Donald Cotter, "The Emerging INF Agreement: A Case of Strategic Regression," *Strategic Review*, Vol. 15, No. 3, Summer 1987, pp. 11–19.

15. Dan Charles, "NATO Looks for Loopholes," *Bulletin of Atomic Scientists*, September 1987, pp. 7–10.

16. "SDI Contractor Study," *F.A.S. Public Interest Report*, Vol. 40, No. 4, April 1987 (hereafter *FAS*). See also in this context Michael Lucas, "SDI and Europe," *World Policy Journal*, Vol. 3, No. 2, Spring 1986, pp. 219–249.

17. *FAS*, ibid.

18. Ibid. A useful source on SDI European contracts is Sheena Phillips, "European Report," in *ADIU Report*; see for example Vol. 9, No. 1, January-February 1987. See also Gerald M. Steinberg, ed., *The Domestic Politics of SDI* (Lexington, Mass.: Lexington Books, 1988); on West German firms and SDI, see Wolfgang Bartels, "Das SDI-Rahmenabkommen und die Interessen der westdeutschen Rüstungskonzerne," in Engels et al., op. cit., pp. 229–247.

19. *Der Kölner Express*, April 18, 1986, reprinted in *Frankfurter Rundschau*, April 22, 1986. An English translation, "The West German–American SDI Participation Agreement," with the accompanying document, "An Agreement of Principles Between the Federal Republic of Germany and the Government of the United States of America," can be found in Ivo Daalder, *The SDI Challenge to Europe* (Cambridge, Mass.: Ballinger, 1987), pp. 111–124.

20. Paul Anderson, "British SDI Still Shrouded in Secrecy," *END Journal of European Disarmament*, No. 21, April–May 1986, pp. 6–7. A detailed overview of the British-U.S. collaboration arrangement can be found in "UK Participation in the US SDI Research Programme—Guidelines," prepared by the British Ministry of Defense in unclassified form for free circulation to "government departments, universities, research organizations and industry in the UK" (mimeo).

21. Hans-Heinrich Weise, "Das SDI-Forschungsprogramm," *Wehrtechnik*, Vol. 18, No. 7, July 1986, pp. 34–36.

22. Lucas, op. cit.; Bernd Kubbig, "Aus militärtechnischer Einbahnstrasse wurde keine Zweibahnstrasse," *Frankfurter Rundschau*, March 16, 1988.

23. Weise, op. cit.

24. Ibid. See also in this context Jean-François Delpech, "New Technologies, the United States and Europe: Implications for Western Security and Economic Growth," *Atlantic Community Quarterly*, Vol. 25, No. 1, Spring 1987, pp. 47–63.

25. Ibid.

26. Sam Nunn, "NATO Challenges and Opportunities: A Three-Track Approach," *NATO Review*, Vol. 35, No. 3, June 1987, pp. 1–7.

27. Michael Gordon, "Nunn Backs Concept of Small ABM System," *International Herald Tribune*, January 29, 1988.

28. Manfred Wörner, op. cit.; see in this context Scheffran, op. cit., Brauch, op. cit.

CHAPTER 4

Several Illusions of NATO's Military Buildup

In February 1988, U.S. Senator Sam Nunn declared NATO had reached a crossroads. "One NATO road," he said, "leads backward down a slippery slope to European denuclearization, American disengagement, and Soviet domination. The other NATO road leads forward to the solid ground of solidarity, stability, and security."[1] In his address to the NATO summit in Brussels, President Reagan expressed similar sentiments, as did other U.S. officials in their comments to West European audiences.

Throughout the postwar period, the United States has periodically tried to shore up NATO solidarity with the introduction of new weapons programs and other signs of U.S commitment to Western Europe's defense. The compensatory measures intended to fill the alleged gaps left by the INF Treaty were seen as an attempt to reaffirm this resolve. But against the backdrop of the historic changes that were occurring in East-West relations, the compensatory approach to NATO's problems was increasingly seen in a number of West European nations, especially in the Federal Republic of Germany, as vaguely anachronistic—a reflection of the postwar approach that was no longer compatible with the dramatically changed realities of Europe. As already noted, public opinion polls in 1987–1988 suggested that the majority of West Europeans no longer regarded the Soviet Union as a military threat,[2] and even those who remained skeptical of Gorbachev's new thinking believed NATO should give him a chance to demonstrate the sincerity of his efforts to reduce conventional arms and restructure Soviet forces into a more defensive posture.[3]

Thus it was already clear at the time of the signing of the INF Treaty that the type of force improvements and burden-sharing arrangements envisioned by the United States would meet growing criticism and political opposition in Western Europe. Indeed, the very seriousness with which these programs were promoted and discussed in the United States and in official NATO circles illustrated that U.S. political leaders were out of touch with political realities in Western Europe and the widespread belief there that a new era in East-West relations had begun. This chapter examines the disparities between the U.S. policy of a military buildup in Western Europe and the political, demographic, economic, and military conditions in European NATO countries. The discussion will attempt to show how these disparities illustrate the incoherence of the policy of NATO modernization and that it is not politically sustainable.

A central component of the U.S. program consisted of calling on NATO members to improve force structures with a new generation of high-tech conventional weapons designed for implementing the FOFA strategy (see Chapter 2). But there were many indications that West European governments would not support the U.S. program to the extent necessary for its integration into NATO force structures.[4] It was becoming clear that European NATO members, while continuing to give Washington minimal support and a good deal of lip service about alliance solidarity, were under a variety of economic, political, and arms control pressures forcing them to reject the notion of a stronger conventional defense in the form envisioned by U.S. security experts.

West European Defense Outlays

Despite considerable efforts by the Reagan administration to convince Western Europe of the need to spend more on defense, only three of NATO's sixteen members met the official alliance goals of 3 percent increases in real terms in 1985.[5] According to NATO officials, figures for 1986 suggested that at least eight NATO countries fell below the 3 percent level. Neither Britain nor the Federal Republic, the most important U.S. allies in NATO, considered the goal to be realistic.[6] For 1988, only Turkey, Norway, Italy, and Luxembourg planned to raise spending by the agreed 3 percent; Britain and West Germany actually planned real reductions. For the first time since West Germany began fielding an army, Bonn's defense budget threatened to fall below 3 percent of gross national product (GNP), an indication of the political constraints facing a conservative West German government once inclined toward a military buildup. The trend in Britain was described as follows:

> Nor can a robust British Army on the Rhine (BAOR) any longer be taken for granted. British defense expenditure is declining in real terms. For the first time in decades defense expediture as a percentage of gross national product is headed downward. These trends, coupled with the Thatcher government's determination to modernize Britain's nuclear deterrent by acquiring the costly Trident, could make a reduction of the 56,000-man BAOR unavoidable. Some German Ministry of Defense officials believe that at least one of the BAOR's three divisions will be withdrawn from Germany within the next ten years.[7]

NATO's official spending prescription had become a polite fiction that the United States insisted on preserving and that European NATO ministers formally approved, though they lacked the intention or the domestic political backing to fill it. This discrepancy was symptomatic of a number of disparities between NATO budgetary planning and West European political, economic, and security realities.[8] These stemmed in part from unrealistic U.S. demands that ignored Western Europe's perceptions of its security needs and the diminution of the Soviet threat. These disparities are also a product of the fact that NATO high-level meetings, where such goals are set, are attended by representatives of West European defense establishments that have a vested interest in increased defense spending by their home governments. Though their aims were not necessarily to buy more U.S. weapons, the annual ritual of approving unrealistic spending goals nevertheless was helpful to West European military-industrial interests to convince their home governments of the need for greater defense spending.

In commenting on the trends in West European defense, François Heisbourg, a security expert and former vice president of the leading French arms producer Thomson, painted a somber picture of the prospects for larger West European defense budgets. He made the following point in 1986 about the "clear adverse shift" in West European public opinion concerning the likelihood of a military confrontation with the Soviet Union: "There is no way in which European defense budgets will increase markedly, especially in a context of persistent unemployment and economic recession."[9]

The unfavorable economic trends for a West European arms buildup were reinforced by demographic trends suggesting that the lack of draft-age men and women would create serious shortfalls in troop levels in the near term.[10] In West Germany, for example, the declining number of young people available for conscription precluded any further buildup of deployed forces and, in fact, suggested a sizable reduction in the Bundeswehr in the 1990s. Even with the most optimistic assessment, the annual number of potential draftees would drop from approximately 300,000 in 1985 to 153,000 in 1994.[11] According to one estimate, the size of the West German army would decrease from 500,000 to 300,000 by the mid-1990s.[12]

None of NATO's largest countries were either in a position or politically disposed to do more for standing forces. Overall, there was a feeling among West Europeans, especially in West Germany and the Benelux countries, that they had made a concerted effort to improve their conventional forces in the 1970s and early 1980s and that it was time to pursue Gorbachev's generous disarmament offers. The demographic bottleneck impeding larger conventional armies was also not helped by the vision of higher costs for a larger number of soldiers who would need training as electronics experts to operate high-tech weapon systems.[13] For the armed forces to retain this personnel, salaries would have to compare favorably with those in the civilian sector. Expected shortages in this high-tech labor market also posed a risk of civilian-military friction if scarce labor were siphoned off into the defense sector.[14]

Moreover, the high and rising costs of the weapons linked to FOFA, ATBM, and near-term SDI suggested growing disparities between expanding West European armies and improving equipment and infrastructures (housing, working conditions) and investing in futuristic weapons systems. This variance has occurred in France, where nuclear modernization has resulted in a serious deterioration in French conventional forces.[15] Although France is noted for the high technological level of its communications systems and Exocet missiles, its tank force in 1991 will be a quarter the size of West Germany's and half of this force will be obsolete.[16] According to official data, France's artillery, air force, and navy will not be significantly increased because of fiscal problems, although their numbers have been officially assessed as insufficient.[17]

Because France did not have the budgetary means to support both its nuclear modernization plans and conventional force improvements, it turned increasingly to battlefield nuclear weapons to replace conventional forces. This strategy included plans to mass produce the neutron bomb and to extend France's role in West European defense,[18] but antinuclear sentiment of its West European neighbors, particularly the Federal Republic, posed political difficulties for this approach.

The pressure to cut military budgets both in Western Europe and in the United States meant that prospects for European purchases of FOFA systems were likely to deteriorate. That some of these were joint U.S.-European programs already in advanced stages of development was no longer a guarantee of their budgetary survival because the real test often comes when particular systems reach the production and procurement stage and the budgetary pros and cons must be discussed and approved by national parliaments. Fiscal and political trends make cancellations and new missile crises more likely. Here it should be kept in mind that cancellations of weapons systems become all the more costly, both fiscally and in terms of U.S.–West European relations, the longer they are put off.

But the problem was not limited to Western Europe. In an Office of Technology Assessment (OTA) study, the authors noted that the critical juncture for FOFA in the United States would arrive when "these programs move from development to procurement." The budget requests "will almost certainly increase, and Congress will face the question of how to finance them."[19]

West European governments were confronted with decisions not only on how much to spend on new weapons but also to what extent they should produce their own high-tech weapons as opposed to collaborating with U.S. firms. In 1984, the *Nouvel Observateur* summed up an early and deep sentiment the French industry held about FOFA: "It is impossible to ignore the American pressure to sell this new generation of weapons to its European allies. The future of the French armaments industry—No. 3 in the world—and hundreds of thousands of French jobs are at stake."[20]

Although France later was somewhat placated by substantial U.S. purchases of French high-tech military equipment, the underlying problems linked to the changing economic environment of intra-NATO defense cooperation and competition remained and have worsened. Important in this context has been the intensifying military-industrial competition between the United States and West European arms suppliers, the international economic slowdown, the crisis of macro-policy cooperation among the OECD economies, and the shrinking international market for military goods.[21]

The outlook for greater West European military spending appeared even more unrealistic in the light of the expected costs of the Carlucci program and the inability or unwillingness of the three largest and most important West European governments to undertake conventional force improvements. Although U.S. officials such as Senator Nunn began to acknowledge the budgetary problems facing NATO countries and to argue for more creative use of NATO resources, they continued to support expensive high-tech programs, such as FOFA and advanced conventional munitions. Cost estimates for FOFA varied widely. The pro-Atlanticist European Security Study Group estimated that FOFA would require $20 billion over a ten-year period. The Defense Research Group of NATO believed no less than $50 billion for the same time period would be necessary. If one tallied up the figures presented in the OTA study of FOFA, which included weapons platforms such as F-15s and F-16s, the total figure was well over $100 billion.[22]

West European and U.S. Views of FOFA

West European misgivings concerning U.S. plans for implementing FOFA as a NATO strategy included serious military objections to its departure from the traditional NATO posture of near-the-border forward defense. The OTA study summarized this view as follows: "The deployment of highly lethal deep attack systems on the Central Front is too aggressive a stance for a defensive alliance such as NATO. Conventional weapons that could reach hundreds of kilometers into eastern Europe are not consonant with NATO's goals, and change the character of the Alliance from defense to that of offense."[23] During the high point of the political debate on FOFA in the Federal Republic in 1984, *Der Spiegel* noted the destabilizing character of FOFA: "Concealed behind the name (FOFA) is the further development of a military doctrine which in the years ahead could saddle the Alliance with a new arms race—thus making the already precarious balance of terror even shakier."[24]

Official NATO arguments for FOFA initially had emphasized that it would replace nuclear weapons with less destructive and more accurate conventional weapons. But this position, put forth on numerous occasions by former NATO commander General Bernard Rogers, was a highly misleading public relations ploy intended at the time to keep the European antinuclear movement at bay. His successor, General Galvin, readopted the traditional NATO nuclear emphasis.[25] With the INF agreement, NATO officials on both sides of the Atlantic again emphasized the importance of expanding nuclear weapons in Western Europe. FOFA would in fact be a mixture of nuclear and non-nuclear systems and would overlap with the U.S. AirLand Battle, a proposal officially adopted by the United States but never approved by NATO.[26]

According to arms control critics, FOFA is an offensive and preemptive approach to warfare that by no means eliminates the risk of nuclear escalation. Although it would make possible the elimination of certain nuclear systems, the risk of instability would increase, according to this view. By appearing to lower the risks of a nuclear war, battle operations based on FOFA would tend to attenuate the force of "self-deterrence" that restrains offensive forays for fear of nuclear escalation. During a crisis this self-restraint, combined with shorter decision times linked to a more automated battle environment, could significantly heighten the risk of a preemptive strike by the other side.[27] Moreover, with the new emphasis on the need for additional battlefield nuclear weapons, critics hold that FOFA would have the effect of lowering the nuclear threshold, not raising it as some FOFA proponents initially claimed.

The offensive character of FOFA has also been criticized as incompatible with the evolving system and spirit of European détente. Josef Joffe, a staunch defender of NATO, has commented on the idea of threatening Eastern Europe with the offensive posture and preemptive strikes linked with FOFA:

> There is now a shadowy political system defined not only by all kinds of economic and political ties but also by a West European *prise de conscience* that regards the East Europeans not as enemies but as hapless victims and even tacit allies . . . With the Federal Republic in the vanguard, the West Europeans will fight tooth and nail against a doctrine that would seek to deter the Soviets by threatening the East Europeans and hence the very ethos of Ostpolitik and détente.[28]

Conclusions

The degree of support that the policy for improving conventional West European defense received in the United States appeared to be the result of a serious misperception on the part of U.S. policymakers about West European political, economic, and demographic trends and public opinion. Even the

OTA study mistakenly characterized FOFA as a "modest success story" in U.S.–West European arms negotiations because it "has evolved from a major political issue within the Alliance in 1984 to quiet negotiations among armament experts in 1987."[29] This assessment neglects the likelihood of new flare-ups of considerable opposition as FOFA programs proceed to the development and procurement stage—at least about systems not canceled for fiscal reasons along the way. One can expect acrimonious parliamentary debates and opposition in West Germany, Belgium, the Netherlands, and other West European countries. Dissension is likely to focus not merely on the costs of FOFA and its overturning of NATO's traditional defensive strategy but also on the fact that its "success story" was a tale of "quiet negotiations" behind NATO closed doors without public or parliamentary approval. This undemocratic way of proceeding has been true of much of NATO policymaking. By assiduously avoiding public discussion of fundamental issues pertaining to the future of West European security, as well as by tinkering with traditional NATO military doctrine in order to impose an offensive posture on East and West and by making "quiet" deployments of FOFA-related nuclear battlefield weapons in Western Europe in the 1980s, the NATO defense establishments on both sides of the Atlantic violated one of the cardinal principles of security policymaking—that the alliance must be supported by a popular consensus to fulfill its political function and be militarily sustainable.[30]

In opting for a secret approach, NATO officialdom merely succeeded in seriously eroding its relationship to the political mainstream. Moreover, it was this head-in-the-sand approach that left NATO officials unable to comprehend the tidal changes that had taken place in West European publics and, indeed, in high-ranking non-NATO policymaking circles throughout Western Europe. This approach in turn helped to generate a Pandora's box of misperceptions and miscalculations on the part of pro-defense West European political figures who seconded the U.S. call for a new arms buildup.

At a deeper level, the problem lies in the historical transition and the inadequacy of the postwar model of security to deal with the post-containment realities of East-West relations. On the one hand, FOFA is in military-technological terms the logical next step in an approach based on the postwar model; FOFA promotes an action-reaction arms race and the bloc-against-bloc struggle between West and East. On the other hand, the crisis of NATO policy and its rejection by large sections of West European elites and publics can be explained by the emergence of a new political and economic environment partially legitimized by the INF Treaty and confirmed by the reform developments in the East. This trend demands a new approach that would systematically integrate disarmament, common security, and deepened détente as instruments to work out solutions to NATO policy dilemmas.

The succession of political defeats of the steel-helmet wing in West Germany in the battle over INF and the victory of their pro-détente, pro–arms control opponents form a pattern that is likely to repeat itself as long as Western defense departments continue to retain their present emphasis in the making of security policy. The failure to rethink the structure and future role of NATO within Western polities will only perpetuate the deepening legitimacy crisis that now confronts the alliance as a result of its failure to articulate a fully adequate and politically credible response to Soviet, East European, or West European arms reduction and disarmament proposals. This deficit is linked to the lack of Western consensus in the debate over the role of conventional and nuclear weapons, over the question of nuclear deterrence versus offensive and offensive-defensive options at the strategic and substrategic level, and over the role of arms control and disarmament in the security policymaking process.

Notes

1. Senator Sam Nunn, "The American/Soviet Disarmament Negotiations and Their Consequences for NATO" (Speech to the Wehrkunde Conference), February 7, 1988.

2. Andrew Nagorski, "A New Page in Relations Between the East and Bonn," *Newsweek*, January 25, 1988; Elisabeth Noelle-Neumann, "Wenn das Gefühl der Bedrohung schwindet," *Frankfurter Allgemeine Zeitung*, July 22, 1988.

3. Ibid.; Robert McCartney, "West Germany Feels the Impact of New Detente," *Washington Post*, January 17, 1988.

4. On the debate on strengthening West European defense, see François Heisbourg, "Conventional Defense: Europe's Constraints and Opportunities," in Andrew Pierre, ed., *The Conventional Defense of Europe: New Technologies and New Strategies* (New York: Council on Foreign Relations, 1986), pp. 71–111; Jean-Francois Ponçet, "The European Pillar," *Atlantic Focus* (Atlantic Institute for International Affairs), No. 1, 1987.

5. David Brown, "European Industry Evolves to Challenge U.S. Leadership," *Aviation Week and Space Technology*, March 9, 1987.

6. Ibid.

7. Jeffrey Record and David Rivkin, Jr., "Defending Post-INF Europe," *Foreign Affairs*, Vol. 66, No. 4, Spring 1988, pp. 735–754.

8. Heisbourg, op. cit.

9. Ibid.

10. Ibid.

11. Ibid.

12. Ponçet, op. cit.

13. Ibid.

14. Ibid.

15. Roger de Weck, "Muss eine Schlact verloren gehen," *Die Zeit*, Vol. 42, No. 40, September 25, 1987.

16. Ibid.

17. Ibid.

18. Ibid.; "Die Partei Giscards für die Neutronenbombe," *Frankfurter Allgemeine Zeitung*, May 30, 1987; George Blum, "Französische Neutronenbombe soll in der BRD stationiert werden, Zweitschlüssel für Bonn,"

Tageszeitung, May 7, 1987; see also the accompanying interviews by Georg Blum and Mycle Schneider with Charles Hernu and Pierre Messner.

19. Office of Technology Assessment, *New Technologies for NATO, Implementing Follow-On Forces Attack* (hereafter *OTA Study*) (Washington, D.C.: Government Printing Office, 1987), p. 4.

20. *Nouvel Observateur*, January 1984, cited in ibid., p. 115.

21. See in this context Michael Brzoska and Thomas Ohlson, "A Buyer's Market: The Arms Trade in the 1980's," *ADIU Report*, Vol. 8, No. 2, March–April 1986, pp. 1–6; Thomas Ohlson and Elisabeth Sköns, "The Trade in Major Conventional Weapons," in *SIPRI Yearbook 1987* (Oxford: Oxford University Press, 1987), pp. 181–200.

22. *OTA Study*, op. cit., pp. 32–33. A frequently cited example of the costs of FOFA is the ill-fated Assault Breaker. As one critic of FOFA has written: "An early star of FOFA, the Assault Breaker missile system, was put on hold in 1984, in a rare display of air force and army unanimity, because it had become too expensive even before the testing phase was completed. According to a study conducted by the U.S. Air Force, the cost of only *one week's* munitions requirements on *one corps front* would amount to $8 billion." Josef Joffe, *The Limited Partnership* (Cambridge, Mass.: Ballinger, 1987), p. 157.

23. Joffe, ibid., p. 119.

24. *Der Spiegel*, Vol. 38, No. 26, June 25, 1984, quoted in ibid.

25. "Former NATO Chief Calls for Force Improvements to Offset INF Cuts," *Aviation Week and Space Technology*, December 14, 1987.

26. On the differences between AirLand Battle and FOFA, see Joffe, op. cit., pp. 170f. For a Soviet discussion of FOFA and the AirLand Battle concept, see Oleg Amirov, Nikolai Kishilov, Vadim Makarevsky, and Yuri Usachev, "'Conventional War': Strategic Concepts," in Institute of World Economy and International Relations, *Disarmament and Security, 1987 Yearbook* (Moscow: Novosti, 1988), pp. 347–369. For U.S. views of the role of nuclear weapons, see the Commission on Integrated Long-Term Strategy, *Discriminate Deterrence* (Washington, D.C., January 1988); Department of Defense, *Support of NATO Strategy in the 1990s* (Washington, D.C.: Department of Defense, 1988).

27. See in this context Jürgen Altmann, "Technical Problems of ATBM Defenses," in Marlies ter Borg and Wim Smit, *Tactical Missile Defense in Europe* (Amsterdam: Free University Press, 1987), pp. 48–63.

28. Joffe, op. cit. pp. 164f.

29. *OTA Study*, op. cit., p. 6.

30. Lynn Davis, "Lessons of the INF Treaty," *Foreign Affairs*, Vol. 66, No. 4, Spring 1988, pp. 720–734.

CHAPTER 5

The Future of NATO: Three Models

In the wake of the INF Treaty, three different models can be extrapolated from the political development and wealth of proposals on the future of NATO and European security.[1] The first consists of more or less preserving the transatlantic status quo of NATO,[2] which would include some form of enhancing flexible response through additional high-tech weaponry linked to tempered versions of FOFA and SDI. The second model is that of building out the European pillar of NATO and thereby making European NATO powers relatively more autonomous from the United States.[3] The third model is the construction of an East-West security system based on détente, common security, and the gradual, phased dissolution of NATO and the Warsaw Pact.

Model 1: Atlanticism and the Classic Dilemma of Nuclear Deterrence and Flexible Response

This model represents a continuation of the postwar model of security. It is based on a combination of preserving the status quo of deterrence and flexible response and at the same time upgrading NATO arsenals with a variety of advanced conventional and nuclear weapons. The erosion of the postwar security order, however, casts considerable doubt on the viability of this model. Misgivings are linked to measures planned to compensate for the systems eliminated by the INF Treaty. For example, additional cruise missiles would be deployed on ships and aircraft. Modernized short-range nuclear and/or conventional missiles below the 500-kilometer range would be deployed. This would include the replacement of the Lance missile, which has a 120-kilometer range, with the U.S. Army tactical missile system, with its range of 480 kilometers, as well as more accurate, dual-capable artillery and other battlefield weapons. The purpose would be to "modernize" flexible response and the NATO threat of first use of nuclear weapons below the strategic nuclear threshold, an approach strongly supported by NATO

Supreme Allied Commander in Europe, U.S. General Galvin, and by the Pentagon. It also corresponds to the U.S. call for more high-tech conventional and nuclear weapons for Western Europe in the framework of FOFA, as discussed in the preceding chapters.

Model 1 raises the classic dilemma of nuclear deterrence and flexible response without offering a solution.[4] Nuclear deterrence is based on the principle that the protagonists deter each other from launching an attack because both are aware that any conflict involving nuclear weapons would result in the mutually assured destruction of both sides as a result of escalation. The dilemma is that deterrence as a military-political instrument loses its credibility because each side knows the other would not launch an attack known to be suicidal. Therefore, according to this reasoning, a gray area of possible conflict opens up on the substrategic level: A potential aggressor could assume that the other side would not respond to substrategic conventional aggression with a suicidal nuclear counterattack. Given this potential substrategic threat, NATO officials draw the inference that the alliance must expand its military strength on substrategic levels with less destructive, more precise high-tech nuclear and conventional weapons systems. These, it is argued, could actually be used in a conflict without unleashing thermonuclear war. But critics of this view argue that such a war-fighting approach is not viable because *any* use of nuclear weapons—or even of roughly equivalent, highly destructive conventional weapons now available—would tend to escalate conflict and thus ignite a nuclear holocaust.[5] The dilemma of deterrence and flexible response lies at the heart of current West European concern about proposals to lower the nuclear threshold with more sophisticated dual-use, offensive-defensive, deep-strike weapons associated with FOFA and to modernize NATO battlefield nuclear weapons.[6] These proposals, according to critics, undermine the stability of deterrence and unacceptably increase the risk of war. They put into question the purpose of deterrence as a strategy of war prevention aimed at maintaining a stable order of peace and security.

Defenders of the Atlanticist model of NATO insist on the viability of the traditional postwar structure of the alliance. But the status quo is in fact being challenged by the following developments, some of which have been discussed in preceding chapters:

1. Economic shifts in the transatlantic relationship that have placed the United States under pressure to reduce its outlays for NATO and have triggered U.S. calls for European NATO governments to increase their defense budgets

2. The new designed-for-NATO weapon systems that lend themselves to an offensive conventional-nuclear strategy, thus putting into question NATO's traditional near-the-border defensive doctrine

3. The declared program of the Soviet leadership to remove the Soviet military threat in Europe
4. The breakdown of elite consensus on NATO military doctrine and policies toward the East
5. Increasing public rejection of deterrence and flexible response as a viable basis for peace, security, and European prosperity in the coming years
6. The popular and elite opposition in West Germany to NATO modernization, including deployment of the proposed replacement for the short-range Lance missile
7. The widespread assumption that the United States will inevitably be forced to reduce its commitment of troops to Western Europe, which has functioned as a delicate lynchpin of the postwar balance of terror and transatlantic unity[7]

In sum, the traditional Atlanticist model has its defenders, but critics argue that its political, economic, and military-technological foundations are so severely eroded that it is no longer a viable framework for the future development of U.S.–West European relations.

Model 2: Europeanist Military Options

The second model, which overlaps in many respects with the Atlanticist model, also prescribes the "strengthening of NATO's European pillar."[8] But here the emphasis has been placed on the loosening of ties with the United States and on establishing greater geostrategic autonomy for Western Europe. The Europeanist approach has been most strongly defended by conservative, pro-defense groupings (see Chapter 1). Like the Atlanticist model, it would involve a relative reduction of U.S. expenditures for European NATO defense and a corresponding increase in fiscal and military-security responsibilities of West European governments. The problems of this model include (1) the changed role of the United States in such a modified system; (2) the thorny question of the articulation of strategic and substrategic nuclear weapons systems of the United States, Britain, and France and their implications for military doctrine and strategy; and (3) linked to (2), the role of West Germany in a more multilateral and potentially more nuclearized Western Europe (or whatever form the strengthened second pillar of NATO would ultimately take).

Although the pro-defense elements in France, Britain, and West Germany promoting West European military projects have been quite aware of their dependence on Washington, they nevertheless no longer wish to tie their destiny exclusively to Washington's ability to push through a new NATO conventional and nuclear modernization program.[9] To do so in the face of domestic opposition and growing public sentiment for disarmament, they calculate, could only further weaken and undermine their domestic political position. To accomplish their aims, they argued in the early post-INF period that Western Europe would become vulnerable to superior Soviet military conventional forces in the future if no steps were taken to compensate for growing weaknesses and the declining credibility of the U.S. nuclear umbrella. They have also used the fear of U.S. abandonment and the threat of U.S. competition to justify their own ambitious high-tech military programs.

Behind French and West German expressions of concern for Western Europe's security fate lay a number of conflicting economic and geostrategic motivations. France made it clear that it was worried about West Germany's seeming drift eastward,[10] particularly its warm embrace of Gorbachev and notions of common security, which raised the specter not only of West German neutralism and denuclearization but also of German reunification. West Germany's expanding economic relations with the Soviet Union were viewed as a potential threat to France's grand project for greater West European economic unity as well as to French hopes that West Germany would buy more French goods, including high-tech military and civilian systems.[11] Both the pro-defense right as well the Socialists in France expressed their apprehension about the crisis in the defense industry, brought on by the escalating costs of the French nuclear modernization program and by the slump in arms exports to the Third World.[12] A closer economic and military-technological alliance with the Federal Republic could ease these problems.

France has viewed Franco–West German military cooperation as a way of simultaneously pulling the FRG "back to the West" and buttressing its own overstretched nuclear and other modernization programs. On the critical importance of this cooperation to France's future, there is a solid consensus in French policymaking circles that is based on an enhanced political role for France as a strategic nuclear power in Europe. The modernization of the French nuclear arsenal, a more self-assertive public posture concerning its nuclear weapons and testing programs and its military cooperation with both Great Britain and the Federal Republic are examples of the French government's effort—particularly evident since the signing of the INF Treaty—to place the French nuclear deterrent at the center of a new European political-security identity.[13]

The prospect of Franco–West German cooperation was warmly welcomed, even encouraged, by U.S. officials.[14] Although wary of European moves that might undermine Washington's grip on NATO, U.S. officials condoned collaboration in part because they believed France could be useful in slowing West Germany's movement toward denuclearization and in promoting an increase in West European defense spending. Beyond this, some analysts saw the Franco–West German connection as the basis for a strong West European pillar of NATO and thus as a way for the region to assume some of the burden for NATO's conventional defense shouldered by the United States. Others, such as former national security advisers Zbigniew Brzezinski and Henry Kissinger, viewed it as the foundation for a far more significant division of responsibilities within NATO: In the future, France and West Germany would take over substantial responsibility for European deterrence and conventional defense—though with the continued backing of the U.S. strategic arsenal[15]—thus freeing the United States to devote more resources to highly mobile conventional and nuclear forces capable of meeting security threats in the Third World where they would be more likely to arise.

The Federal Republic, France, and Nuclear Weapons

The construction site of the planned nuclear reprocessing plant at Wackersdorf in Bavaria was the scene of repeated violent demonstrations by the antinuclear movement until the suspension of the project in 1989.[16] The virulence of the protests stemmed not merely from objections to nuclear power but more acutely from the apprehension that the plant could have provided West Germany with large amounts of nuclear material for a possible military nuclear option.

These fears were not allayed by the scandal in 1987 over the illegal transport of high-grade radioactive plutonium waste from Belgium into the Federal Republic. The "Nukem Affair" shook the credibility of the West German nuclear industry in a number of areas, including the management of nuclear firms, the transport of nuclear waste, and suspected criminal violations of West German nuclear law.[17] It also raised questions concerning West Germany's export of nuclear equipment and its responsibilities as a signatory of the Nuclear Non-Proliferation Treaty.

The Federal Republic is proscribed from developing or possessing nuclear weapons under the Allied arrangements made following World War II in the framework of the WEU and the conditions under which the FRG was permitted to join NATO. Despite this proscription, however, the Federal Republic today is a major producer and exporter of civilian nuclear power plants. The West German electric ultility RWE is also a consortium partner in the French Superphénix fast-breeder reactor, a source of nuclear material for French weapons programs, despite the fact that such participation can be interpreted as a violation of West German non-nuclear status.[18] Moreover, West German firms have exported dual-use nuclear materials, know-how, and equipment to Pakistan, which is reported to be in a position to manufacture military nuclear devices by the early 1990s.[19]

The popular concern in West Germany over the country's future nuclear options also was fueled by the Federal Republic's expanding defense collaboration with France. The current moves to intensify this cooperation illuminate the contradictions and nuclear dilemmas of a "Europeanized" second pillar of NATO.

Whereas France has expressed an interest in structuring Franco–West German security cooperation in the framework of a French-dominated, more Europeanized security system, the Federal Republic has repeatedly expressed its loyalty to NATO and declared the United States its main alliance partner.[20] In this context, Bonn has preferred to interpret Franco–West German security cooperation as a symptom that France is moving closer to NATO and could at some future point rejoin the military integration of the alliance. France left NATO as a full military member in 1967 and developed its own nuclear deterrence doctrine based on national defense of French territory.

The major differences in the French and West German perspectives on their joint military efforts were put into relief by the "Bold Sparrow" military exercise in September 1987.[21] This joint war game, which was supposed to be a symbol of rapprochement and future military cooperation, was marked by political differences concerning its purpose and organization. Bonn wanted the maneuver to document France's move in the direction of rejoining NATO.[22] This was supposed to be the upshot of the demonstration exercise designed to test French ability to use helicopters to launch a counterattack in the framework of NATO's forward, near-the-border defense strategy against invading tank divisions. But the French forces, to the surprise and irritation of their hosts, took the opportunity to emphasize the French security doctrine and independence of NATO by practicing nuclear military strategy based on use of atomic weapons to counter an enemy attack.[23] This change in the program was not announced in advance to the press or to the West German General Staff because it would have caused considerable controversy and embarrassment for the West German government and might have led to the event's cancellation.[24]

Although France insisted on testing its traditional military strategy in Bavaria, it has nevertheless made noteworthy concessions in order to woo West Germany as a military partner. In the fall of 1987, President Mitterrand announced that France would not use its short-range Pluton prestrategic missile in or near the Federal Republic. This pledge represented a major shift in French military doctrine, which specifies that short- and intermediate-range missiles are supposed to be fired onto West (or East) German territory as a "last warning" to an invading force before France launches strategic nuclear weapons.[25] This doctrine reproduces the basic flaw of flexible response: France in a conflict would risk destroying what is supposed to be protected. By triggering nuclear explosions on its doorstep—in West or East Germany—it would thereby risk a nuclear war that would destroy Western Europe.

In the discussion about joint cooperation, a main focus of West German political and defense circles was that the French nuclear targeting of the

Federal Republic was politically and militarily an unacceptable basis for security cooperation; no West German chancellor could even consider a formal military cooperation agreement based on the French status quo version of flexible response designed to protect French territory. In recognition of this dilemma as an obstacle to Franco–West German cooperation, a new political-military consensus emerged in France in which the model of restricting French nuclear defense to its national territory would be abandoned in favor of a more "Europeanized" security system in which the French "nuclear sanctuary" would be extended to cover West German territory as well. This new definition was the essence of Mitterrand's announcement and similar subsequent pronouncements audible across the French political spectrum. But these statements in themselves did not solve the problem: As West German security experts pointed out, the change in strategic doctrine signaled by Paris must be logically followed by actually eliminating the French short-range nuclear Pluton missile (range: 120 kilometers) and halting the development of the Hadès missile (range: 450–480 kilometers) that is scheduled to go into service in 1992. The dual-capable Hadès, whose first flight test took place in November 1988, can carry a 10–20 kiloton nuclear warhead or a conventional warhead. As a major component of French prestrategic forces, it will be able, according to official sources, to be fired either as a nuclear warning to an invading forces or into enemy territory as a deep-strike weapon.[26] Halting the development of the Hadès remained unlikely.

An overlapping problem that would have to be resolved in a formalized Franco–West German security relationship concerns access to decisionmaking on the deployment of nuclear weapons in a crisis. In this context, there have been tentative proposals by Paris to "consult" with Bonn if there is sufficient time. Certainly, as long as French weapons are aimed at German territory, a West German chancellor could not officially sanction France's launching its nuclear weapons at German territory without "violating his oath of office in the most extreme manner."[27]

Even if the French systems that threaten the two Germanies were eliminated and French military doctrine adjusted to accommodate West German security concerns, there would still remain the equally serious problem of the precise role of the Federal Republic in a Franco–West German security axis. The dilemma here also involves the status of West Germany vis-à-vis the French military nuclear command structure. On the one hand, it is a widely held consensus that France would not share its "nuclear button" with a West German government, despite a number of French proposals that suggested the contrary.[28] On the other hand, an integrated Franco–West German security system nevertheless implies at least some form of consultation. But even the suggestion of a "secondary access" of West Germany to nuclear weapons, whatever form this might take, could generate major domestic and external political problems, given West German geography between Eastern and Western Europe and the memory of Germany's role during World War II. Even a partially nuclearized West Germany would be politically unacceptable for many nations in both East and West.[29]

In a different but related context, a Franco–West German brigade resides in West Germany, although a fully combined force is not permitted by either the West German or the French constitution.[30] Even without this obstacle to military cooperation, there would remain the equally thorny problems of whether such a force would be under French or West German command and which military doctrine it would serve—French national defense or the West German–NATO doctrine of forward, near-the-border defense.[31] This dilemma raises the issue of the Federal Republic's obligation to NATO and to the United States because West German forces cannot be under NATO and Franco–West German command at the same time. These fundamental problems have continued to provoke West European skepticism about the military significance of the Franco–West German cooperation. As the *Financial Times* succinctly put it: "It is all very well establishing a joint Franco-German brigade, but it can never be employed effectively until Paris and Bonn reconcile their defense doctrines."[32]

Similarly, there is the additional question of the position of other European NATO powers concerning a "strengthened European pillar" based on a Franco–West German axis. Britain, the Netherlands, and Italy have expressed serious misgivings about the proposals for greater Franco–West German security cooperation because of its implications for the cohesion and the future of NATO.[33]

Former French Defense Minister Charles Hernu made the unexpected proposal that Paris should consider stationing French neutron bombs in West Germany and give Bonn "double-key" coresponsibility over their deployment.[34] France has been developing the neutron bomb, the enhanced radiation weapon (ERW), since the early 1980s for possible use on the Hadès missile. Hernu's proposal, put forth in the context of a possible French–West German military axis, raised many of the same problems previously discussed. It posed the question of the possible relationship between French and NATO strategy and whether the two viewpoints, considered from a purely military perspective, are mutually compatible. If the proposal to station French neutron bombs in West Germany is seen in the framework of the U.S. and NATO campaign for FOFA (deep strikes into the Warsaw Pact, as opposed to defense on West German territory), then the purely military solution of the dilemmas can be perhaps discerned. For FOFA proponents, the logical solution would lie in moving the battleground farther east into Warsaw Pact territory with the aid of new conventional and battlefield nuclear weapons and the FOFA doctrine of offensive and preemptive defense. President Mitterrand during his visit to the Federal Republic in October 1987 sought to assure his hosts that France would not fire its short-range nuclear missiles at an invading force once it entered West German territory. But as a group of security experts point out:

> German officials welcomed Mitterrand's carefully worded suggestions that France should not use its Pluton missiles against West German territory, even though the weapon's 120-km range makes them unsuitable for any other purpose. The Hadès, which would have a range of 480 km, would be able to reach the GDR (as well as Eastern Czechoslovakia). However, Bonn takes little comfort at this statistic and believes that France should not use nuclear weapons over German territory, east *or* west.[35]

A French strategy that would attempt to reconcile the FOFA concept and the French model of including West (and possibly East) Germany in its nuclear sanctuary would thus generate a new set of predicaments for both France and the Federal Republic, not to mention European NATO as a whole. If France were to implement this model—for example, by stationing short-range missiles along the German-German border—it would raise questions concerning West Germany's official non-nuclear status and would also collide with West German domestic opposition to any proposal for additional nuclear weapons on German soil. Given public attitudes in West Germany, no political party could expect to be elected or retain office on a program based on greater militarization and nuclearization, a position reflected in the Kohl government's decision to postpone approval of the U.S. plan to replace the short-range Lance missile, a major item in NATO's modernization program.[36]

The French military and political establishment would view the option of the Hadès and neutron bomb as a fiscally more palatable alternative to raising the number of French troops in West Germany if, for instance, the United States withdrew several of its divisions and France were asked to fill the gap. This option would allow for savings on conventional equipment, an important consideration because the French military budget has come under pressure from shrinking military export markets, the general condition of the French economy, and heavy French military investment in recent years.[37] The deployment of French neutron bombs could also help to legitimize French nuclear weapons in a Franco–West German alliance and would thus offer some protection against the denuclearizing tendencies of U.S.-Soviet arms control accords reinforced from below by the world's antinuclear movements. But what appears to be an elegant solution for the French political establishment would be politically unacceptable for any future West German government.

The other military option reportedly considered by Paris was for France and West Germany to build a long-range missile capable of reaching the Soviet Union. This joint project, which could be modeled after the Ariane missile, was the more likely option in the opinion of Dr. Alfred Mechtersheimer, a former Bundeswehr officer and member of the Bundestag on the Green Party list.[38] According to Mechtersheimer, innovations like the Franco-German brigade are merely camouflage for a joint Franco-German strategic Euromissile—a weapon nominally French but in effect Franco–West German because West Germany would share in the targeting. Members of the CDU-CSU steel-helmet faction, such as CDU faction leader Alfred Dregger, were reported to be sympathetic to such a project,[39] and, as already noted, the late CDU leader Franz-Josef Strauss had defended a West German accession to nuclear weapons and argued for years in favor of a Europeanized nuclear deterrent.[40]

Both these options are linked to the political-economic relationship between France and the Federal Republic. On this level as well, a military alliance could easily become a pregnant source of political tensions and instabilities. The ambiguity of France's motives in undertaking such a joint project illuminates why this would tend to be the case. As already mentioned, France wanted to curtail what it sees as West Germany's drift toward "neutralism" and closer economic ties with the East.[41] France hoped that by extending its nuclear sanctuary to West Germany it would be able to use its nuclear assets as a political instrument to maintain its political-military bargaining power vis-à-vis an economically and, in terms of conventional forces, significantly more powerful Federal Republic. At the same time, France needs West German fiscal and military resources to modernize its force structure if it is to play a larger role in West European defense and at the same time help to upgrade the region's political and military bargaining power vis-à-vis the United States (and the Soviet Union). France would also like to use this leverage to influence West German economic policy. But to accomplish this volatile bundle of aims, Paris would have to retain the commanding position in a Franco–Western German alliance, which would most likely prove difficult for the following reason: A strategic nuclear but economically weak France in a military alliance in which the Federal Republic is supposed to be subordinate to Paris would not be a recipe for West European stability.[42] West Germany would come to dominate what would become a very lopsided relationship because its superior economic and military-industrial strength would increasingly assert itself. In an environment characterized by militarizing policies drawn along the traditional lines of the postwar model of security, the stage would be set for a West German shift in the direction of acquiring more military cards, including the possible accession to the status of a military nuclear power. For economic and political-military reasons, West Germany would tend to become more involved in the French production cycle of nuclear weapons. As this cooperation increased, the voices of the West German nuclear lobby calling for a West German nuclear military status in the middle 1990s could grow louder.[43]

The upgrading of the role of West European nuclear weapons as a result of a Franco–West German suballiance also would tend to put further pressure on the Nuclear Non-Proliferation Treaty (NPT) by giving new stimulus to Western Europe's nuclear industries. This increased activity in turn would pose the problem of nuclear proliferation and would set a poor example for Third World countries that would like to possess atomic weapons to upgrade their military-political status. The NPT expires in 1995.[44] If First World states such as the Federal Republic decide not to prolong their non-nuclear status, "threshold" nuclear states in the Third World might be less likely to renounce their own military nuclear ambitions. Conversely, as more Third World countries become military nuclear states, the political and industrial nuclear lobby would be in a stronger position to call for a West German nuclear weapons status. A West German proponent of nuclear weapons, Hubertus Hoffmann, echoed the thinking of this lobby in his statement that the Federal Republic "should not avoid the nuclear responsibility."[45]

A Western Europe of Suballiances

In the context of Western Alliance politics, it would remain to be seen where a Franco-German alliance would situate itself within the West European security landscape beside NATO, a reactivated WEU, and the various other security policymaking and consultative bodies that have increased in the 1980s. Also, given the economic balance of power between France and the Federal Republic, the ambitions of the West German pro-military right, and the fact that the Federal Republic today has the largest and best-equipped conventional army in Western Europe, it would probably be only a matter of time until West Germany came to dominate and have increasing policymaking say over a more "Europeanized" French or Franco–West German nuclear strategic force.

The prospect that the European pillar of NATO would be strengthened thereby is doubtful because there would likely be "European pillars" ambiguously cooperating and competing with one another. Such a configuration would constitute a fragmentation of West European defense into different, albeit overlapping, suballiances. These could easily fall prey to transatlantic and nationalist friction as large and small European powers, in East and West, begin to worry about (1) a militarily more powerful West Germany; (2) the erosion of coherence in Western defense, strategy, and doctrine; (3) the direction and aims of West European high-tech civilian-military industries; and (4) the effects of the various European pillars on the future of East-West relations.[46]

The scenario sketched here of the Europeanist model and its assumption of the postwar model of security can be judged as problematic, given the daunting political, economic, and military problems linked to it. Yet the tendencies and contradictions that underpin it are real and are competing with policies that would be based on the post-containment model of security. Although the West German pro-defense right has been weakened by the INF agreement and by Moscow's policies of perestroika, glasnost, and arms reductions, it is far from being defeated. The steel-helmet wing would receive new support, for example, if the Soviet threat were seen to be reviving and if, consequently, détente were to suffer. Domestically, this grouping could experience a political comeback if the current popular right-wing resurgence in the wake of the 1989 West Berlin elections continued to grow in the 1990s as a result of slow economic growth and rising unemployment. It should also be remembered that members and supporters of the steel-helmet wing continue to occupy key positions within the West German government and military. If the United States pressed Western Europe with an intensified global military policy (including NATO nuclear and conventional modernization) and at the same time attempted to ease its military overextension by suddenly shifting some of its forces out of Western Europe to shore up its regional interventionary position, West Germany's military interests would also be given a boost. The fear of U.S. abandonment in the context of NATO modernization and unrest in Eastern Europe and the Third World could be a combination that would push West Germany back onto a more military-oriented path.

Détente in French Policy

The watershed of French foreign policy that has placed it in a gray-area transition between the postwar and the post-containment models of security is reflected in the fact that although President Mitterrand has championed a new Eurodefense identity under French leadership, he began in the late 1980s to more actively expand the role of détente in French foreign policy. This new focus was reflected not only in French-Soviet economic and scientific cooperation (see Chapter 10) but in events such as the historic welcome of East Germany's head of state Erich Honecker in Paris and Mitterrand's trip to Eastern Europe and the Soviet Union in 1988.[47] The Honecker reception in Paris marked the opening of a new chapter in French foreign policy.[48]

Mitterrand's new course in the nonmilitary side of French foreign policy is important for three reasons. First, it demonstrated how, contrary to widely held views in the United States, acceptance of the postwar division of Germany and the legitimacy of East European regimes on the basis of the Helsinki Final Act has gained greater importance as the appropriate way to achieve genuine progress in European East-West relations and at the same time to promote peaceful reform in the other half of Europe. Second—and more important in the context of the prospect of a Franco–West German military suballiance—Mitterrand's political gesture to Honecker was a sign that the politics of détente, as opposed to anticommunism and the enemy image of the Soviet threat, has taken on greater weight in French policy. If this trend continues, it could tilt French industrial and technological planning in a decidedly more civilian-oriented direction in the 1990s. Such a shift would naturally affect domestic military programs and the government's response to the deepening economic troubles of French military firms. These could either be bailed out with additional, costly defense contracts, be scrapped (unlikely), or, in certain selected cases, be encouraged through appropriate government programs to pursue a more civilian-oriented high-tech strategy. The last alternative would allow France to take more effective advantage of the opening not only of the unified Common Market in 1992 but also the huge East European and Soviet market, which is predicted to boom in the mid-1990s. A combined East-West strength of over 700 million consumers may make an economic course based on a more resolute détente policy irresistible. Third, Mitterrand's more active détente policy recalled in important respects de Gaulle's vision of a pan-Europe extending from the Urals to the Atlantic, in which France would assume a more active role in mediating between East and West and overcoming the postwar division of the continent.

Notwithstanding these signs of a more détente-oriented course, a prime interest of France is to maintain strong relations with the United States, which remains its main partner within the Western Alliance. In the unofficial view of the French political class, French Atlanticism remains an indispensable counterweight to an increasingly powerful West Germany. Traditional French fears of its economically mighty neighbor continue to mandate U.S. ties, even as France calls for greater West European autonomy.

Against the backdrop of these complex and contradictory aims in French foreign relations, it becomes clear why détente and a policy based on the post-containment model of security might be a politically and economically more stabilizing perspective for France than the development of a Franco–West German suballiance. A policy more centrally based on East-West military disengagement and mutual reductions would have the advantage of not encouraging the slumbering potential of a new German (in the guise of a Franco–West German) military buildup. It could at the same time upgrade the French role in the expansion of East-West economic relations. But such a transition could not be made without the United States. Given France's postwar political culture, military-industrial high-tech lobby, and current military policies, it is highly unlikely that France would or could adopt this course unilaterally without a major shift on the part of the United States.

Model 3: The Policy Road
of Arms Reduction and Demilitarization

Both the Atlanticist and the Europeanist models are fraught with contradictions that put into question their viability as a foundation for NATO policy. The legitimacy crisis of nuclear deterrence, the positive prospects of the disarmament process, the changing economic-political relationship of the United States and Western Europe, the Soviet reform process and its opening to the West, the deepening of European détente, and the unification of the Common Market are some of the factors that suggest the postwar Atlanticist world is passing into history. The Europeanist model can be interpreted as a response to its demise, but is plagued with too many unresolved problems to become a viable alternative.

The contradictions of both the Atlanticist and the Europeanist models suggest the need for the alternative principles of the post-containment model for constructing a new European security system. This model would provide a road to resolve the military-related dilemmas of the Atlanticist and the Europeanist models through a far-reaching restructuring, gradual thinning out, and long-term dissolution of NATO and the Warsaw Pact. The demilitarizing dimension of this model is implied in many of the proposals for arms control and disarmament that have been developed over the past two decades and that are now being taken seriously in official negotiations and policy research circles. The core elements of these initiatives include large reductions of deployed nuclear and conventional forces; a shift from offensive to structurally defensive military doctrines, strategies, and force postures; and a transition to common security and nonmilitary forms of economic and political cooperation.[49] The demilitarizing dimension of such a European security order would in turn provide the groundwork for East-West interaction not based on military force or the threat of force, but on peaceful competition and cooperation and on continuing negotiations to settle conflicts, lower tension, and create structures to deepen East-West economic, cultural, ecological, and humanitarian intercourse. Chapter 1 briefly discussed a number of disarmament and confidence-building proposals, such as nuclear and chemical weapon-free corridors in central Europe, large troop and equipment reductions from the Atlantic to the Urals, and structurally nonoffensive defense. In the CFE and other conferences in the CSCE framework, such proposals will play an increasingly vital role both in reaching agreements and in creating a new basis for long-term economic and political development in Europe. The CSCE is legitimizing nonmilitary forms of security based on more intensive East-West interaction, a topic addressed in Chapter 11.

Conclusion: A Franco–West German Suballiance and the Policy Challenge to the United States

Given its key position in the West, the United States is likely to remain a centrally important force in the evolution of Franco–West German relations into the next century. But as long as the main power in the alliance refuses to relinquish its postwar model of security—in which military arsenals and strategic doctrines are the dominant component and the principal mechanism regulating East-West competition—its weaker allies may be condemned to continue on this path, albeit with diminished allegiance to their transatlantic partner. The current U.S. NATO policy of a more militarized Western Europe would likely bring instability without benefit to collective Western interests, but a timely shift on the part of Washington toward a carefully phased scaling down of the military component of the East-West conflict would facilitate Western Europe's following a similar path and would dovetail with current European trends in this direction.

If the United States does not alter its present game plan of a military buildup for Western Europe, the result could be a half-continent of unstable, overlapping, and competing sub- and pseudo-alliances. West European states might be forced to rely more on their national military-political bargaining chips to regulate their intraregional rivalries and to vainly seek external security through a destablizing mixture of offensive and defensive arms racing. Together with flagging economic growth and increasing levels of unemployment, such a security landscape would not bring stability or unity to the Western Alliance.

The result could be different if Washington were to choose the path of demilitarization and active East-West cooperation. This approach could help to establish the necessary alliance umbrella for a collective Western policy of common security and disarmament for Western Europe that would enable the region to ease out of its postwar nuclear dilemmas in a nonconfrontational manner, reaffirm and recraft its attachment to the United States as its main partner, and achieve forms of European integration and détente that would bring more security and well-being to both continents.

Although the cooperative path would appear to be the appropriate course for the United States to overcome the deepening crisis of transition of the transatlantic alliance, adopting it cannot be reduced to the simple question of forging a new NATO consensus. U.S. policy toward its allies is firmly rooted in the structures and functioning of the U.S. economy. There are three important linkages in this context that are relevant to the analysis of this book:

1. The use of military spending as an instrument of macroeconomic management
2. The organization of much of U.S. R&D under the ideological and political-economic umbrella of technological-military competition with the Soviet Union
3. U.S. security controls on export trade with communist countries

These structural links between the U.S. economy and U.S. security policy suggest that a major change of U.S. NATO policy would necessarily entail significant changes in the running of the U.S. economy. Part 2 of this analysis will examine these underpinning aspects of U.S. NATO policy. Chapters 6 and 7 will show that the watershed of U.S.–West European relations and the crisis of the postwar model of security are also reflected in the decline of the U.S. economy, in the emergence of new technologies, and in the impact of new technologies on Western economies. Chapter 8 will discuss the lack of transatlantic consensus on the question of exports of high technology to the Soviet Union.

Notes

1. Werner Weidenfeld, "Neuorganisation der Sicherheit Westeuropas," *Europa-Archiv*, Vol. 42, No. 9, 1987; Wolfgang Ischinger, "Jenseits der Abschreckung? Nuklearwaffen, Rüstungskontrolle und die Zukunft Europas," *Europa-Archiv*, Vol. 43, No. 12, June 1988, pp. 339–348; Peter Schlotter, "Konzepte und Perspectiven der sicherheitspolitischen Zusammenarbeit in Westeuropa," *Die Neue Gesellschaft Frankfurter Hefte*, Vol. 34, No. 11, November 1987, pp. 999–1005. On the INF Treaty and its relationship to détente, see Wolfgang Zellner, "Die Null-Lösung—Öffnung zu einer zweiten Phase der Entspannungs-politik," *Blätter für deutsche und internationale Politik*, Vol. 32, No. 7, July 1987, pp. 876–892.

2. The British position on NATO can be characterized as the most Atlanticist among U.S. allies: On modernization of NATO, see British Information Services, "The NATO Summit: The British View" (Policy Statement), March 4, 1988. For an overview of British views on nuclear modernization in the wake of the INF Treaty, see Foreign Affairs Committee, *The Political Impact of the Process of Arms Control and Disarmament* (House of Commons, July 20, 1988), pp. 14–20ff. Josef Joffe in *The Limited Partnership* (Cambridge, Mass.: Ballinger, 1987) defends the Atlanticist argument that despite the structural problems that NATO throughout its history has confronted and the forces of change that appear to put the alliance into question today, the future of U.S. and West European security and peace lies in the preservation of NATO in its present form. He presents a host of traditional, frequently heard arguments to defend nuclear deterrence and flexible response and maintains they must remain the basis of the transatlantic relationship. Among the central points he makes to support his case are these: (1) Nuclear deterrence has provided an effective strategy in the past and guaranteed peace and security in Europe for four and a half decades; (2) the various models of Western security based on an independent West European nuclear defense (such as an all–West European strategy or a Franco–West German alliance) are untenable in the light of postwar history and, more importantly, the reluctance of France to share control over its nuclear deterrent forces with non-nuclear states, particularly the Federal Republic; (3) the conventional defense of Western Europe with emerging technologies suited for FOFA-type strategies as a replacement for flexible response is not feasible, given the prohibitive costs of this approach and its operational-military requirements; and (4) a decoupling of West European defense from the United States would revive age-old nationalistic rivalries among West European powers that would risk generating West-West tension and disunity and East-West political-military instability. Echoing the views of François Mitterrand

and other West European heads of state, Joffe argues that no West European power could replace the U.S. security guarantee. He concludes his analysis with a plea against any U.S. flirtation with "nuclear isolationism" based on a nuclear disengagement from Western Europe and a retreat into a "Fortress America."

Joffe's prescription for the future of the Western Alliance can be reduced to the proposition that things must remain as they have been. Although he provides cogent arguments against proposed alternatives to extended deterrence, such as "conventionalization" in the form of FOFA, his argument for the preservation of the NATO status quo falls short in several essential respects. He fails to consider the more fundamental premises of NATO, which are for him and other traditional Atlanticists so self-evident that they remain unreflected assumptions, although events have in fact put them into question. Joffe's omissions in this respect include (1) the failure to discuss adequately the diminishing Soviet threat in the light of the current plans of the Moscow leadership to radically reduce Soviet armed forces and to restructure them on the basis of the notions of "reasonable sufficiency" and "nonprovocative defense"; (2) the failure to take up the fact that economic realities make it impossible for the United States or the Soviet Union to continue to support the military standoff of NATO and the Warsaw Pact as they have done in the past; and (3) how this fact is forcing major reductions in military outlays and political adjustments in both alliances.

The signs of the economic-military crisis in East and West have been evident from the onset of the Reagan military buildup and, certainly, in the case of the Soviet Union, since the announcement of the Soviet reform program. These changing economic realities raise not only the question of viability of FOFA, which Joffe correctly rejects on economic and other grounds, but also the perpetuation of the postwar East-West military conflict as such. Moreover, although Joffe recognizes the new realities of détente, he fails to draw their full implications for the future of West European security. Somewhat blinded by over forty years of Atlanticism and the Soviet military threat, he fails to address the changes in the international security environment as a result of "new thinking" in the Soviet Union and the signing of the INF Treaty. Symptomatic of a certain myopic dismissiveness regarding current developments, Joffe scornfully rejects the notion of "structural inability to attack" (strukturelle Nichtangriffsunfähigkeit) as an "untranslatable shibboleth" (p. 152); in fact this notion has received serious attention in Western Europe and in the Soviet Union, where it has become a key concept in the program to restructure Soviet forces and to remove the Soviet military threat from Europe. (On the importance of this concept, see Chapter 1, note 35.) Finally, although Joffe rejects FOFA, he does not deal with the problem that most of the advanced weapons programs (which presumably would continue if NATO were to remain as it is) exemplify the main characteristics of the FOFA concept—offensive defense with the capability of deep strikes into Warsaw Pact territory. This fact clearly suggests that the traditional model of NATO is being superceded by the technological dynamics of the arms race and the present course of military R&D. Moreover, it is precisely this offensive dimension of NATO modernization that has become a major factor in the decline of public support for NATO policies, as Joffe himself eloquently suggests in his damning criticism of FOFA as a threat to détente (pp. 164–165).

3. David Buchan, "UK and France to Talk on N-Missiles," *Financial Times*, December 14, 1987. Karl Kaiser and Pierre Lellouche, eds., *Deutsch-*

französische Sicherheits politik. Auf dem Wege zur Gemeinsamkeit (Bonn: Europa Union Verlag, 1986), Part 3, pp. 113–142. David Calleo, in *Beyond American Hegemony: The Future of the Western Alliance* (New York: Basic Books, 1987), argues the opposite position from Joffe (see preceding note). Calleo believes that changing economic, political, and military realities today make possible and necessary a U.S. disengagement from West European defense. He convincingly demonstrates that the United States—with its debtor status, declining growth rates, lower rate of productivity growth, and federal trade and budget deficits—is no longer in a position to support its Atlantic commitments. At the same time, Western Europe, with increased economic strength (partly a result of postwar arrangements), is in a position to assume the economic and military burdens of its own defense vis-à-vis the Warsaw Pact. Calleo, acknowledging the nuclear dilemmas taken up by Joffe, argues in contrast to the latter's strong criticism of a denuclearized, conventional defense, that Western Europe, with the aid of high-tech conventional weapons to implement FOFA, could defend itself with a combination of conventional weapons and a West-Europeanized nuclear deterrent. Calleo can be considered a "Europeanist" insofar as he argues that Western Europe should become relatively autonomous from the United States in security policy. His position is contrary to Joffe's traditional Atlanticism, but both authors share an inability to envision non- and demilitarizing security arrangements. Both authors raise the central problems of East-West security in Western Europe, but neither provides an adequate framework for understanding the role of disarmament and the Soviet reform process in having radically altered the terms of the East-West debate. Nor do they give sufficient weight to the international perception of a diminishing Soviet threat. Calleo carefully documents the process of U.S. hegemonial decline and the unfolding of a more plural world, yet his analysis is weak because he fails to think beyond the military straitjacket of postwar arrangements. In this respect, the full implications of his main thesis—that the postwar world's military arrangements have become unsustainable for both systems—are not drawn. Having failed to do this, Calleo offers only military solutions and the conclusion (which appears to have been disproved by the INF Treaty) that "arms-control negotiations will probably remain what they have become— the diplomatic obligato to the relentless Soviet-American buildup of arms" (p. 214). Another less serious but nonetheless symptomatic weakness of Calleo's analysis is his failure to consider "Europe" as more than its Western portion. Thus the term "pan-Europe," which in Europe today (West and East) has come to mean from the Urals to the Atlantic, is used by him to refer exclusively to Western Europe or, even more restrictedly, to European NATO powers.

4. Horst Afheldt, *Atomkrieg* (München: Hanser, 1984); Ulrich Albrecht, *Kündigt den Nachrüstungsbeschluß!* (Frankfurt: Fischer, 1982).

5. Afheldt, ibid. Albrecht, ibid.

6. Ibid.; Jürgen Altmann, "Technical Problems of ATBM Defenses," in Marlies ter Borg and Wim Smit, *Tactical Missile Defense in Europe* (Amsterdam: Free University Press, 1987), pp. 48–63.

7. See in this context Calleo, op. cit., pp. 82–109; Paul Kennedy, *The Rise and Fall of Great Powers* (New York: Random House, 1987).

8. See in this context Zellner, op. cit.; Walter Schütze, "Der 'Erbfeind' als Ersatzfreund," *Blätter for deutsche Politik und internationale Politik*, Vol. 33, No. 1, January 1988, pp. 25–36; Pascal Boniface and François Heisbourg, *Les Puces, les Hommes et la Bombe: L'Europe face aux nouveaux*

défis technologiques et militaires (Paris: Hachette, 1986), Part 2, pp. 213–278.

9. See in this context Ernest Conne, "Europe Talks Up a Self-Reliant Defense," *Los Angeles Times*, November 3, 1987; Michael Howard, "A European Perspective on the Reagan Years," *Foreign Affairs*, Vol. 66, No. 3 (*America and the World 1987–88*), pp. 378–493; Boniface and Heisbourg, ibid.

10. See in this context Ingo Kolboom, "Im Westen nichts neues? Frankreichs Sicherheitspolitik and die deutsche Frage" in Kaiser and Lellouche, op. cit., pp. 68–89; Karen Elliot House, "Europessimism Takes Turn for the Worse," *Wall Street Journal*, January 27, 1988; Calleo, op. cit.; pp. 171f.

11. Phillip Revzin, "French Fight to Anchor Germany in West," *Wall Street Journal*, January 21, 1988.

12. Joseph Fitchett, "National Security Gives Protectionists a Weapon," *International Herald Tribune*, December 16, 1988; Jolyon Howorth, "Die französische Verteidigungspolitik im Widerstreit zwischen Abrüstung und Abschreckung," *Europa-Archiv*, Vol. 43, No. 12, 1988, pp. 331–339.

13. William Arkin et al., "Nuclear Weapons" in *SIPRI Yearbook 1989* (Oxford: Oxford University Press, 1989), pp. 3–48. On French nuclear strategy see Kaiser and Lellouche, op. cit., Part 2, pp. 57–109. See also Fréderic Tiberghien, "Puissance et rôle de l'armament préstratégique français," *Le Monde Diplomatique*, Vol. 34, No. 395, February 1987, pp. 14–15; "Kohl: Paris kann Nuklear-Garantie nicht übernehmen," *Süddeutsche Zeitung*, June 24, 1987; Ian Davidson, "Mitterrand Explains N-Weapons Policy," *Financial Times*, October 23, 1987.

14. "NATO Chief Backs Paris-Bonn Accord," *Financial Times*, February 11, 1988.

15. Commission on Integrated Long-Term Strategy, *Discriminate Deterrence* (Washington, D.C., January 1988), Chapter 3. Both Kissinger and Brzezinski are among the authors of this report.

16. On the Wackersdorf reprocessing plant, see Arbeitsgruppe Atomindustrie, *Wer mit Wem im Atomstaat und Grossindustrie* (Frankfurt: Verlag 2001, 1987); on the political demonstrations in Wackersdorf, see Manfred Bissing, "Wo Recht zu Unrecht wird," *Natur*, No. 25, August 1986; Klaus Lange, "Über den neuen Widerstand" in ibid.

17. The Nukem scandal has been reported in detail by the West German news media. On the development of the affair, see Klaus Brill, "Allmählich fügt sich das Puzzle zusammen," *Süddeutsche Zeitung*, January 15 and 16, 1988. See also the numerous articles in *Der Spiegel*, Vol. 42, No. 2, January 4, 1988, and No. 3, January 11, 1988.

18. Georg Blum, "Französische Neutronenbombe soll in der BRD stationiert werden," *Tageszeitung*, May 7, 1987.

19. Charles van Doren, "Pakistan and Congress," *Arms Control Today*, Vol. 17, No. 9, November 1987, pp. 6–9; Lewis Dunn, "Non-Proliferation: The Next Steps," in ibid., pp. 3–5; "Die Katze schnurrt in Kahut," *Der Spiegel*, Vol. 42, No. 3, January 18, 1988.

20. Calleo, op. cit., Chapter 10; see also the essays in Kaiser and Lellouche, op. cit.

21. Schütze, op. cit.

22. Ibid.

23. Ibid.; Ian Davidson, "A Little Local Difficulty," *Financial Times*, December 22, 1987.

24. Schütze, op. cit.

25. Davidson, "A Little Difficulty," op. cit.

26. Arkin, op. cit.; François Heisbourg, "The British and French Nuclear Forces," *Survival*, Vol. 31, No. 4, July/August 1989, pp. 301–320. Howorth, op. cit.; Berthold Meyer and Peter Schlotter, "Deutsch-französischer Sicherheitsrat soll die Abrüstungsbereitschaft Frankreichs fördern," Press Release, Peace Research Institute Frankfurt, January 18, 1988.

27. Meyer and Schlotter, ibid.

28. See in this context Egon Bahr, *Zum europäischen Frieden, Eine Autwort auf Gorbatschow* (West Berlin: Siedler, 1988).

29. Ibid.; Meyer und Schlotter, op. cit.

30. Schütze, op. cit.

31. Ibid.; Thomas O'Boyle, "Nuclear-Missile Talks Lend a New Urgency to Paris-Bonn Amity," *Wall Street Journal*, June 12, 1987; David Marsh, "Paris and Bonn to Create Joint Defense Council," *Financial Times*, September 25, 1987.

32. "Franco-German Co-operation," *Financial Times*, November 17, 1987.

33. Tim Carrington, "Kohl Stance on Nuclear Arms Intensifies Allied Concern About European Defense," *Wall Street Journal*, February 8, 1988.

34. "Die Partei Giscards für die Neutronenbombe," *Frankfurter Allgemeine Zeitung*, May 30, 1987. For a detailed documentation of French plans concerning the neutron bomb, see Blum, op. cit.; see also the accompanying interviews by Georg Blum and Mycle Schneider with Charles Hernu and Pierre Messner.

35. William Arkin et al., "Nuclear Weapons," in *SIPRI Yearbook 1988*, (Oxford: Oxford University Press, 1988), pp. 23–64.

36. Carrington, op. cit. The decision by Chancellor Kohl can be interpreted as an attempt to exclude the issue of Lance modernization from the 1990 national elections. The failure to reject modernization outright, however, in the opinion of the West German SPD, will probably keep the Lance in the center of the campaign.

37. Howorth, op. cit.

38. Diana Johnstone, "After U.S.-Soviet INF Pact Europe May Build Own Missiles," *In These Times*, February 24–March 8, 1988.

39. Ibid.

40. Weidenfeld, op. cit. For an overview of the failed plans for a West European nuclear multilateral force (MLF), see Joffe, op. cit., pp. 55–60.

41. Calleo, op. cit., pp. 183ff.

42. See in this context the concluding chapter in Joffe, op. cit., pp. 189–209.

43. See in this context ". . . und dann ist es die deutsche Bombe," interview with Robert Jungk, *Die Zeit*, Vol. 43, No. 5, January 29, 1988.

44. Arkin et al., op. cit., 1988; Leon Spector, "Nuclear Proliferation, Who's Next," *Bulletin of Atomic Scientists*, Vol. 43, No. 4, May 1987; Dunn, op. cit.

45. Hubertus Hoffmann, *Atompartner Washington-Bonn* (Koblenz: Bernard and Gräfe, 1986), as cited by Robert Jungk in interview, *Die Zeit*, op. cit.

46. Joffe, op. cit., pp. 200–202.

47. For detailed coverage of Honecker's visit to Paris, see *Neues Deutschland*, January 8, 9, and 10, 1988. On relations between France and the GDR and the economic motives of Mitterrand's policy, see Friedhelm B. Meyer

zu Natrup, "Frankreich und die DDR," *Europa-Archiv*, Vol. 43, No. 11, 1988, pp. 311–320.

48. See in this context Günter Gaus, "The Two Germanies, Don't Over-React to Mr. Honecker's Visit," *Financial Times*, September 2, 1987; Günter Gaus, "Berlin in Germany: Foundation of Europe's Peace," *International Affairs*, Vol. 63, No. 3, Summer 1987, pp. 439–448.

49. See in this context Bahr 1988, op. cit.; Karsten Voigt, "Von einer Zone der Hochrüstung zu Schritten der regionalen Abrüstung: Europa am Scheideweg," *S + F, Vierteljahresschrift für Sicherheit und Frieden*, Vol. 5, No. 3, 1987, pp. 170–177 and Christian Krause, "Strukturelle Nichtangriffsfähigkeit im Rahmen europäischer Entspannungspolitik," in same publication, pp. 183–194.

PART 2

The Economic and Technological Challenge of Post-INF Europe

CHAPTER 6

The Erosion of Postwar Military Production and the Future of the U.S. Economy

The decline of the postwar model of security and the policy watershed it has opened up are reflected in the economic and technological challenges that the United States had to confront during the Reagan era. The Reagan administration failed to reverse the erosion of U.S. military and economic power through its massive military spending program.

The purpose of this chapter is to examine this failure and to suggest that it is a powerful demonstration of the main hypothesis of this book— that the United States and the Western Alliance as a whole have reached a turning point in which the postwar model of security is collapsing as a viable military, political, and economic foundation of Western policy consensus. The failure of using military expenditures for economic development—the policy the United States has practiced throughout the postwar period—is forcing both the United States and Western Europe to begin an uneven shift in the direction of disarmament, détente, and East-West economic-political cooperation. This reorientation reflects not only the political realities discussed in Part 1 but also the imperatives of economic recovery and the need to reforge security policymaking on a demilitarizing foundation compatible with the new realities of the global economy.

In this chapter I link the erosion of the postwar model of security to the decline of the postwar model of economic growth and the resulting search by all major Western economies for new technologies to enable them to produce more efficiently and remain internationally competitive. Although Western Europe's response to the collapse of postwar growth (discussed in more detail in Chapter 7) has been more civilian- and market-oriented, the United States looked to the postwar model of security and its corollary in military spending for a stimulant of aggregate demand and technology innovation. I will also argue that the failure of the Reagan military program to accomplish its initial aims suggests that the structural adjustment of the U.S. economy in the coming years will depend on a conscious delinking of industrial planning from military spending.

The Decline of the U.S. Economy

The early claims of the Reagan administration that its large military budgets could be fiscally sustained and would also spur economic growth were not borne out. The Reagan era came to an end against the backdrop of annual federal deficits of over $200 billion, trade deficits on the order of $150 billion, and the widespread agreement across the domestic and international political spectrum that the U.S. military budget of $300 billion could no longer be sustained.[1] The urgency of budgetary retrenchment and a shift of priorities was accented with the worldwide stock market crash in October 1987.

Despite the never-say-die claims by the outgoing president to the contrary, the U.S. economy dramatically deteriorated during the 1980–1988 period. Lloyd Dumas, writing in 1987, listed the following economic indicators to demonstrate this point:

> - *a halt and reversal in the growth of average real income*—purchasing power earned per hour worked has been flat during the 1980s and it fell 3 percent between 1978 and 1985;
> - *twenty-year highs in the poverty rate*—peaking at 15.2 percent in the "strong recovery" year, 1983;
> - *hundreds of bank failures*—more than 300 since 1981 and a post-Depression record of 120 in 1985 alone;
> - *a doubling of the national debt* in the last six years, with 1985 interest service alone absorbing roughly $130 billion—approximately the personal income tax collections from all Americans living west of the Mississippi River; . . .
> - *a worsening trade-off between unemployment and inflation,* with both averaging, in the first half of the 1980s, more than twice their average rate in the last half of the 1960s;
> - *deteriorating rates of productivity growth*—the average annual rate having dropped by 33 percent in the business sector as a whole and 73 percent in manufacturing, between 1965–69 and 1980–84;
> - *a gigantic trade deficit* that by 1985 had more than doubled the record-breaking $69.4 billion figure set only two years earlier. This turnaround followed a string of continuous trade surpluses from 1894 to 1970.[2]

The declining performance of the U.S. economy and its effects on competitiveness have been assessed by Stephen Cohen and John Zysman. They take as their criteria the following economic indicators: trade deficits in manufactured goods; share of export markets; rates of productivity increases; profit margins; real wages; increasing price elasticities of imports; and position in high-technology markets. They conclude that "American industry confronts a severe problem of competitiveness such as it has never known before. Each measure has its limitations and can perhaps be explained away, but, taken together, they defy easy dismissal and portray a serious, long-term problem."[3]

Cohen and Zysman emphasize the link between U.S economic decline and the failure to introduce on a wide scale automatic control technologies such as CAD and CAM (computer-aided design and manufacturing) in the manufacturing sector. The U.S. ability to compete, they point out, also suffered as a result of low-cost labor in newly industrializing countries, whose firms have therefore been able to penetrate the markets of advanced economies. In addition, U.S. producers moved their production facilities offshore in order to find cheap labor, to be in closer proximity to foreign markets, and to reduce the cost of products they sell in the United States.[4] Such

"de-industrialization" has been encouraged by developing countries which have adopted policies favorable to setting up export platforms and other benefits for U.S. capital. The cumulative effect of this process is the loss of manufacturing ability itself and the disappearance of supply and service infrastructures over several generations of product and process innovation.[5]

Also in a sobering vein, the economist C. Fred Bergsten has warned of the worsening of the U.S. financial position. He points out that U.S. debt is likely to exceed $1 trillion by 1989 and rise by $300 billion or so annually thereafter.[6] Already by 1985 the United States, over a period of just two years, lost its position as the world's largest creditor and became the largest debtor. By 1989, Bergsten predicts, "U.S. external debt could exceed the total external debt of all the developing countries."[7]

The Origins of Military Keynesianism

In order to understand the current decline of the U.S. economy, it must be placed within the broader context[8] of (1) the historical decline of the postwar model of growth; and (2) the U.S. response to this decline in the form of massive military outlays amounting to over $2 trillion during the Reagan era. This spending has been linked to the following broad goals: (a) increasing aggregate demand; (b) technologically regenerating the U.S. economy; and (c) improving military security.

The postwar boom, based on major investment in industries such as automobiles, manufacturing, petrochemicals, jet aircraft, computers, shipbuilding, and nuclear power, petered out in the late 1960s. This long cycle of growth is linked to Keynesian policies of stimulating effective demand in Western market economies through government spending, which has led to creation of a growing public sector and, in the case of the United States more so than in other major Western economies, defense outlays.

In its U.S. form, the postwar model of growth was linked to the assumption of the compatibility of a relatively high level of military spending with healthy economic performance. Since the 1950s, "Military Keynesianism"[9] has been a central component of U.S. economic policy, and it has formed the historical root of the large deficit-based military budgets of the 1980s. Military Keynesianism has been defined by Hugh Mosley as a more or less explicit concept of economic policy that "entails the use of military expenditures to promote economic stability and growth within a broadly Keynesian framework."[10] The five basic elements of this approach are

1. A demand management perspective on the economy and a concern with the problems of insufficient aggregate demand.
2. The willingness to use government fiscal and monetary policy to stimulate aggregate demand to maintain employment and spur growth.
3. The willingness to engage in planned deficits to support continued or expanded countercyclical government demand, in contrast to the older fiscal orthodoxy of the necessity for balanced budgets.
4. Reliance on government military expenditures to create such demand.
5. The assumption that the government-subsidized high-technology component of military-industrial production contributes significantly to innovation and growth in the economy as a whole.[11]

After World War II, the success of "war socialism"[12] had led top economists and government advisers to believe that military expenditures would be a well-suited instrument for economic management. This was the reasoning: First, through defense expenditures the federal government can expand the public sector without competing against the private sector or undermining business confidence. Second, military expenditures are "highly flexible because there is no readily conceivable general state of oversupply of military goods with a rapid rate of technological obsolescence in a competitive arms race. That is, the United States can have too many schools, hospital beds, or even highways, but military spending for national security is subject to no such manifest limits."[13] Third, military spending is highly elastic and can be increased or contracted to conform to the short-run requirements of economic policy. Finally, defense purchases of goods and services stimulate the economy in a direct and immediate way. The economic effect

begins as soon as contracts are let or "obligations incurred," in contrast to the more indirect stimulation of a tax cut, reduced interest rates, or increased transfer payments, all of which take much longer to affect employment. Because defense purchases of goods and services account for more than two-thirds of all federal purchases, this instrument is ready at hand for U.S. policymakers.

[Fourthly,] . . . in contrast to increased consumer spending and to many government social programs, military demand is particularly focused on the stagnation-prone capital goods sector because of the high ratio of hardware and construction in military spending and the specialized and shifting channels of final demand.[14]

In the late 1940s, Military Keynesian principles were incorporated in the National Security Council's Memorandum 68 (NSC-68), which was to form the policy foundation of postwar foreign policy.[15] NSC-68 called for a massive buildup of U.S. military forces in order to combat what it alleged to be the aggressive and expansive foreign policy of the Soviet Union. It contrasted the high levels of economic production during the war and the slowdown of the U.S. economy with the recession of 1949 and argued that large military outlays would sustain economic health. Its economic principles were controversial and became the subject of an internal policy debate.[16] But the outbreak of the Korean War produced the popular support the Truman administration needed to have NSC-68 officially adopted in 1950. It became a central policy rationale for U.S. rearmament and, as Mosley points out, was "not only the source of militarization of foreign policy and of the corresponding new military strategy of defense through the maintenance of large peacetime forces, but also the beginning of the militarization of economic policy."[17]

The use of military spending as an economic stimulus has continued uninterrupted throughout the postwar era. With the decline of the postwar boom, the allegedly positive effects of Military Keynesianism have been put into question but without essentially affecting U.S. policy. On the contrary, the decline of U.S. economic performance was a central rationale for the Reagan military spending program, but the result was a general economic decline, particularly in the military sector.

Signs of Deterioration of the U.S. Military Economy

Prospective defense spending cuts in the United States[18] and in other Western and Eastern economies have been briefly discussed in preceding chapters. The need for adjustment of various sorts can be linked to several factors.

Costs, military trade-offs, and mismanagement. The significantly increased cost of military research, development, and production of new weapons systems has created significant trade-offs between state-of-the-art advanced weaponry and general military preparedness (personnel, training, infrastructures, and logistics).[19] These problems have been exacerbated in the United States by large cost overruns in military programs; poor project management; extensive waste of defense industrial resources, increasing environmental damage; unchecked interservice rivalry;[20] lack of coherent long-term planning; widespread padding of contracts (known as "gold-plating"); and criminal violations by defense contractors.[21]

Procurement and technological obsolescence. The procurement cycle for new weapons lags behind the fast pace of high-technology development. It is more often the case today that military establishments procure weapons that quickly become technologically obsolete.[22] A related problem is the mismatch between hardware and software—SDI is an example. The rush to produce battle management hardware led to technologically premature designs that were already outdated because they were incompatible with researched but still undeveloped types of software considered necessary for SDI's mission.[23]

Secrecy versus openness. The penchant for secrecy and restriction of information by military R&D laboratories conflicts with the need for openness and expanding networks of communication among scientists working on the frontiers of military and civilian technologies.[24] The stunting effects of secrecy are cogently illustrated in the case of information technology, a driving force of the civilian and military technological revolution. The advance of the R&D in this field depends on a number of external factors, such as collaboration between laboratories and firms, expansion of networks of data banks and hardware systems, accommodation of faster and larger data flows, and increased numbers of expert and nonexpert end users in the public and private sectors. The attempt, through policies of classification and information restriction, to reserve a special domain of the international diffusion of civilian information technology for exclusive use in U.S. military projects conflicts with the general advancement of information technology. It also conflicts with the strategy of multinational firms throughout the world, which are accelerating cooperation through international licensing agreements, coproduction, joint ventures, and communications networks with universities and research laboratories. Given this trend, it is not surprising that U.S. insistence on restrictions has generated friction between civilian and military interest groups in different areas of advanced technology.[25]

Civilian innovations and security export controls. In contrast to earlier phases of the postwar era, nonmilitary R&D of advanced technology has now established a substantial lead over military R&D. Defense departments have become dependent on civilian technology innovations, which led the Reagan administration at the behest of the Pentagon to impose qualitatively more stringent security controls to restrict the domestic movement and export of potentially dual-use high technology and a wide range of scientific data. These actions were defended by the U.S government on military-technological and economic-competitive grounds and have formed a central thrust of U.S. policy.[26] The Reagan administration envisioned qualitatively expanding the military-technological edge of the United States over the Soviet Union and restoring U.S. technological leadership in the world economy. That this strategy backfired is suggested by the worsening of U.S. economic performance and the absence of any clear signs that the United States has approached an undisputed qualitative superiority over the Soviets. Moreover, as U.S. security controls increased, they evoked mounting skepticism concerning military R&D in a highly restricted environment as an effective instrument of technology development.[27]

Civilian economic priorities. Advanced industrial economies locked into the race for emerging nonmilitary technologies are under fiscal and other economic pressures to reduce their military outlays, which put at risk nonmilitary priorities.[28] Although there is no scholarly consensus on the effects of military spending on the civilian economy, a growing body of evidence suggests that defense outlays do not result in sufficient spin-off to justify the use of military R&D as an effective instrument to generate nonmilitary technological innovations. This conclusion derives in part from the increasing divergence in design specifications for civilian and military goods.[29] Military equipment must be designed for the extreme conditions of the nuclear battlefield, which is technologically far removed from markets for nonmilitary consumer and capital goods. The failure to take account of this divergence and sundry other related trade-offs between civilian and military investment is linked by some experts to the long-term slippage in key economic indicators of countries such as the United States and Britain. These nations have devoted a relatively higher percentage of their R&D resources over the past forty years to military production, partly with the expectation and rationale of large amounts of spin-offs moving from the military to the civilian sector. By contrast, military outlays of export giants such as Japan and the Federal Republic throughout the postwar period have been significantly smaller as a percentage of GNP than those of the United States.[30]

Given the relatively large U.S. commitment to military R&D, one could reasonably expect that the efficiency of the major U.S. manufacturing industries would correspondingly improve—or at least maintain a relatively constant level—if in fact the standard arguments concerning the positive effects of military spending on the civilian economy hold. Since the early 1960s, however, U.S. high-technology industries have lost ground to Japan and Western Europe in competition for shares of both the U.S. and international markets. In 1984 the U.S. balance of trade in high technology showed a deficit for the first time, despite the fact that in the 1980–1988 period federal outlays for R&D increased by 26 percent (in constant U.S. dollars). The significance of this statistic becomes clear when it is also noted that defense outlays for R&D increased 83 percent during this period, while civilian R&D fell 24 percent.[31] This shift of resources from the civilian to the military sector was made with the expectation that it would enhance the U.S. high-tech position in international trade. The evident decline of military R&D as an efficient driving force of nonmilitary innovation and market success has led to a still-limited reappraisal in the United States of military R&D planning and of the relationship between the military establishment and the nonmilitary industrial sector.[32]

Saturation of the arms market. The expansion of the international arms market during the 1970s and early 1980s was plagued by the worldwide economic contraction. Most severely affected were the nations of the Third World, which are major clients of First World arms suppliers. Slow growth, falling prices for raw materials, falling exports, and rising debt reduced the ability of many Third World states to purchase large stocks of sophisticated arms, which in turn intensified international competition among suppliers and generated surplus capacity and overproduction. Exacerbating the problem was the emergence of new state-sponsored suppliers among the newly industrializing nations. In the struggle of arms exporters to maintain their respective market shares in a period of defense budget contraction, the Iran-Iraq war provided a welcome and lucrative outlet. The result was a spectacular increase in illegal exports of a wide range of weapons systems to both sides, including missiles, aircraft, and chemical and biological weapons.[33] The documented use of these weapons in the war and their gruesome mass destruction of human life highlighted the political problem of the proliferation of non-nuclear weapons. It also focused worldwide attention on the ability of suppliers to circumvent controls easily and to violate with impunity domestic and international law to assure sales in an increasingly out-of-control global market.

Arms exports and Third World debt. The vicious cycle of arms production and pressure on Third World states to provide market outlets has become an obstacle to overcoming the debt crisis of the Third World. Because they have hindered a more constructive allocation of scarce economic resources, arms sales to the Third World have had the overall effect of exacerbating the debt problem. This resulted in the 1980s in mounting pressure on the financial institutions and economies of the First World as the aggregate debt mass continued to grow.[34]

Military Spending as "Industrial Policy"

Although the United States does not have a genuine industrial policy, large military outlays and the economic weight of the defense sector raise the question of to what extent military expenditures constitute a "pseudo-industrial" policy. Ann Markusen, echoing a well-established view, argues that U.S. military spending functions as a "de facto industrial policy"—but one in which the distortions "brought about by this reliance on military-led investment and innovation" have led to poor economic performance.[35] She discusses the following characteristics that qualify U.S. defense spending as a de facto industrial policy.

> It targets specific sectors in the economy that are believed to possess longterm potential for promoting growth in employment and output. It provides substantial research and development funding to firms in those sectors. It offers large-scale incentives for technological innovation and funds for major investments on favorable terms. It provides for the government to act as a large and dependable customer through special procurement arrangements. It utilizes trade policies, such as trade promotion and protection, to favor certain industries. And it provides adjustment assistance for displaced workers and communities through retraining of personnel and conversion of idled facilities.[36]

In elaborating on these characteristics, Markusen explains the role of research programs like the Defense Advanced Research Projects Agency (DARPA):

> The government channels substantial resources to a rather small set of large, heavily defense-dependent firms in high-tech industries like aircraft and missiles, communications equipment, and electronics. It provides a protected market for their products by acting as the single largest buyer in crucial early commercialization stages and by . . . efforts to adapt numerically-controlled machine tools, CAD/CAM (computer-aided design/computer-aided manufacturing) systems, and other automating technologies to the production of military hardware. It builds and leases or sells plants to defense contractors at bargain rates. . . . It offers lifetime job and income security to military personnel, as well as retraining services for retired officers.[37]

Military spending as a motor of R&D for nonmilitary commerical technology. In the 1960s, a number of Pentagon programs were successful in encouraging nonmilitary competitiveness and the technological advancement of U.S. high-tech industries. In that phase of postwar economic and technological development, military spending in the form of investment in R&D and in procurement appeared to have positive results. As Jay Stowsky points out:

> In the case of early Pentagon involvement in areas such as aircraft and microelectronics, for example, . . . military programs aimed explicitly at advancing the technological state-of-the-art, encouraged competitive product development and efficient, generalizable

production technologies, provided outlets for stable volume
production that enabled manufacturers to realize learning curves and
large economies of scale over long production runs. . . . [This]
occurred at an early state in each industry's development (before the
direction of commerical development had been defined and confirmed
by investment), and permitted relevant military advances to diffuse
into commercial applications. In both of these cases, the Pentagon
clearly assisted in the creation of a beneficial and competitive
trajectory of development for the affected industries.[38]

The positive results of Pentagon involvement described above did not occur,
however, in the case of numerically controlled machine tools:

Defense programs have focused on the development of specific
military product applications, relied on sole-source suppliers and
cost-plus contracts, underwritten the use of expensive, specialized
production batches, involved industries whose commercial priorities
were already well-established and confirmed by a pattern of
investments, and did not permit dual-use technologies to diffuse into
the commercial sector. In these cases, the Pentagon has clearly
contributed to the evolution of a militarily dependent and
uncompetitive industry structure.[39]

The result of this failure of Pentagon intervention has been the rapid
decline of U.S. competitiveness in this important industrial branch. As
Stowsky notes:

Although the total number of NC machine tools almost doubled
between 1978 and 1982, imports as a share of the value of U.S.
consumption rose from a little over 23 percent in 1980 to more than
35 percent in 1983, almost 90 percent of them from Japan. In 1984,
two-thirds of the numerically controlled turning machines and three-
quarters of the NC machining centers installed in U.S. firms were
bought from foreign firms. During the first seven months of 1985,
more than 50 percent of all NC tools used in the United States came
from overseas.[40]

The Pentagon and the weakening of the individual firm. In his
investigation of the effects of Pentagon involvement in the commercial
workings of the firm, Stowsky (echoing similar findings by Melman) points
out that the firm's competitiveness is often sharply reduced as it turns away
from market signals and begins to "mimic the bureaucratic structure of the
Pentagon."[41] This imitation occurs as the firm quite naturally strives to
communicate and deal with Pentagon officials more effectively. In summing
up the dangers of Pentagon dependence, Stowsky concludes that the Pentagon
"can use explicitly uncompetitive incentives . . . to structure the organization

of production to suit its own purposes."[42] He does not label Pentagon involvement as necessarily good or bad, but feels the potentially beneficial effects of Pentagon support for a firm—R&D subsidies, diffusion of innovations by defense-trained personnel, volume premiums, and so on—degrade easily into damaging forms of protectionism, sole-source dependence, cost-plus contracts, technological oversophistication, narrowly applied R&D overspecialization, and export controls.[43]

Military spending as a mask of true economic performance. One of the effects of military production in the United States has been the misperception of economic performance, particularly during the Reagan era. To demonstrate this point, Markusen cites the "recovery" of 1983 in which military spending obscured how poorly nonmilitary sectors were doing: The recovery was largely the result of deficit military spending and the limited economic stimulation it produced.[44] Markusen also cites another example of this phenomenon by correlating the 1985 output of consumer goods and business equipment (no increase) with the production of military and space goods (an increase of 11 percent). While demand for military equipment increased 45 percent in January 1986, other factory orders fell by 1 percent. A similar pattern was visible in trade: Net exports of capital goods fell from $42 billion in 1980 to $12 billion in 1984. During this same period, net exports of military-type equipment tripled, increasing from $5.7 billion to $16.5 billion.[45]

The Decline of Postwar Keynesianism

As growth rates slowed during the 1960s, the mainstay industries of major Western economies no longer attracted sustaining levels of investment. They had reached the stage of maturity and their rate of return had permanently declined. The standard postwar cure of stimulating more aggregate demand proved unable to crank up the sluggish motors of industrial growth. Keynesian inputs only further bloated public deficits without stemming the tide of sliding profits, heavy import penetration, lost markets, and deindustrialization resulting from migration of production capacity (and know-how) to low-wage enclaves abroad.[46] Rationalization policies were introduced that placed the welfare state, employment, and the traditional position of organized labor under mounting pressure. The need for major restructuring was increasingly felt. Tulder and Junne have described the search for new technologies as a consequence of this structural contraction:

> The world economy is actually undergoing a massive restructuring. This is a reaction to the economic crisis in the 1970s and the early 1980s. Western Europe has been more affected by the crisis than

either the United States of America or Japan. While economic growth (of the Gross National Product) in Japan still averaged 4.4% in the period 1974–1984, the United States only realized 2.7% and Europe only 1.8%. And while official unemployment never reached more than 2.7% in Japan and 9.5% in the United States, it climbed to 10.8% in the European Community.[47]

In an effort to reverse these trends, programs were launched to cut capital costs, raise productivity, improve competitive position, and create new markets, particularly for high-value consumer products. New technologies were sought to achieve these goals. According to this strategy, larger investment by industry and government in R&D would create new means of production to bring about an economic upswing and a new long wave of prosperity.[48] The diffusion of emerging technologies, it was hoped, would place the industrial base on a new foundation that would streamline the production of goods and services. Technological breakthroughs and their expeditious product application, according to this vision, would provide additional growth opportunities and, in the same dynamic upswing, remove the bottlenecks that had brought postwar growth to a halt.

Postwar Decline and Technological Renewal

A major consequence of the economic decline was the rise in unemployment, which contributed to the erosion of the traditional postwar relationship among government, organized labor, and management in the advanced industrial countries. The institutionalized structures established between organized labor and management, together with guarantees of the welfare state, formed the social architecture that helped sustain postwar prosperity based on standardized mass production and consumption markets. The decline of the "Fordist" model of production was accompanied by signs of fragmentation of the power of organized labor, particularly in the United States and Britain, throughout the 1970s and 1980s.[49] The rise in structural unemployment reflected both the decline of the traditional technological base of postwar production and the introduction of rationalization in the form of automation and new production technologies, which radically reduced the number of necessary workers in a wide range of industries and service sectors. These trends have been linked by Tulder and Junne and by Roobeek to the evolution of the production process as follows:[50]

1. During the 1960s and 1970s, the cost of labor increased as the rate of productivity growth slackened and was no longer able to keep pace with the regularly negotiated wage increases that were the hallmark of the codified cooperation between organized labor and corporate management during most of the postwar period.

2. To compensate for rising wages, large firms introduced automatic

equipment, but it could only produce a single product on the model of centralized mass production. In order to produce with a high rate of return, larger economies of scale were introduced through high-volume production, which in turn required larger, more centralized factories and thus resulted in higher overhead.

3. The attempt to compensate for the falling rate of return and intensified competition through larger, more centralized production units, together with other factors, substantially increased levels of pollution and other forms of environmental damage.

4. Increasing energy consumption produced geopolitical tensions as well as major financial and ecological problems.

5. Increasing demand for particular raw materials, especially oil, and the periodic loss of easy access to raw material sources posed the recurring problem of scarcities capable of disrupting the production cycle.

6. Because of extensive investments in fixed automation, large over-centralized mass production units, and complex environmental regulations to manage increasing pollution levels, equipment tended to become increasingly inflexible.

To overcome these bottlenecks, companies and governments looked to the research and development of new technologies that would reduce the cost of labor, limit capital needs, have less detrimental effects on the environment, consume less energy and other raw materials, and provide for more flexibility. This investment in R&D came at a time of emerging technological breakthroughs. The result has been the current global race for new technologies.

The potential of new technologies: several examples. In analyzing technologies, which they see as the prospective basis of a new economic upswing and restructuring, Tulder and Junne concentrate on "core technologies" such as microelectronics and biotechnology.[51] These have spawned a wealth of new products, processes, and services and are having an across-the-board restructuring impact on the international economy.

Microelectronics and biotechnology have also been characterized as "technology clusters" around which individual technologies are being further developed and are linking up in "technology webs."[52] This process is occurring in the R&D phase of emerging technologies and in the phase of their integration into existing and newly emerging industrial systems.

Microelectronics can reduce labor spent in production by cutting the time necessary for assembly of a product or lowering the number of moving parts. In the form of word processors, numerically controlled machines, and robots, this technology can replace large numbers of human workers on an assembly line. The cost of employing a robot is estimated at $6 per hour in the United States, whereas the wage of an auto worker doing a similar or the same task would be about $19 an hour.[53] Moreover, because robots are run on digital information, they can be linked up with other divisions of a production complex, such as a warehouse for raw materials and half-finished products, or with administrative offices or other geographically distant divisions of large firms.

Similarly, telecommunications technologies based on the microchip can boost productivity among workers. Improved communication through more efficient and more rapid flow of information from one place to another means this technology can often substitute for the transport of goods and people, thereby reducing traveling time and commuting.

Other capital- and labor-saving benefits that can be derived from application of microelectronics include improved organization of production, avoidance of duplication, and the reduction of waste and errors in the work process. An important example of lowering capital costs is the displacement of large mainframe computers in many spheres of production by personal computers, which are as work-efficient as the older mainframes. Similarly, capital goods have also been greatly cheapened by becoming programable. A machine that can be reprogramed can perform with greater versatility. Different models of the same product can be more easily manufactured by a single machine. Machines equipped with the necessary software can diagnose their own breakdowns and repair themselves, thus avoiding costly down-time and the need to call in repair personnel. Reprogramable machines also make it possible to change models more efficiently and rapidly—for example, in the auto industry—which can lead to investment savings of 60 percent over fixed automation and thus make it unnecessary to write off costly machinery once the particular model in production is retired.

Biotechnology, the other technology cluster, will make it possible to replace or eliminate a broad range of ecologically dirty and costly petrochemical processes. Whereas petrochemicals must be "cooked" at high temperatures and under high pressure, biotechnological processes take place at low pressure and naturally occurring temperature.[54] Because equipment does not have to be exposed to extreme conditions, capital costs can be significantly reduced. Biotechnology has extraordinary potential for application across sectors, with revolutionary implications for agriculture, medicine, the physical and natural sciences, and many other fields.

An emerging new paradigm of work. The far-reaching impact of new technologies has led a number of analysts to postulate a new paradigm of the production and labor process that differs from the model of centralized mass production that has dominated during the postwar period. This evolving paradigm is radically altering (a) the nature of the production process; (b) the relationship of workers to their instruments of labor; and (c) the worker's function and specific quality of labor input in the production process. This paradigm, known as "flexible specialization" and based on technologies such as CAD and CAM, can bring automation to very small production runs ("batch production") of a large variety of different goods. It is linked to

> more specialized, higher-valued products—goods that are precision-engineered, that are custom-tailored to serve individual markets, or that embody rapidly evolving technologies. Such products will be found in high-tech segments of more traditional industries (specialty steel and chemicals, computer-controlled machine tools, advanced automobile components) as well as in new high-technology industries (semiconductors, fiber optics, lasers, biotechnology and robotics).[55]

Robert Reich argues that production based on "flexible specialization" assumes that the worker participates in key strategic activities of the firm. These include planning for rapid changes in product line and the introduction of process innovation in response to constantly changing market conditions. He cites several examples of existing flexible enterprises in the following description of the labor process linked to the concept:

> Wherever such enterprises are found—in many Japanese factories, in the sogo shosha (trading companies) of Japan, in a few American companies producing high-technology goods, in Israeli kibbutz industries, in several Swedish and West German firms, in the plants of the Mondragón region of Spain—there are many of the same attributes: The salaries, benefits, and status of senior managers are not vastly different from those of junior employees; employees are relatively secure in their jobs; and important company decisions contribute to widespread consultation and negotiation. These features contribute to increased productivity . . . because they enhance the organization's capacity to adapt quickly to novel situations.[56]

The worker as transmitter of knowledge to industry. In their analysis of industrial policy, Walter Zegveld and Christien Enzing view reindustrialization as the "structural transformation of industry into higher added value, more knowledge-intensive sectors and product groups, and the creation of major new technology-based industries serving new markets."[57] They emphasize that to attain these goals, science and technology are necessary but by themselves insufficient. They stress the role of the worker as one of the essential ways in which the transfer of knowledge to industry takes place and the role of coupling with the commercial market as an important element of industrial policy:

> "Knowledge" as an input-factor is transferred to industry in two main ways. The first way is that knowledge is incorporated in the labour supply to industry via the labour market. The currently perceived importance of education and training can well be illustrated and

measured by the considerable financial allocations in this area; the financial means in question represent a significant share of overall government budgets. At the same time, relatively little attention is being paid to the development of coupling mechanisms between the educational system and its "clients," an important client being industry. The second technology transfer path consists of direct knowledge and hardware transfers to industry from the co-financed technical and scientifc infra-structure.

Within the framework of industrial technology policy, it is clearly important to restructure the pattern of allocation of public funds, skilled manpower supply and public R&D facilities in such a way that better match the requirements of the market sector.[58]

Conclusion: The Military Keynesian Response

The Reagan era experienced an accelerated decline of the U.S. economy unprecedented in the postwar era. The $2-trillion U.S. military spending program was designed to generate new prosperity, introduce new technologies, and prosecute a geopolitical strategy based on a more confrontational military-technological competition with the Soviet Union. The economic dimension of the Reagan defense outlays is emphasized by Markusen as follows:

> Though federal military spending has long influenced the course of U.S. industrial development, no administration has so explicitly used it for this purpose as the current one. Indeed, the Reagan administration has acknowledged that its . . . military buildup is not only aimed at improving defense preparedness, but is expected to tackle the problem of U.S. economic competitiveness as well. In its rationale for the Strategic Computing Initiative (SCI), for example, the administration has unambiguously set forth the dual goal of "national security and economic strength." The $600-million strategic computing and artificial intelligence research project contains a commitment to industrial development—specifically, to stimulating new computer concepts, encouraging industrial funding, generating new computer-based applications, and pioneering new techniques in software development and methodology. In this way, the administration has closely tied commercial concerns to military ones—a policy designed not only to justify the enormous escalation in military-related research commitments, but also to hasten the adaption of Pentagon-subsidized innovations for commercial uses.[59]

The shift to massive military spending to develop new military and nonmilitary technologies raises the complex question of whether this effort will in the end duplicate the early successes of the Pentagon during the 1960s or whether it will replicate the U.S. failure to develop an internationally competitive numerically controlled machine tools industry. Although it may be too early to pass final judgment, the fact remains that the decline of the U.S. economy has not been reversed. A pessimistic view of future prospects is suggested by the military-oriented form of several major U.S. high-technology projects. Two important programs in this context are the VHSIC (very high speed integrated circuit) program and the Strategic Computing Initiative, mentioned by Markusen. Stowsky offers the following evaluation:

> The VHSIC program and the Strategic Computing Initiative . . . tend to replicate the series of actions which typically have led to a pattern of *negative* outcomes. This is not necessarily because these programs are poorly designed, at least from a defense perspective. Rather, it follows from the fact that military needs are no longer in the mainstream of industrial evolution in many high-technology sectors. Unlike many of the programs of the 1950's and early 60's, current defense procurement policies are actually inhibiting the discovery and especially the diffusion of new commercial technologies.[60]

The Reagan program can be viewed as a political-economic response to the end of the postwar cycle of growth and as an attempt to rejuvenate the U.S. economy. To meet the double challenge of its economic slippage and the technological revolution, the United States adopted the traditional policy of military spending as the favored macroeconomic instrument of change. On the demand side, the Reagan administration's massive defense outlays were intended to stimulate aggregate demand, though they displaced many nonmilitary, social, and infrastructure programs in this Keynesian function. On the supply side, an important aim was to subsidize high-tech R&D investment to promote technological innovation. Vast amounts of government aid in the form of military contracts and tax breaks went to selected high-tech military-industrial and other corporate interests. This assistance proceeded simultaneously with an accelerating process of deindustrialization, in which many traditional manufacturing industries were neglected, allowed to emigrate, or simply left to go under. The driving vision was not so much a modernization of U.S. industries in order to make the existing industrial base more innovative, productive, and competitive than an attempt to generate a brave new world of flourishing high-tech industries with the help of a Military Keynesian strategy. These companies were supposed to materialize out of the military R&D and weapons projects of military-industrial firms and their subcontractors. The resulting industrial and service sectors, according to the Reagan vision, would somehow replace many of the traditional manufacturing industries and would sweep across an economic landscape pressed into the service of intensified technological-military competition and a new cold war. The diffusion of R&D innovations throughout the economy did not materialize to the degree and in a form that could bring about self-sustaining economic growth, improved international competitiveness, the retraining of large sections of the work force, or far-reaching technological renewal. As a result, public infrastructures further declined along with the standard of living of most Americans. Millions of jobs were created, but the overwhelming majority of these were low-paid, unskilled, and part-time.

Although it is premature to offer a fully satisfying or comprehensive explanation for the failure of the Reagan reindustrialization program, several factors can be posed on the basis of the foregoing analysis.

1. The concentration on military-related systems, strategies, and goals that exemplify the postwar model of security, which is no longer viable as an effective instrument for economic or technological development

2. The commercially paralyzing effects of security requirements dictated by this approach

3. The influence of Military Keynesian ways of thinking concerning macro- and microeconomic change

4. The overall mismatch of the Military Keynesian approach to the commercial, political, and technological conditions of the international economy as it becomes more integrated, politically pluralistic, and less defined by the divisions of the postwar era

In contrast to the United States, Western Europe and Japan have pursued strategies of high-tech R&D aimed more explicitly at fitting emerging technologies to the existing manufacturing base in order to make it more productive, more relevant to the skilled work force, and internationally more competitive. The result is reflected in the domestic and international success, for example, of the Japanese and West German economies. In the United States, the Military Keynesian method of promoting new technologies has tended to make them less linkable and less relevant to the broader production apparatus, the market, and the work force. Many of the innovations developed are either technologically unsuited for these purposes or too costly because they have been developed through a military perspective and noncommercial, sole-source dependence. Moreover, the very industries in which new technology might have been appropriate are in many cases no longer to be found in the United States, or they are simply not in a favorable position to be coupled easily to new technologies, even if such coupling were a major priority of official U.S. policy.

Technological innovations that have been developed have tended in many cases to be subject to too many security-related barriers to reach the nonmilitary economy at the expeditious tempo and in the appropriate form to generate the desired nonmilitary economic effects. In this sense, one could argue that the Reagan strategy combined the worst of two worlds: On the one hand, the exclusivity of the military practice of reserving innovations strictly for the military in order to regain a substantial technological-military edge over the Soviets tended to lock out the very nonmilitary firms, small companies, and pioneering entrepreneurs so important to diffusing new technology and making it relevant to the economy as a whole. On the other hand, by allowing the traditional manufacturing industries to deteriorate further, the United States shunted aside a significant receptor of new technology and an essential economic multiplier of emerging innovations. The net result was a largely aborted Military Keynesian program that, unlike the early postwar military spending programs, ended not by genuinely stimulating a new type of economic growth that could be self-sustaining but by pushing the economy further into industrial and infrastructural decay and out-of-control deficits and debt.

Finally, it should also be mentioned that even as a method of developing new weapons systems, the Reagan program is open to serious question. Apparently here too the obsolete models and thinking of a bygone postwar era have dominated and generated economically and technologically flawed results. In the strategic domain, much of the exotic hardware and software originally envisioned for SDI has not materialized and never will. Not only has much of the technology been put into doubt on the basis of scientific and technological criteria, but there is also widespread agreement that the macroeconomic costs of such an enterprise would be prohibitive. In the domain of conventional weapons, the costs of many of the high-tech conventional weapons initially planned render their development and deployment similarly unlikely.

In sum, military expenditures wielded as a blunt instrument of industrial planning point toward macro- and microeconomic failure. The conclusion that must be drawn is that without a radical change in approach, the United States will not be able to overcome its deepening economic malaise. Change must entail not merely a drastic reduction in military expenditures— it must also entail abandoning the Military Keynesian approach in favor of genuine industrial and technology policy that would directly target the nonmilitary economy and implement the "euthanasia" of the military economy.[61] Such an agenda would aim at setting up a true industrial planning structure that could replace the de facto planning mechanism of the Pentagon.

The Reagan era is an example of the major barriers to moving beyond the faulty policy approach of Military Keynesianism. It once again demonstrated the strength of economic and political interests that are cemented into the postwar military-industrial order and its ideology of security. At the same time, however, the Reagan administration did embrace disarmament and the notion of ending the nuclear arms race. One interpretation of the INF Treaty suggests that the administration came vaguely to recognize the need to find a political path on which East and West could move beyond the postwar order. Aside from political-security considerations, the economic failure of trying to make butter from guns appeared to become painfully clear. If this awareness continues to deepen—as it must in the coming years—the search for a political-economic alternative will become a central political issue. The disarmament process, Soviet military disengagement, the reform movement throughout Eastern Europe, the Soviet Union, and China, and the achievement of the INF Treaty are perhaps creating the historical context for the United States to move beyond the era of Military Keynesianism.

Notes

1. Michael Moffitt, "Shocks, Deadlocks and Scorched Earth," *World Policy Journal*, Vol. 4, No. 4, Fall 1987, pp. 443–582; Jeff Faux, "The Post-Reagan Economy," *World Policy Journal*, Vol. 3, No. 2, Spring 1986, pp. 183–218; Felix Rohatyn, "The Debtor Economy: A Proposal," *New York Review of Books*, Vol. 31, No. 17, November 8, 1984, pp. 16–21. Proposals for defense budget cuts are to be found in Congressional Budget Office, *Reducing the Deficit: Spending and Revenue Options, A Report to the Senate and House Committee on the Budget—Part 2* (Washington, D.C.: Government Printing Office, 1987).
2. Lloyd Dumas, "National Security and Economic Delusion," *Challenge*, Vol. 30, No. 1, March/April 1987, pp. 28–33. (Author's emphasis added.)
3. Stephen Cohen and John Zysman, "Can America Compete," *Challenge*, Vol. 29, No. 2, May/June 1986, pp. 57–64. See also their more detailed discussion, Cohen, Zysman, David Teece and Laura Tyson, *Competitiveness* (President's Commission on Industrial Competitiveness, *Global Competition, The New Reality*, Vol. 3, published as separate working paper, Berkeley, Calif., 1984).
4. Cohen and Zysman, ibid.
5. Ibid. According to Bluestone and Harrison, between 1950 and 1980 direct foreign investment of U.S. corporations grew from $12 billion to $192 billion. Over the same period, gross private investment grew less than half as rapidly, from $54 billion to about $400 billion. By the end of the 1970s, overseas profits accounted for a third or more of the overall profits of the 100 largest multinational producers and banks in the United States. Barry Bluestone and Bennett Harrison, *The Deindustrialization of America* (New York: Basic Books, 1982) p. 42; Mario Pianta, *New Technologies Across the Atlantic* (Sussex: Wheatsheaf, 1988), p. 39.
6. C. Fred Bergsten, "The Second Debt Crisis is Coming," *Challenge*, Vol. 30, No. 6, Anniversary Issue 1987, pp. 50–57.
7. Ibid.
8. There is a growing literature on the decline of U.S. hegemony and the changing role of military spending in the U.S. and international economy. On the role of military production and spending in the early postwar period, see Fred Block, *The Origins of International Economic Disorder* (Berkeley: University of California Press, 1977); James Cypher, "The Basic Economics of Rearming America," *Monthly Review*, Vol. 33, No. 6, 1981, pp. 11–27. See also Michael Lucas, *Die Politische Ökonomie der amerikanischen Hegemonie*

unter besonderer Berücksichtigung der Rolle von Rüstung im internationalen System der Nachkriegszeit (Diplomarbeit, Freie Universität Berlin, 1983). On the growing economic-political problems of military production, see Seymour Melman, *Profits Without Production* (New York: Alfred Knopf, 1983); Robert DeGrasse, Jr., *Military Expansion, Economic Decline: The Impact of Military Spending on U.S. Economic Performance* (New York: M. E. Sharpe, 1983); Lloyd Dumas, *The Overburdened Economy* (Berkeley: University of California Press, 1986), henceforth Dumas, op. cit.; Mary Kaldor, *The Baroque Arsenal* (London: Abacus, 1982); Michael Lucas, "Die Vereinigten Staaten von Amerika und die Krise des Kalten Kriegs-Systems," *Prokla*, Vol. 12, No. 48, March 1982, pp. 119–154; Michael Lucas, "US-Rüstungspolitik: Wirtschaftliche Folgen und Hintergründe," in *Anti-Militarismus Information*, August 1982. pp. 72–79. On the subject of hegemonial decline, see Robert Gilpin, *War and Change in World Politics* (Cambridge: Cambridge University Press, 1981); Paul Kennedy, *The Rise and Fall of Great Powers* (New York: Random House, 1987); Mario Pianta, op. cit. On the onset of the economic crisis in the West, see André Gunder Frank, *Crisis: In the First World* (London: Holms and Meier, 1981); Robert Ballance and Stuart Sinclair, *Collapse and Survival: Industrial Strategies in a Changing World* (London: George Allen and Unwin, 1983); Rob van Tulder and Gerd Junne, *European Multinationals and Core Technologies* (New York: John Wiley, 1988). On the relationship of cycles of economic growth and specific technologies and their interaction, see J. J. van Duijn, *The Long Wave in Economic Life* (London: George Allen and Unwin, 1983), Chapter 1, and Part 2.

9. On the concept of "Military Keynesianism," see Hugh Mosley, *The Arms Race: Economic and Social Consequences* (Lexington, Mass.: Lexington Books, 1985), pp. 5f. See also Cypher, op. cit.

10. Mosley, ibid., p. 5. While Mosley and Cypher characterize U.S. military spending policies in the postwar era as "Keynesian," Alan Wolfe (*America's Impasse*, New York: Pantheon, 1981) argues the case that they represent a form of "counter-Keynesianism." Wolfe maintains that the power of political conservatives and business interests in the late 1930s and after World War II was strong enough to block legislation that would have given government the power required to impose genuinely Keynesian reforms. Wolfe points out that although Keynes was no socialist, he envisioned that the state would assume vital economic functions. He cites the following passage from Keynes: "No obvious case is made out for a system of State Socialism which would embrace most of the economic life of the community. It is not the ownership of the means of production which it is important for the state to assume. *If* the state is able to determine the aggregate amount of resources devoted to augmenting the instruments and the basic rate of reward for those who own them, it will have accomplished all that is necessary." John Maynard Keynes, *The General Theory of Employment, Interest and Money* (New York: Harcourt, Brace and World, 1936), p. 378, cited in Wolfe, op. cit., pp. 50f. Similarly, Wolfe maintains that Keynes's position on the failure of capitalism and the radical reforms necessary to save it from its worst vices is summed up in the British economist's observation that "the outstanding faults of the economic society in which we live are its failures to provide full employment and its arbitrary and inequitable distribution of wealth." Keynes advocated an economy committed to full employment, a redistribution of wealth, and lower interest rates to stimulate investment. These policies would reduce the rewards to holders of capital and bring about the "euthanasia of the rentier, and, consequently, the euthanasia of the cumulative power of the capitalist to

exploit the scarcity-value of capital." Keynes, ibid., p. 578, cited in Wolfe, ibid., pp. 51f. Wolfe shows that in the U.S. debate over postwar economic policy, the U.S. Keynesians who called for an application of Keynes's idea in the form of conscious economic planning were forced to adopt a watered-down form of Keynesianism that reversed the central relationship between business and government in Keynes's conception. The state failed to place itself in a position to guarantee full employment and failed to arrogate the power to regulate investment and profit. "If Keynesianism," Wolfe observes, "implies the use of government to influence and direct decisions made in the private sector, then postwar economic planning could only be defined as counter-Keynesianism: the use of the private sector to influence the scope and activities of the government" (p. 54). The outcome of the debate included the setting up of the Council of Economic Advisers, which was claimed as a victory of U.S. Keynesianism. But the new body was fully beholden to the private sector to pursue fiscal and monetary policies that would guarantee growth of the U.S. economy but not the kind of changes Keynes envisioned. Ibid., pp. 53. Wolfe also points out that the choice of military spending as one of the mechanisms to stimulate demand had obvious political advantages for its Democratic proponents: (1) It played to the public mood of anticommunism that was made popular by the Truman administration; (2) because the main proponents of Keynesian military spending were Democrats, it provided them a means to counter the charge that they were soft on communism; and (3) it also brought powerful military interests over to the side of the Democrats. Ibid., pp. 61f; Block, op. cit., p. 103.

11. Mosley, ibid., p. 5.
12. "War socialism" refers to the extension of government controls over the economy that occurred during World Wars I and II. See in this context Paul Mattick, *Marx and Keynes* (London: Merlin Press, 1969), pp. 137–139. See also Dumas, op. cit., pp. 118–119.
13. Mosley, op. cit., p. 5.
14. Ibid.
15. The authors of NSC-68 maintained that increased military spending could result in a

> substantial absolute increase in output and could thereby increase the allocation of resources to a build-up of the economic and military strength of itself and its allies without suffering a decline in its real standard of living. . . . From the point of view of the economy as a whole, the program might not result in a real decrease in the standard of living, for the economic effects of the program might be to increase the gross national product by more than the amount being absorbed for additional military and foreign assistance purposes.

Foreign Relations of the United States 1950, Vol. 1, pp. 258, 286, as cited in Mosley, op. cit., p. 8. On NSC-68, see also the detailed discussion of this and other passages in Jerry Sanders, *The Peddlers of Crisis* (Boston: South End Press, 1983), Chapter 1. The authors of NSC-68 also suggested that their proposed military spending program was necessary to prevent a relapse into the type of economic stagnation that had occurred during the interwar years.
16. The Bureau of the Budget questioned the comparison in NSC-68 of the U.S. economy in 1949 to the conditions prevailing at the height of World War II when the nation was in the heat of wartime economic mobilization.

Skepticism was also expressed concerning the possible effect of heavy military spending on the durable goods sector and fear that this pressure would require "a diversion from present civil purposes either through inflation or through taxes or direct controls" of economic activity; ibid., p. 304, as cited in Mosley, op. cit., p. 11. This debate was never resolved and was overshadowed by the prosecution of the Korean War and its legitimation of rearmament. The controversy over the economic effects of military spending has continued throughout the postwar era. The Bureau of the Budget's early criticism anticipated recent discussion of military programs and their draining of material and human resources from the civilian economy. See in this context Dumas, op. cit., pp. 207–222. One could note in this context that the defense sector is the single largest component of the public sector. John Kenneth Galbraith commented in discussing the role of defense spending and the public sector: "If a large public sector of the economy is the fulcrum for the regulation of demand, plainly military expenditures are the pivot on which the fulcrum rests. . . . Military expenditures are what now makes the public sector large. Without them the federal government would be rather less than half its present size. It is most unlikely that this would exercise the requisite leverage on the economy." John Kenneth Galbraith, *New Industrial State* (New York: New American Library, 1968), pp. 238–239, 240, as cited in Mosley, op. cit., p. 14. This suggests that the so-called Reagan revolution of reducing the role of the state in the economy did not really get off the ground under Reagan. By massively increasing military spending, he in fact significantly augmented the political role of the state in the most vital sectors of the economy. Galbraith's comment also suggests some of the problems that the Bush administration will have if in fact it cuts back substantially on military spending. The economic function of military spending would have to be replaced by genuine industrial planning mechanisms, but such moves would likely provoke political opposition from the military and political conservatives representing powerful business interests.

On the size of the military as an economic factor, Douglas Lee points out that the defense industry

> represents about 73 percent of federal government purchases and about 28 percent of federal spending. Defense production is 6.8 percent of our total domestic product and represents almost 20 percent of the equipment produced in the United States. Defense equipment shipments worth $7 billion to $8 billion every month represent about 22 percent of the manufacturing shipments in this country. At present the industry has a $150 billion backlog. About 5.5 million people are directly employed in the defense effort, including 4 million active military personnel and civilians employed by the Department of Defense and another 1.5 million employed directly by the defense industry. This does not include jobs generated in the secondary supplying industries.

L. Douglas Lee, "Time to Rethink Defense," *Challenge*, Vol. 30, No. 1, March–April 1987, pp. 15–20. For another estimate of the size of the defense industry, see Melman, op. cit., pp. 83. On the methodological problems of estimating the size of the defense industry and military expenditures, see the detailed discussion in Mosley, op. cit., Chapter 1.

17. Mosley, ibid., p. 10.

18. Congressional Budget Office, op. cit.; Walter Pincus and David Hoffman, "Bush Is Said to Seek Cuts at Pentagon," *International Herald Tribune*, November 29, 1989. If substantial cuts do occur, it is likely that they will not come from the White House but from the Congress. On the budgetary problems and cuts of the SDI program, see also Irwin Goodwin, "SDI: Losing Momentum over What is Affordable and Possible," *Physics Today*, January 1987, pp. 47–51; George Wilson, "U.S. Panel Makes Deep Cuts in Reagan Request for SDI Funds," *International Herald Tribune*, April 4-5, 1987; See also Joshua Epstein, *The 1988 Defense Budget* (Washington, D.C., 1987).

19. See in this context Jean-François Delpech, "New Technologies, the United States and Europe: Implications for Western Security and Economic Growth," *Atlantic Community Quarterly*, Vol. 25, No. 1, Spring 1987, pp. 47–63; Stephen Alexis Cain and Gordon Adams, "Reagan's 1988 Military Budget," *Bulletin of Atomic Scientists*, Vol. 44, No. 3, March 1987, pp. 50–52. On economic imperatives for defense spending cuts in the context of arms control and disarmament, see Lee, op. cit.

20. For a detailed analysis of defense cost overruns and their causes, see Melman, op. cit., pp. 135–137ff; on poor management practices of the Pentagon, see in particular Chapter 5; see also Jacques Gansler, *The Defense Economy* (Cambridge, Mass.: MIT Press, 1980). Gansler, who formerly worked for the Pentagon, provides a good overview of the differences between the operation of the military and nonmilitary economies. On rising costs of weapons procurement, see Gordon Adams, *Controlling Weapons Costs* (New York: Council on Economic Priorities, 1983). On some of the environmental problems linked to nuclear weapons production in the United States see William Arkin et al., "Nuclear Weapons" in SIPRI Yearbook 1989 (Oxford: Oxford University Press, 1989), pp. 3–38. For examples of cost overruns, see John Barry and Tom Morganthau, "The Defense Dilemma," *Newsweek*, January 23, 1989; for an analytical discussion of the costs of SDI, see Rosy Nimroody, *Star Wars: The Economic Fallout* (Cambridge, Mass.: Ballinger, 1988), pp. 25–49; Barry Blechman and Victor Utgoff, "The Macroeconomics of Strategic Defenses," *International Security*, Vol. 11, No. 3, Winter 1986–87, pp. 33–70. For an overview of the problems of military production in their political-technological context, see Pianta, op. cit., pp. 46–57.

21. Melman, ibid., Nimroody, ibid. SDI is a salient example of the lack of coherent defense policy planning. See also in this context Douglas Waller, James Bruce, and Douglas Cook, "SDI: Progress and Challenges" (Staff Report submitted to Senators William Proxmire, J. Bennett Johnston, and Lawton Chiles, March 17, 1986); Nimroody, op. cit., Chapter 2. Zegveld and Enzing, following Waller et al., point out that from the onset SDI planners received conflicting advice from the different advisory panels and failed to reconcile the different views concerning the program's goals, chances of success, technological challenges, and meaning for the future of U.S. and Western security planing. Walter Zegveld and Christian Enzing, *SDI and Industrial Policy: Threat or Opportunity* (New York: St. Martin's, 1987), p. 9.

22. National Academy of Science, Committee On Science, Engineering, and Public Policy, *Balancing the National Interest: U.S. National Security Export Controls and Global Economic Competition* (Washington, D.C.: National Academy Press, 1987), p. 56; Delpech, op. cit.

23. Eastport Study Group, *Summer Study 1985: A Report to the Director, Strategic Defense Initiative Organization*, December 1985 (mimeo), p. 9. See

also David Parnas, "Software Aspects of Strategic Defense Systems, *American Scientist*, No. 73, September–October 1985.

24. For a detailed discussion of the broader pros and cons of military classification of scientific data, see David Dickson, *The New Politics of Science* (New York: Pantheon, 1984); Warren Davis, "The Pentagon and the Scientist," in John Tirman, ed., *The Militarization of High Technology* (Cambridge, Mass.: Ballinger, 1984), pp. 153–180. Classification and restriction of the flow of scientific information have been a major issue in the SDI debate on both sides of the Atlantic in academic, business, and government circles. Many of these issues are taken up by Dickson and Davis. See also in this context William Hartung and Rosy Nimroody, "Star Wars: Pentagon Invades Academia," *CEP Newsletter*, January 1986.

25. Hartung and Nimroody, ibid.; Fred Kaplan, "3,700 Scientists Refuse SDI Funds," *Boston Globe*, May 14, 1986; John Holdren and F. Bailey Green, "Military Spending, the SDI, and Government Support of Research and Development: Effects on the Economy and the Health of American Science," *F.A.S. Public Interest Report* (Journal of the Federation of American Scientists), Vol. 39, No. 7, September 1986, pp. 1–17; Peter Schulze, "Internationale Wettbewerbsfähigkeit, militärische Zukunftsprogramme und Aspekte der Rüstungskooperation im Hochtechnologiebereich am Beispiel von SDI" in Hartmut Elsenhaus et al., *Frankreich, Europa, Weltpolitik* (Opladen: Westdeutscher Verlag, 1989).

26. See Chapter 8.

27. See Chapter 8; Dumas, op. cit., pp. 208–217; Nimroody, op. cit., pp. 119–144; Holdren and Green, op. cit.; Pianta, op. cit., pp. 87f.

28. Melman, op. cit., Chapter 7; Kaldor, op. cit., Chapter 1; Already in 1974 the National Academy of Engineering concluded that "With few exceptions the vast technology developed by federally funded programs since World War II has not resulted in widespread 'spinoffs' of secondary or additional applications of practical products, processes and services that have made an impact on the nation's economic growth, industrial productivity, employment gains, and foreign trade," cited in Dumas, op. cit., p. 214. Zegveld and Enzing in their analysis of SDI conclude that

> There is evidence to suggest that the military industrial complex is depriving the civilian market-oriented sector of many of the country's "top brains" in such crucial areas as computing and electronics. Large amounts of human capital are being "locked in" to rather esoteric projects that do not have significant or apparent civilian spin-off potential. Finally, defense procurement is featherbedding some suppliers due to inadequate quality control procedures and lack of accountability. In short, it is being suggested that military R&D spending is seriously distorting the broad thrust of American technological development along paths dictated by military requirements and away from the current and future needs of world markets for civilian goods.

Zegveld and Enzing, op. cit., pp. 76–77. On the ongoing discussion in the press, including official views that defend the thesis of civilian spin-off from military funding, see "SDI Commercial Spinoff," *Current News* (special edition), No. 1709, April 5, 1988. For a more analytical approach, see Nimroody, op. cit., pp. 119–144; Zegveld and Enzing provide a good overview and analysis of spin-off from the point of view of industrial innovation. On West European views of possible spin-off from SDI, see also Michael Lucas, "SDI and Europe," *World Policy Journal*, Vol. 3, No. 2, Spring 1986, pp. 219–249, and Chapter 7 in this book.

29. Melman, op. cit.; Pianta, op. cit., pp. 87f.

30. In 1984, for example, "defense spending as a percentage of GNP was 6.9 percent in the United States, 4.1 in France, and 3.3 percent in Germany. Per capita, Germany spent $334 on defense in 1984, France $367, and the United States $1,057." David Calleo, *Beyond American Hegemony: The Future of the Western Alliance* (New York: Basic Books, 1987), p. 113; data cited from Secretary of State for Defense (Britain), *Statement on the Defense Estimates 1985, No. 1* (London, Her Majesty's Stationery Office), p. 36. For an analysis of the pattern of relatively higher defense budgets of the United States and Britain during the postwar period, see Chapter 7 in Calleo, ibid. Calleo takes up this problem in the context of U.S. fiscal deficits and their relationship to U.S. geopolitical strategy. He sees the problem of U.S. budgetary deficits not merely as a result of relatively higher military outlays and U.S. imperial strategy but also of the domestic political constraints on the federal government in financing military expenditures through higher taxes. These are, politically speaking, relatively more unpopular in the United States than in Western Europe, where there are higher taxes on income but also generally better public services. In contrast to Calleo, Melman and Dumas focus more directly on military production itself. For a comparison of economic performance of the United States, West Germany, and Japan in the context of the disavantaging effects of U.S. military production, see Melman, op. cit., Chapter 10. On comparative economic performance of the United States and other major economies in general, see Ira Magaziner and Robert Reich, *Minding America's Business* (New York: Vintage, 1983), in particular Chapters 2 and 3; Pianta, op. cit., pp. 21–42.

31. Figures are from "Research and Development FY 1989," American Association for the Advancement of Science, Report 13, 1988, Table 3. According to the National Academy of Science's earlier estimates, U.S. high-tech trade surplus fell from $26 billion in 1980 to $7 billion in 1985. See Department of Commerce, *1986 U.S. Industrial Outlook: Prospects for Over 350 Manufacturing and Service Industries* (Washington, D.C., 1986).

32. The increased militarization of R&D in the early and mid-1980s met with increasing criticism concerning the civilian spin-off of R&D projects sponsored by the Pentagon. This led to the Federal Technology Transfer Act of 1986 and the Competitiveness Initiative of January 27, 1987. Both were designed to strengthen cooperation between federal laboratories and with universities and industries. Commission of European Communities, *First Report on the State of Science and Technology in Europe* (Brussels, November 29, 1988), p. 47. See also in this context Michael Yoshino and Glenn Fong, "The Very High Speed Integrated Circuit Program," in Bruce Scott and George Lodge, *U.S. Competitiveness in the World Economy* (Boston: Harvard Business School Press, 1985), pp. 176–184.

33. On the export of chemical and biological weapons during the Iran-Iraq war and a comprehensive list of states and firms directly or indirectly involved in the production of poison gas in Iraq, see Andreas Zumach, "Supermächte halfen Irak bei C-Waffenproduktion," *Die Tageszeitung*, January 26, 1989. On recent developments in conventional weapons exports, see Michael Klare, "The Perils of the Arms Trade," *World Policy Journal*, Vol. 6, No. 1, Winter 1988-89, pp. 141–168. On arms exports of the Federal Republic, see Herbert

Wulf, "The West German Arms Industry and Arms Exports," *Alternatives*, Vol. 12, 1988, pp. 319–335. On the boom in West German arms exports, see "Beispielloser Boom beim Waffenexport," *Süddeutscher Zeitung*, January 23, 1989. On Third World debt and military spending, see Dumas, op. cit., pp. 241f.

34. Dumas points out that "expressed in terms of U.S. currency, from 1960 to 1981 the less developed countries (LDCs) of the world spent a total of more than one trillion dollars on their militaries. . . . In 1960, the LDCs accounted for about 10 percent of worldwide military spending; five years later their share was under 12 percent, . . . by the end of the 1970s, their share was more than 23 percent." Dumas, ibid., pp. 242f.

35. Ann Markusen, "The Militarized Economy," *World Policy Journal*, Vol. 3, No. 3, Summer 1986, pp. 495–516; Gerd Junne, "Das amerikanische Rüstungsprogramm: Ein Substitut für Industriepolitik," *Leviathan*, Vol. 13, No. 1, 1985, pp. 23–37. John Tirman provides an overview of the discussion on defense spending and industrial planning; see "The Defense-Economy Debate," in Tirman, op. cit., pp. 1–32; see also Robert Reich, "High Technology, Defense and International Trade," pp. 33–43 in ibid.; Pianta, op. cit., pp. 101ff. Zegveld and Enzing also view U.S. military programs as sharing many of the goals of industrial policy. In their discussion of SDI, they pose the question of whether the structural transformation process can sufficiently advance in the absence of national industrial technology policies. Their answer is yes based in part on the existence of strong market-driven forces in the United States. They nevertheless argue, similar to Markusen, that the United States, through the Pentagon, practices an informal type of industrial planning. This occurs on the supply side through highly defined R&D programs and the promotion of specific technological trajectories and on the demand side through the mechanism of military procurement; see Zegveld and Enzing, op. cit., pp. 72f.

36. Markusen, ibid.; Nimroody, op. cit., pp. 142–144. On industrial policy in a more general and international comparative context, see Magaziner and Reich, op. cit., Parts 3 and 4; Ballance and Sinclair, op. cit.; Chalmers Johnson, *The Industrial Policy Debate* (San Francisco: Institute for Contemporary Studies, 1984).

37. Markusen, ibid.

38. Jay Stowsky, *Beating Our Plowshares into Double-Edged Swords: The Impact of Pentagon Policies on the Commercialization of Advanced Technologies*, Research Report, Berkeley Round Table on the International Economy, 1986.

39. Ibid.; Melman, op. cit., Chapter 5. See also David Noble, *Forces of Production* (New York: Knopf, 1984).

40. Stowsky, ibid.

41. Ibid.; Melman, op. cit., Chapter 5; Pianta, op. cit., pp. 84–88.

42. Stowsky, ibid.

43. Ibid.

44. Markusen, op. cit.

45. Ibid.

46. Cohen and Zysman, op. cit.; Bluestone and Harrison, op. cit., pp. 170–178; see also Bluestone and Harrison, *The Great U-Turn* (New York: Basic Books, 1988).

47. Tulder and Junne, op. cit., p. 1. Zegveld and Enzing in their discussion of the economic slowdown of the late 1960s stress the fact that by then a large number of postwar industries entered the maturity- and market-

saturation phase of their life cycles. Characteristics of this phase are increasing rationalization, growing automation, higher manufacturing unemployment, and stiffer price competition. Under such conditions, they argue, the traditional postwar policies of macroeconomic management based on maintaining full employment and controlling financial flows through demand management are no longer effective. Innovation becomes necessary in order to initiate new products and to "enable industries to enter the first phase of a next generation of growth cycles." Zegveld and Enzing, op. cit., p. 67.

48. Tulder and Junne, ibid.; Annemieke Roobeek, "The Crisis of Fordism and the Rise of a New Technological Paradigm," *Futures*, Vol. 19, No. 2, April 1987, pp. 129–154. On the theory of long waves in economic development, see van Duijn, op. cit.; Ballance and Sinclair, op. cit., pp. 4–6.

49. Bluestone and Harrison, 1982, op. cit., Chapter 2. Bluestone and Harrison note that during the 1970s, 32–38 million jobs were lost in industry. In more recent research summarized in "The Grim Truth about the Job Miracle," *New York Times*, February 1, 1987, they show that in the period 1979–1985, 9.3 million jobs were created in the United States, 44 percent of which were, however, low-paying and in the service sector.

50. Tulder and Junne, op. cit., pp. 2–4; Roobeek, op. cit.

51. Tulder and Junne, ibid., p. 6. A useful source on new technologies are the Annexes in European Communities, *First Report*, op. cit.

52. Tulder and Junne, ibid.

53. Ibid, p. 20.

54. Ibid, p. 24.

55. Robert Reich, *The Next American Frontier* (New York: Penguin, 1984), p. 13.

56. Ibid., p. 257.

57. Zegveld and Enzing, op. cit., p. 68.

58. Ibid.

59. Markusen, op. cit.

60. Stowsky, op. cit.

61. See in this context Dumas, op. cit., Chapter 12.

CHAPTER 7

Technology R&D in Western Europe: The Civilian-Military Interplay

In contrast to the United States, West European governments adopted a relatively more civilian- and market-oriented approach to technological-industrial policy than the United States. This chapter will examine several transatlantic differences concerning civilian versus military R&D and the catalyzing influence of SDI on West European research programs and will suggest that the different approaches reflect a technological watershed in West European policy. Here two policy alternatives compete and overlap: (1) the continuation of East-West technological-military competition corresponding to the postwar model of security; and (2) the use of R&D and new technologies as an instrument to promote détente, disarmament, and East-West cooperation. On the one hand, the technological revolution has increased the threat of a new arms race in the coming years. On the other hand, it has opened up a new potential for disarmament, for more effective verification regimes, and for prevention of a serious technological division between Eastern and Western Europe in the 1990s and beyond. Because the production of new weapons systems is intertwined with the development of nonmilitary technology, the pursuit of military R&D programs could result in reducing the potential civilian economic benefits of new technologies. This loss could also hinder West European economic and political integration and East-West détente, a possibility that puts into relief the need to impose arms control constraints on military R&D.

Western Europe and the Technological Revolution

John Marcum, the director for science, technology, and industry of the Organization for Economic Cooperation and Development (OECD), wrote the following in 1984 on the nature of contemporary technological development:

Today we stand on the threshold of a new era—an era driven by rapidly changing technologies. . . . The major technologies—electronics, telecommunications, industrial materials, production automation, bio-technology, artificial intelligence and the more specific fields of fiber optics, composite materials, CAD/CAM, robotics—promise to alter significantly the economies of all countries.[1]

The specific challenge to Western Europe of the forces Marcum described were summed up in 1986 in a European Community study: "The new technologies are one of the greatest challenges of our time. . . . There is, however, great and wide-spread concern that Europe is lagging behind and must struggle even to hold its ground in the face of its major competitors, the United States and Japan."[2] The study gives the following reasons for Western Europe's difficulties:[3]

1. The lack of a large unified market, which would reduce production costs
2. The fragmentation of the public purchasing market
3. The duplication of research work
4. The failure to expeditiously exploit research findings in processes and products
5. The insufficient contribution of small firms as a result of numerous bureaucratic and economic obstacles, including the lack of risk capital

Margaret Sharp and Claire Shearman view West European collaboration and the unification of the Common Market in the larger framework of the competitive pressures generated by increasing global integration. They cite in this context the following factors:[4]

1. Rising development costs, tighter profit margins, and the need for larger economies of scale
2. Deregulation and the more active role of U.S. and Japanese firms in West European R&D, production, and markets
3. The strengthening of controls on export of Western high-tech goods made with U.S. components to communist countries
4. The efforts of military-industrial firms and defense ministries to lessen their dependence on imports of U.S. weapons and military high technology by promoting "made-in-Europe" weapons systems

In a similar vein, André Danzin has described the economic problems that the European Community faces in the domain of microelectronics and information technology (IT):

Marked deterioration in the trade deficit of the ten in electronics, information technologies and telecommunications: Following a small positive balance in 1979, the export-import ratios have been negative since 1980 and are expected to reach 10 to 12 billion Ecus annually from 1985 to 1987;

Serious loss of jobs in a job market already plagued with under-employment: In 1982 it was estimated that 2 to 4 million jobs were lost as a result of increasing inability to compete in information technology;

The threat of technological dependence, particularly in the domain of microelectronics and certain classes of high-speed devices: It has been pointed out by European analysts that this weakness is particularly conspicuous in the ability to design military equipment and certain classes of software;

An across-the-board delay in Europe in comparison to the U.S. and Japan in the transformation of industries, services and education as a result of the slow rate of introducing and applying information technology.[5]

Danzin links the problems of the microelectronics sector to the current restructuring of the world economy and the technological revolution. He and other analysts view the need for adjustment as more acute in Western Europe because of its relatively higher unemployment compared with the United States and Japan.[6]

The Interaction of Military and Civilian R&D

The race for new technologies to enhance competitiveness during the 1980s has led to increased state promotion of technology projects in the military and civilian sectors. R&D funds are funneled to firms, for example, in the form of military contracts for high-tech development, which has raised a number of questions concerning the relationship of military to civilian technology development. In the debate on the role of military R&D as a source of spin-off for the nonmilitary commercial sector, there are a variety of different considerations of costs and benefits and no clear expert consensus.

The Dual Orientation of High-Tech Firms: The French Example

Pierre Dussauge, in an examination of French military-industrial firms, describes the interplay of military and civilian funding of R&D projects:

State financing of a large part of the expenses of research and
development of military programs allows the firm in charge of
carrying out these programs to acquire know-how and specific
competence without having to make large investments. The civilian
activity pursued on the basis of this know-how will require
considerably less investment than corresponding activities developed
in an autonomous fashion and will result in appreciably less cost for
the firm.[7]

Besides lowering investment costs, arms production and technological
programs linked to military R&D "will allow the firm to acquire a
technological head-start vis-a-vis competitors whose activities are limited to
merely civilian production."[8] To demonstrate this claim, Dussauge gives the
following example: "Airbus, which Aerospatiale produces, has been able to
benefit from highly advanced technological processes (notably in the domain
of new materials) developed in the framework of military programs."[9]

Dussauge develops the notion of "technological capital" that is generated
in the military-industrial firm by state subsidies. But he also notes that "the
technological synergies between military and civilian activities are indeed
very variable: while they can be very pronounced in certain areas such as that
of helicopters in the case of Aerospatiale and aircraft turbines in the case of
Snecma, they can be very weak in other areas such as tanks, self-propulsion
or submarines."[10] Dussauge cites in this context the example of aircraft in
which the "synergy" of developing combat aircraft and large passenger aircraft
is limited. This was confirmed by the failure of the nonmilitary Mercure
program undertaken by the military aircraft manufacturer Dassault.[11] These
two types of aircraft were therefore constructed by two different firms,
Aerospatiale and Dassault.

Dussauge heavily qualifies his main argument by stating that the
synergy produced by the combination of military and civilian production
within the same firm is a special case, an unusual phenomenon. The
military-civilian synergy, when it does occur, does not materialize in
products having both a civilian and military application but rather as a result
of military activities of a firm and the public financing granted the firm for
this purpose. Technological competence is either created or further developed
and can then be exploited for civilian production. Dussauge here cites the
example of Matra, whose highly sophisticated military missiles have little
immediate technological relevance to the world of commercial products.
Matra's military research programs nevertheless absorb a large part of the
overall expenses of laboratory facilities and the research centers of the firm,
thus indirectly subsidizing civilian activities.[12]

Another important dimension of the interaction of civilian and military
production is military exports, which often have the effect of leading to sales
of nonmilitary goods. "Arms exports," Dussauge points out, "have helped
the export firm to get a better footing in the client country," and military

contracts can open the way to nonmilitary commercial projects.[13] The French firm Thomson, for example, secured contracts for its civilian air surveillance equipment partly as a result of its military contracts in the field of air defense.

Military exports can be particularly beneficial financially for major industrial firms. Military activities of a firm

> as a rule generate important financial resources. Because of the manner in which prices are determined, provisioning the French armed forces with equipment is almost by definition a profitable activity; the profitability of exports is, in general, even considerably higher. Moreover, as a profitable activity, arms production does not require large financial input from the defense firms themselves. Firm-financed military projects, although not negligible, are, in most cases, small. The research in such projects, generally financed from internal funds stemming from other domains in the firm's activity, is largely administrated by the state; industrial development and investments are almost entirely financed by the D.G.A. [Délégation Générale pour l'armement]. . . . In effect, the orders, especially for export, give rise to large advance payments which are spread out up to the time of final delivery of the ordered equipment.[14]

Dussauge points out, however, that the financing function of arms production can be a double-edged sword because a diminution in orders for military equipment (particularly from foreign clients) can have the effect of lowering production and thus raising the problem of idle capacity.[15]

The cash input into military-industrial firms, according to Dussauge, leads enterprises "almost naturally to seek avenues of diversification allowing them to absorb their financial surpluses while developing new activities. The strategy Matra adopted during the 1970s was based on this model of diversification, which was made possible by financial resources generated by arms production.[16] Dussauge also points out that in the case of some firms such as SNPE, the cash surplus is such that "not being able to reinvest its cash flow in its traditional activities which engendered the latter, [it] is led to pose the question of a genuine diversification beyond armaments production."[17]

In generalizing his research findings, Dussauge contends that

> Military activities appear in the firm's portfolio of activities as "cash cow"-type activity which is atypical: On the one hand, this development demands considerable and continuous investments, particularly because of the importance of technology; on the other hand, they provide the firm with large financial resources which are massively reinvested in arms production. . . . Military activities, whatever their stage of development and their rhythm of growth, thus generate resources; at no moment, or almost no moment, do they demand large investments of the firm. They do not consume cash flow.[18]

The West German View

Hans-Hilger Haunschild, a state secretary in the West German Ministry of Research and Technology, emphasizes the close relationship between civilian and military research and the consequences of this fact for the Federal Republic's evolving R&D policies:

> In the light of the significance of modern technology for military as well as civilian applications, the Ministry of Research and Technology (BMFT), responsible for civilian R&D, and the Ministry of Defense (BMVg), responsible for military R&D, work closely together in certain areas. For example, they are coordinating their planning for the future development of electronic components and data processing.[19]

Haunschild makes several additional points:[20]

1. The participation of West German firms in SDI, besides involving the development of new weapons, will involve the development of data processing systems for management and the interfacing of human beings in high-grade automatic systems.
2. The distinction between civilian and military research—and between their respective rationales as separate areas of endeavor—should not be blurred or confused.
3. The success of West German nonmilitary research in the postwar period played an essential role in the reacceptance of the Federal Republic in the international community. Its credibility vis-à-vis other nations was based on an explicit and clear separation of civilian and military R&D.
4. It is "absolutely necessary" to clearly separate the discussion of civilian from military application of R&D expenditures.
5. The Federal Republic and Japan have both demonstrated during the postwar period that civilian R&D does not require the detour of military R&D to be successful.
6. The U.S. style of organizing its large R&D projects and NASA contracts is in many cases not a viable approach for the Federal Republic, which has neither the same financial resources nor the same role in the NATO alliance to justify or allow such an approach.

SDI

Konrad Seitz, the director of planning in the West German Foreign Office, suggested in 1985 that SDI research programs could produce a quantum jump of the U.S. economy into the twenty-first century and leave Western Europe in the dust of technological dependence. Seitz compared the potential of SDI to the Manhattan Project and the mobilization of the U.S. scientific community in response to the Sputnik shock of 1957.

> Military research has become the driving force of most advanced technologies, since the extreme technological requirements of new weapon systems impose themselves in civilian sectors. The first computers served military purposes. The first communication satellites were military satellites and the first—and very expensive—integrated circuits were dependent on demand from the U.S. Department of Defense and NASA. SDI should be viewed in a similar context.[21]

Seitz's view that considerable spin-off could be expected from West German participation in SDI was not shared by much of West German industry. West German military-industrial interests were divided over the question of participation in SDI. The head of research at Siemens summed up the prevailing skepticism: "Siemens and other firms are not wild about SDI contracts. West German industry is not waiting spellbound for a technological leap from military space projects. A firm such as Siemens is being challenged by major projects in civilian R&D in such fields as optics, fusion, magnetic suspension transport systems and communication."[22]

Taking a similar view, the conservative *Frankfurter Allgemeine Zeitung* editorialized that "to await non-military technological advances from SDI is to over-estimate its civilian spinoff" and, echoing a widespread West European view, estimated that costs to develop civilian innovations through military R&D programs such as SDI would be ten times greater than if R&D funds were used directly for nonmilitary ends.[23]

These views on spin-off reflect the lack of a clear expert consensus on this complex problem. Yet they also reflect the prevailing view in Western Europe—relatively more skeptical than in the United States—of using military R&D to promote nonmilitary industrial development. This skepticism, however, has not led to any definitive separation between military and civilian R&D. On the contrary, the two have become, on the whole, more closely tied to one another—a linkage that has raised the question of the political and economic direction of West European R&D efforts and, in particular, what role the competition for new military technologies will play in determining the R&D and defense policies of West European economies in the coming years.

New Technologies and the Arms Race

Despite the new climate of détente and the flowering of East-West cooperation, it still remains unclear to what extent the technological revolution in Western Europe will come under the pressure of the competitive arms race, given the absence of constraints on military R&D.[24] As argued in Part 1 of this book, the risk of a new arms race that would severely hamper the new era of détente cannot be dismissed. The revolution in new technologies is transforming the technological basis of the arms race by linking it more closely to basic research, to nonmilitary and dual-use R&D, and to the commercial diffusion of new products, processes, and services that have dual-use characteristics. Microelectronics, telecommunications, and other high technologies are being incorporated into weapons systems and in the process are exponentially increasing their lethality, precision, speed, and range of operations.

On the Dual Nature of New Technologies

The dual nature of many new technologies forms a central aspect of the policy debate on what priority should be given to military or civilian goals in West European technology programs. One side of the Janus-faced, new technologies is beckoning to a new spiral of arms racing and proliferation. The other side points toward the potential of new technologies for opening up a new economic era and qualitatively more effective technologies for the verification of disarmament and arms control agreements. Several new technologies have this dual potential.

Genetic engineering has the potential for opening up a new era in health care and prevention of disease; in understanding biological processes; in diagnosing, monitoring, and correcting ecological disorders; and for creating new branches of industry, agriculture, and science. It also has the potential for developing systems to detect biological, chemical, and other kinds of weapons for the purpose of verifying arms control and disarmament agreements.[25] But genetic engineering can also be used to develop a new universe of weapons systems potentially more dangerous than the postwar generation of atomic bombs and ballistic missiles. It is a technology that under conditions of competitive arms racing has the potential of endangering the evolutionary future of humankind and, if ever used to develop weapons of mass destruction, the potential of unleashing a sub-cellular race to oblivion. Finally, there are many highly complex nonmilitary ethical problems posed by genetic engineering. These will tend to be exacerbated and remain largely impervious to satisfactory resolution as long as the door to the military use of this technology remains open.

Lasers have a wide transsectoral field of potential application in industry, agriculture, science, medicine, and many other areas. They are also highly versatile as range finders, can be deployed as weapons of mass destruction, and have potential application in a myriad of military-related activities. *Advanced visible infrared sensor technology* can be used in industry, for scientific investigation, and for arms control detection purposes. But it has also vastly improved the military capability to detect targets at night and under adverse observation conditions.[26]

Millimeter wave technology makes it possible to see through smoke, fog, and dust. It can thus be used to detect and exterminate enemy forces and to refine terminal homing missiles and self-guided artillery ammunition. But it can also be applied in fire fighting, outdoor rescue work, protection of the environment, weather forecasting, and for countless other nonmilitary uses. Similarly, *very high speed integrated circuits* (VHSIC) are building blocks with an enormous range of potential applications in nonmilitary spheres of social life and are opening up new vistas of technical invention. But they are also the building blocks for automatic target recognition, analysis and integration of battlefield data, and assistance in battle management and tactical decisionmaking. *Robots and artificial intelligence* can replace many of the forms of drudgery that have plagued the human race since time immemorial, but they also permit the analysis and organization of military data and can replace humans in combat.[27]

Challenge for Arms Control

These few examples illustrate a major trend that is rapidly transforming the nature and risks of military violence, weapons proliferation, and the purpose and function of disarmament. Marek Thee has concisely summed up the significance of the military use of new technologies for the arms race:

> The massive application of modern military technology in armaments has signified a basic shift in the centre of gravity of the arms race, from quantity to quality. This marks a fundamental change in the parameters of the arms race and, consequently, also in the requirements to halt and reverse this race. Yet the arms control exercise has done little to adjust to the new situation. The qualitative arms race has found no place on the agenda of the arms control negotiations.
>
> One of the effects of the qualitative competition has been a vigorous intensification of armaments, very much extraneous and unyielding to control efforts. Previously, when the arms race was predominantly quantitative in nature, responses to the adversary's armament could have been tailored proportionately. They could have been kept on a moderate level, taking into account the quantitative saturation of military arsenals and high costs of the weaponry.[28]

Thee goes on to describe how the scientific-technological race escalates:

> Things tend to become uncalculable. With the long lead-times of weapon development projects far into the future, and the parallel fear of technological breakthroughs by the adversary, stimulants to the

arms race are invigorated. Less notice is taken of existing arsenals, while more attention is paid to weapons on the drawing table and in the pipeline. Also, cost inhibitions are reduced, as no price seems too high for the achievement of technological advantages. The outcome is a state of nervousness in the arms race, constantly stimulating overreaction and exceeding real challenges. The arms race has become virulent indeed.[29]

Thee's description of the effects of new technologies on the arms race also poses the question of the extent to which the intra-Western competitive search for new weapons technology impacts on the nonmilitary dimension of technology development and policy.[30] SDI and West European R&D programs provide an example of several aspects of this interplay.

SDI and the Technological-Political Origins of EUREKA

The initial announcement of SDI as a $26-billion R&D research program intensified West European fears of a brain drain of scientists to U.S. shores and of falling permanently behind in the competitive race for new technologies.[31] Although it was only one among several factors, SDI mobilized West European R&D collaboration programs, particularly during the 1983–1986 period, and reinforced ongoing efforts to create a unified Common Market and transborder infrastructures for high-tech products and services.[32]

The perception in Western Europe of SDI as a multifaceted challenge can be gleaned from the following description of the birth of the research program EUREKA (European Research and Coordination Agency) by *Le Monde*'s defense editor, Jacques Isnard, in June 1985:

> Confronted with the project for defense in space launched by the American president in 1983, the Europeans, in fact, want to respond to the triple—political, strategic and technological—challenge posed by the U.S. decision to devote $26 billion in five years to an attempt to set up a defensive network in space against nuclear missiles.
>
> Let us look at the SDI's technological challenge. The most advanced and most promising aspects of tomorrow's technology will be systematically explored: all types of sensors, lasers and particle beams, as well as large-scale and high-speed data processing. These are the so-called critical technologies which touch on electronics, physics, computers, fusion and mechanics. 18,000 people in the U.S. are already involved in the research under the overall direction of the Strategic Defense Initiative Organization, headed by Lt. Gen. James Abrahamson at the Pentagon, a "machine" to coordinate the work of industrial enterprises, university laboratories and research centers, not only in the U.S., but also in the allied countries wishing to participate.[33]

Isnard points out that although critics of EUREKA reduced the program to an attempt to come up with a response to SDI, EUREKA was more complex, having the aim of "reserving a front row seat for Western Europe in the acquisition of technologies which include fifth-generation computers, artificial intelligence, optronics, lasers and space."[34] Moreover, the French EUREKA proposal

> to constitute a "technological Europe" does not prejudge the answer to the U.S. proposals for European participation in anti-missile space defense. It is rather an invitation to the Europeans not to answer the Americans in dispersed fashion and to create a sort of common coordinated technological front in substance. France is saying that the Europeans should formulate their own requirements and express them first before embarking on any collaboration with such a powerful partner.[35]

A modus vivendi with Bonn. The official French view of EUREKA was not shared by the Federal Republic, which registered a mixture of interest in EUREKA but also apprehension so as not to be viewed as refusing SDI and thus offending the United States as the leader of NATO. Isnard attributed the early difficulties that EUREKA had in getting off the ground "in part to the misunderstanding between Bonn and Paris on the nature of EUREKA and the issue of cooperation between Europe and the United States on the American program."[36]

Linked to what Isnard calls the "misunderstanding" between Paris and Bonn were a number of unsettled questions. For example, would participation in EUREKA exclude participation in SDI for French and/or other West European firms? Similarly, did the French government intend to use EUREKA as an instrument to design its programs in such a manner that the United States would feel rebuffed and challenged?

France took pains to reassure its West European partners. The modus vivendi that was worked out and became part of the structure of the French program can be summed up as follows: (1) French firms participating in EUREKA were given the green light to join SDI on a contract basis with the Pentagon and U.S. military-industrial firms; and (2) EUREKA would consist of civilian and dual-use programs but would be given a predominantly civilian emphasis and would receive the greater part of its public legitimation as a civilian-oriented set of projects.

These characteristics of EUREKA provided a framework for a strong West German participation. Had EUREKA been given a predominantly military emphasis, the West German government would have had to overcome greater domestic opposition to participation from liberal business-oriented interests, from liberal-left, peace-oriented factions within West Germany's political parties, and from its politically powerful peace movement. Bonn would also have had to deal with the problem that a significantly upgraded French–West German military cooperation would have raised in the eyes of the United States and NATO. France is not a full member of the NATO alliance, and although Washington does not oppose French–West German defense collaboration, it would like to maintain West Germany's close ties to U.S. military-industrial interests. The Kohl government saw its "special relationship" with the United States as a major element in its military-industrial and NATO strategy. This influence continued to be reflected in its reluctance to radically expand its defense relationship with France and in the failure of a number of important French–West German defense projects to get off the ground.[37]

That EUREKA was at least in part a response to SDI is also made clear by numerous official and unofficial documents and statements in France before and after creation of the program. An influential study by the French Forecasting and Analysis Center (CAP) of the Ministry of External Relations examined the technological and political-economic risks of French and West European participation in SDI. It cautioned against the approach embodied in SDI of using military R&D to develop civilian economic spin-off. The study posed these main conclusions:[38]

1. Participation in SDI would not be an effective way to meet the technological challenge to France and Western Europe.
2. SDI-related R&D cannot be expected to have significant short-term consequences for nonmilitary sectors of the economy.
3. Caution must be exercised by West European firms that consider collaborating on SDI projects, given U.S. practices of classification of scientific and technical data.
4. It would be logical for the SDIO to want to cooperate with West European military-industrial firms in areas in which Western Europe already enjoys a leading position and not in fields in which the United States is stronger relative to Western Europe, such as lasers, microcomputers, and space technologies.
5. As a response to SDI, EUREKA offers a larger field of potential technological and commercial applications than the U.S. program.

The study also recommended that because of U.S. and Japanese superiority in computer technology, Western Europe would be well-advised not to enter into competition with those countries in all areas of computer technology but instead to try to marshal its cooperative potential to develop mainframe computer systems tailored specifically to European conditions and technological needs. A similar recommendation was made in the case of West European R&D in artificial intelligence.

EUREKA's civilian emphasis. The director of the French Center for the Study of Advanced Systems and Technologies (CESTA), Yves Stourzé, in discussing the importance of the nonmilitary thrust of EUREKA, summed up a widely held view among the program's West European proponents. They consider EUREKA a specifically civilian response to SDI and its predominantly military focus: "I am profoundly convinced that the future lies with civilian technology. Certainly, the question of defense is indeed fundamental, but the technological infrastructure in today's world is, for the most part, based on a civilian grid."[39] Stourzé stresses the importance of building a civilian technological base as the proper foundation for a strong defense: "I would tend to say, without referring to the military domain, that our independence, our security as Europeans, is based on the reinforcement of our technological base."[40]

Stourzé's further comments on the reasons EUREKA was created reinforce the thesis that EUREKA is indeed a response to SDI, while at the same time a program that has adopted a path and set of instruments different from those of SDIO and the Reagan administration. In this context, the ambiguity of Stourzé's position on the civilian and military dimensions of technology policy should be kept in mind: EUREKA represents not a rejection of a defense orientation but a view that the military technology of the future will be based on currently emerging civilian technological advances and planned infrastructures. Therefore, Stourzé concludes, EUREKA should have a predominantly civilian mission, at least for the time being. While championing the civilian thrust of EUREKA, he clearly leaves the door open for a militarizing redirection of EUREKA or subsequent military spin-off in the future.

On the question of technology development and cooperation, Stourzé made the following points in the same interview concerning SDI's polarizing effect on transatlantic relations:[41]

1. The tendency in the United States to restrict data and information by classifying it for security reasons is a form of U.S. withdrawal from cooperation with Western Europe and Japan.
2. This practice leads to greater technological cooperation among West Europeans and, at the same time, to greater caution in cooperation negotiations with the United States in order to guarantee, as much as possible, a fair partnership.
3. West European cooperation, independent of the United States, is indispensable, given the risk that it could in future classify or otherwise restrict technological data or hardware and thereby obstruct West European plans for transborder cooperation and standardization.

It should be pointed out that Stourzé made these comments in July 1985 when the French government was particularly critical of SDI. By early 1986 French official attitudes toward Star Wars changed significantly as French high-tech firms began to take on SDI work.

The Lack of Western Political
Consensus on the Direction of R&D

Notwithstanding early criticisms of SDI, West European governments subsequently became more interested in the U.S. project, particularly in contracts with potential spin-off for West European military programs.[42] The changed response reflects their ambiguous relationship to U.S. military programs. While not subscribing to SDI's longer-term military-political goals, most West European governments have signed SDI agreements or, having declined a formal accord, have nevertheless given national firms the green light to enter into contracts with the SDIO.

This ambiguity not only reflects transatlantic differences on the strategic aims of SDI but also can be linked to the lack of consensus within national policymaking elites on how to adjust to the watershed political climate and disarmament breakthroughs that materialized in the period following the Reykjavik summit of 1986. These factors include the INF Treaty, the subsequent unilateral Soviet and East European disarmament measures, and the declared Soviet intention of removing a large portion of its armed forces from Eastern Europe.

Linked to this uncertainty is the problem of the importance of military R&D programs in technology and security policy. Long-term policy goals of major West European powers and setting priorities to achieve them must be carried out in a climate of minimal consensus on the future development of the East-West conflict and, accordingly, on the respective roles to be assigned to military competition, nonmilitary technological cooperation, and disarmament. As already discussed, this consensus no longer exists. Reestablishing it, moreover, has become more complicated, in part because of the expanding role of dual-use technologies in international trade and their military potential. The risk of dual-use technologies being used for military ends could obstruct the process of economic integration and international cooperation, both of which fundamentally depend on a stable environment of trust and confidence suitable for long-term investment. Creating such conditions implies the reduction to a minimum of sources of potential political tension and military violence.

Besides the political-military aspects of dual-use technologies, there is the related question of the cost benefits of military R&D. At the national and European Community level, for example, there is a recognized need to structure more coherently the relationship between civilian and military R&D programs in order to use more effectively scarce scientific labor and financial resources.[43] This reorganization is viewed as necessary to reduce waste resulting from duplication and overlap of programs. Improving coordination is made difficult, however, as a result of differences in methods and organization as well as national fragmentation of military and nonmilitary R&D programs.

Another relevant problem in this context is that military R&D programs, when linked to civilian R&D programs, can drive up the costs of the latter,[44] which has led to attempts in Western Europe and the United States to separate military and civilian programs more carefully and at the same time to create more effective technology transfer conduits between them. These measures tend, however, to reproduce financial and other trade-offs between military and civilian R&D.[45]

The problem of overlap, duplication, and rising costs resulting from military R&D is evident both at the national and the European Community level. At the EC level, the problem becomes more complicated by additional political-military factors: Cooperation in dual-use R&D raises the question of to what extent an individual EC member is willing to participate in cooperative R&D that may have been initiated partly for the purposes of national defense under conditions of a globally competitive arms race, or to share civilian R&D that could have military applications in the future. The problem is further exacerbated by the EC policy of deepening economic and scientific cooperation and exchange with non-EC states, including the European Free Trade Association (EFTA) and COMECON nations and countries of the Third World. An example here is the GDR, which has become an associate member of EUREKA.

The shadow of the possible military use or military spin-offs hangs over dual-use technologies that are integral to trade in capital goods and to economic development in general. These technologies include, for example, sensor and signal/image processing, complex system design and information management, human-machine interfaces, vehicle technology, advanced design and manufacturing technology, microelectronics, optoelectronics, bioelectronics, energy conversion, advanced materials, and mechanical engineering. The risk of their direct or indirect military application thus has the potential to complicate cooperation by generating political uncertainties and raising the specter of weapons proliferation. This uncertainty can cause economic losses if firms or governments hesitate to export particular dual-use technologies because of possible political consequences or legitimation crises. Firms might find themselves under pressure to forgo entire classes of exports if, after entering into contracts for delivery of particular dual-use goods, they then become the object of international criticisms and sanctions because of a client's open or clandestine military activities.[46]

The scandals in 1989 involving West German firms, which had exported dual-use technologies related to nuclear and chemical weapons production to Libya, Pakistan, and other Third World nations,[47] is a particularly clear-cut case of the proliferation problem linked to dual-use technologies. In an international environment with an increasing number of such new technologies, the problem would tend to take on new dimensions and thus would be difficult to avoid without international constraints.

The preceding brief analysis suggests that the military factor inherent in dual-use technologies has the potential of deleteriously complicating EC efforts to achieve overall macroeconomic aims of lowering costs, unifying the Common Market, and becoming a terrain of increased East-West and North-South economic cooperation. The dual-use problem in this context poses the question of the military and civilian components of European Community R&D programs. Although these are nonmilitary in nature, there is an ambiguous interplay of military and civilian factors in their research design and prospective development.

West European R&D Programs: A Brief Overview

Current European Community cooperation is underpinned by the commitment in the Single European Act to (1) strengthen the scientific and technological basis of West European industry; (2) encourage and support cooperative efforts among industry, research centers, and universities; and (3) adopt the EC guideline known as the "Framework Programme" as a medium-term planning mechanism.[48] The three largest EC projects in this context are ESPRIT (information technologies), BRITE (new materials), and RACE (telecommunications). Other EC programs and their goals are the Biotechnology Action Program (BAP), to promote the application of biotechnology to industry and agriculture; SCIENCE, to promote cooperation and exchanges of research scientists; ERASMUS, to encourage greater student mobility and cooperation between higher education institutions; COMETT, to promote partnerships in training projects between enterprises and universities; EUROTRA, to lower language barriers and thereby ease the transborder circulation of information within the EC; and SPRINT, to create more favorable conditions for innovation and technology transfer in general.[49]

Funding

The EC's R&D programs receive annually approximately 1 billion ECU (European Currency Unit). The ECU is a basket currency based on the currencies of all EC member states. One ECU equals $1.09 (August 1989). The 1 billion ECU, even with planned increases will remain relatively small compared with the total 35 billion ECU spent per year by individual member states on R&D.[50] The total costs of programs supported by the EC equal about 4 percent of estimated public and private civilian research funding, about 50 billion ECU per year. The greater part of R&D outlays in Western Europe is thus allocated in respective national frameworks.[51] By way of comparison, it should be noted that Western Europe's R&D funding as a percentage of GNP and in absolute values trails significantly behind the

United States and Japan. U.S. funding for R&D is 1.75 times the total of all EC members.[52] R&D in the EC amounts to 1.9 percent of GNP, in the United States 2.8 percent of GNP, and in Japan 2.6 percent.[53] Even when military R&D is omitted, U.S. outlays are still clearly in the lead. Only the Federal Republic, with R&D expenditures of 2.8 percent of its GNP, can compare with the United States and Japan.[54] Within the EC itself, R&D expenditures are dominated by the Federal Republic, England, and France, which combined provide 75 percent of the total.[55]

As already noted, EC programs are criticized for their failure to achieve a higher degree of coordination and effectiveness in efforts to eliminate duplication of research and waste of limited resources. Problems in achieving higher levels of cooperation include the different national levels of R&D funding, the differential funding for military and civilian projects in individual countries, the respective academic traditions in higher education, and conflicting priorities of member states in economic and social policy.[56] Factors considered important to improving coordination include better information flows concerning current programs and R&D policy of the different members and improved consultation in the form of expert commissions of the different framework programs.[57]

A Unified Common Market by 1992

The goal of achieving a European Common Market is acting as an important political-economic push-and-pull force in promoting greater R&D and technological cooperation in the "Europe of the 12" and among the EC, EFTA, and COMECON economies. Besides enlarging the market for West European products, a unified market presupposes and promotes greater liberalization of public procurement rules; common standards in industrial, marketing, and research activities; and new public and private infrastructures. All these will tend to increase aggregate demand, raise employment, and stimulate investment.[58]

The process of West European integration and the advancing globalization of West European firms is also eroding the political division of Europe. Common Market unification tends to extend EC activity across East-West borders and, as a result, to increase the pressure to remove existing iron curtains, which hinder the opening up of Eastern markets for Western high-tech goods and services. A more detailed discussion of the advances in East-West economic cooperation can be found in Chapter 10.

The European Research and Coordination Agency (EUREKA)

Organized in 1985, EUREKA forms the umbrella for 213 transborder high-tech projects.[59] Its funding amounts to about 1 billion ECU annually, 50

percent of which comes from EC programs, although EUREKA is not under
EC direction. There are 800 organizations, two-thirds of them firms, from
over 19 countries involved.[60]

EUREKA's goals. A major priority of EUREKA is to harness emerging
technologies to improve macro- and microeconomic efficiency. In this
sense, the program has little in common with the military spending approach
to technology development embodied in SDI. Its main thrust is civilian
R&D, joint production, and the creation of transborder high-tech
infrastructures to regionalize West European economies and improve their
productivity.[61] Toward this end, new products, systems, and services are
being promoted in a variety of fields, including computers, telecommunications, industrial lasers, robotics, new materials, biotechnology, flexible
production systems, high-definition television, environmental protection, and
transportation.

Other goals of EUREKA include pooling resources among West
European economies in order to eliminate the waste of R&D duplication and
go-it-alone national policies; developing computer-telecommunication
networks to link research institutes and firms in different countries; and
using public financing to stimulate private investment in specific high-
tech projects.[62] Government subsidies to participating firms are gauged
according to how soon a particular project can come on stream as a
marketable product.

Cooperation within the EUREKA framework is not confined to
countries belonging to the European Community; the program is open to all
West European states. This is in part intended to prevent growing
technological disparities between large and small, more and less advanced
European economies. Cooperative projects with COMECON countries are
also on EUREKA's agenda; as previously noted, the GDR is now an
associate member.

Critics of EUREKA argue that its scale is too modest to achieve the
mobilization of resources that the technological challenge facing Western
Europe requires and that the programs could be better distributed between
participating countries.[63] It is also maintained that many of the projects
would have been organized in any case within the framework of the European
Community. Defenders of EUREKA have stressed that the program is a
useful addition to EC activity.

The military potential.   Although EUREKA is a civilian-oriented
program, it does not exclude research that could be applied to either current or
future military ends. Many of the programs involve research of dual-use
technologies and thus can be viewed as having both a military and civilian
potential. Because there is no arms control monitoring of R&D, it is difficult
to assess with any precision the size or potential growth of EUREKA's

military dimension. It is worth noting in this context, however, that prominent French and West German political and military figures have repeatedly called for a militarization of EUREKA, emphasizing its potential contribution to West European air defense, ATBM capability, and other current military efforts.[64]

One of the central questions that haunts EUREKA is to what extent it will retain its civilian spirit or, under the pressure of French and NATO modernization plans, the WEU, and U.S. high-tech defense programs, be increasingly pulled into the global race for emerging military technology. Given its basic structures, EUREKA could not be easily transformed into a West European military counterpart of SDI, but it could be burdened with an increasing number of explicitly military projects if, for example, the governments and firms currently supporting it decide to shift their priorities away from civilian- and market-oriented goals. Because EUREKA is not under the auspices of the European Community, it is less visible and accountable to the public concerning its individual projects. Questions therefore arise about the possible military aims and potential military spin-offs of programs and whether they should be open to EC expert assessment regarding the potential military use of their results. A report by the European Parliament has discussed this issue:

> Sceptics have pointed out that the French "fall silent when they are asked about the military spin-off." EUREKA's drive for fifth or sixth generation computers capable of thirty gigaflops per second, for example, is unlikely to "widen Europe's grip on world markets," since the market for such machines "will scarcely run into double figures." The main users will be the military.[65]

European military-industrial interests have called for a European counterpart to the U.S. Defense Advanced Research Projects Agency (DARPA) in order to upgrade West European military R&D. Boniface and Heisbourg have commented on the military potential of EUREKA—and by implication on other European R&D programs:

> [T]he primary effect of creating a European sphere of technology will be to reinforce the capacity of European states to modernize their defense at the best price, given the fact that the high-technology firms are engaged in both civil and military technology development. The technologies that are being considered for development in EUREKA are often amenable to military applications, just as the Bessemer blast furnaces of the 19th century were able to supply steel interchangeably to civilian building sites or to the manufacturers of armor plate.[66]

The European Strategic Program of
Research in Information Technology (ESPRIT)

ESPRIT is the single largest framework programme of the European Community. It was started in 1984 with the goal of making West European information industries internationally competitive in the 1990s. The first half of the ten-year program was funded with 1.5 billion ECU, 50 percent from the EC and 50 percent from industrial firms joining the project. The second phase of ESPRIT has a budget of 3.5 billion ECU.[67] While the first phase concentrated on precompetitive research in microelectronics, information systems, and application technologies (including flexible production, office systems, and artificial intelligence), the second phase also includes basic research. Two important ground rules for selecting projects and firms for participation are that the research must be carried out by several teams in different countries of the EC and that projects must combine basic research with the goal of achieving new applications of the technologies developed.

The role of firms. In 1984 Western Europe's external trade balance in IT showed a deficit of $10.6 billion.[68] To correct this imbalance, major West European firms undertook concerted action, including the setting up of ESPRIT, and have markedly improved their economic performance since then: The six largest IT firms have had an annual growth rate of 25 percent, while the world market growth rate in IT has been only 15 percent.[69] Moreover, in the West European market, these firms have increased their market share from 33 percent to almost 50 percent.[70]

Despite these gains, however, the high-tech problems described at the beginning of this chapter are far from having been removed. West European firms that manufacture information systems still have a relatively small share of international markets—only 15–25 percent of their volume of sales.[71] The industry is still highly dependent on foreign producers for electronic components and important classes of peripheral devices. There is also a lack of skilled labor and other personnel.

A major concern of ESPRIT is to connect the academic world and public nonprofit research facilities with the private interests of small and medium-sized firms. During the first eighteen months of ESPRIT's existence, it approved 173 projects with 1,700 researchers, 478 organizations, 104 universities, and 81 research institutes.[72] The first phase of ESPRIT was hailed by its sponsors as a demonstration that cooperation among Western Europe's multinational firms is a viable road to strengthen transborder West European technology. Supporters point in this context to the national breakdown of the projects: Of the organizations that participated in the pilot phase, 27 were located in Britain, 21 in Germany, 10 in the Netherlands, 8 in Belgium, 4 in France, and 2 in Italy.[73]

ESPRIT is also designed to establish greater commonality of West

European standards. This could enable firms to develop systems that can be readily integrated into products of a larger number of manufacturers within the EC.

ESPRIT's critics maintain that the program, despite its success in getting off the ground and committing its initial funds, suffers from a "Eurocratic" manner of operating, with the result that its research grants "will not add up to a critical mass of scientific endeavor."[74] Underlying this viewpoint are the traditional problems of national rivalries, bureaucratization within the European Community, entrenched firm-to-firm and national competition, and the disparity of interests and influence between large and small firms. In the past, these problems have repeatedly hindered West European cooperation.

Although these criticisms merit serious attention, they may be premature, given ESPRIT's successful first phase, the current positive echo within the West European business and political community, and the international competitive forces driving the region's current high-tech cooperative efforts. Moreover, ESPRIT should be seen not as an isolated project but in relation to other R&D efforts with which it is interacting. Finally, because it is a young program, it is also capable of changing course along its learning curve.

The military potential. ESPRIT, like EUREKA, illustrates how West European programs pursued as civilian R&D projects are also creating a new military-technological base. Many of ESPRIT's basic research programs are related to dual-use technologies, and many of the leading firms participating in ESPRIT are high-tech military-industrial corporations involved in military production.

Research in Advanced Communication in Europe (RACE)

Officially set up in August 1985, RACE is an EC project aimed at promoting R&D in advanced communication technology. Its goal is to "strengthen Europe's position in order to overcome the weakness of the Community vis-à-vis the United States and Japan in the field of new basic information technologies."[75] To achieve this aim, RACE has an ambitious agenda aimed at creating the technological base for introducing the Integrated Broadband Communications Network (IBCN) throughout the EC. Its projects have a broad range: creating new communication infrastructures, defining relevant R&D fields, providing less-developed regions of the EC better access to emerging advanced high-tech infrastructures, and developing service networks.

By 1995 RACE backers hope to make it possible for Western Europe to overtake the United States in telecommunications by eliminating current incompatible software standards in the transmission of data.[76] This would address the problem of fragmentation of West European standards and norms due in part to national monopoly-type postal and communication systems.

European Programs and the United States

Transition to a unified market with continental reach also raises the central problem of the role of large U.S. firms like IBM. On the one hand, programs such as ESPRIT, RACE, and EUREKA are designed to allow Western Europe to keep firms like IBM at bay long enough to catch up in areas where Western Europe is technologically weak. Besides the competitive rationale behind these efforts, there is also the military-security aspect: The United States, following patterns set by the Reagan government, could see fit to restrict West European high-tech exports if the goods are manufactured with U.S. components.[77] As will be discussed in Chapter 8, U.S. security exports and classification practices linked to them are encouraging West European firms to "decouple" from U.S. companies in order to avoid falling under the jurisdiction of U.S. and COCOM restrictions on goods or services sold to Eastern countries. On the other hand, many West European firms will take such risks because they want greater access to U.S. technology and have extensive and expanding relations with IBM and other U.S. high-tech giants.[78] These firms are already strongly represented in Western Europe and in many cases are eager to collaborate with European firms across a broad range of R&D, production, and marketing activities.

Conclusions

Western European governments, in contrast to the United States, are relatively more sensitive to the risks of extra costs and technological distortions created by militarizing R&D programs. They have examined and drawn important lessons from the U.S. experience and view programs such as SDI partly as a continuation of an R&D approach that they generally reject. The West European perspective is that it is considerably less costly, technologically more effective, and politically more acceptable to develop commercial technology if research is not organized under the umbrella of military programs.

Because they have the option of more direct forms of industrial policy and planning, West European governments and industries, acting both nationally and on a multilateral and/or EC basis, are generally able to do more with considerably less financial input and to target more precisely nonmilitary economic goals. This capability stems in part from the fact that Western Europe is not burdened with the constraints of an institutionalized Military Keynesian approach to state-funded industrial programs. As a result, the process of technology development is less subject to the military-related security controls and classification laws that constrain U.S. R&D programs, which gives West European governments and firms distinct advantages in a number of different areas, including organizing transsectoral cooperation, moving into Eastern markets, and establishing R&D and other forms of cooperation with Eastern countries.

Politically and ideologically, West European governments at the national and EC level see a premium in emphasizing the civilian, job-creating, and détente-promoting potential of the development and diffusion of new technologies. They resist framing technological advancement in terms of military security and achieving an edge in military-technological competition. In the Federal Republic, which enjoys the largest GNP of Western Europe, orienting R&D programs toward military security or using this as a public selling point would meet with considerable opposition.

The differences in approach between the United States and Western Europe are creating transatlantic friction—tension that could increase because the technological revolution has become a driving force of both the militarization of R&D and greater civilian cooperation across traditional postwar military-political boundaries. Transatlantic disputes over exports of high-technology goods to the East reflect and exacerbate the controversy over asking Western Europe to spend more on defense. The high-tech export debate also highlights differences within NATO on arms control and the future of East-West relations.

The differences between the U.S. and West European R&D programs in terms of their respective military potential are significant but should not be overemphasized. Many of the West European research programs are dual-use in character and at the level of basic and applied research are creating a technological environment that will offer qualitatively new possibilities for weapons development and competitive arms racing. In addition to R&D for straightforward military ends, R&D programs that appear today as more civilian-oriented in their organization and goals are providing firms and national defense establishments with know-how and hardware for arms development.

New technologies pose the need for new forms of disarmament constraints that would cover not merely existing types of weapons but also the process of weapons invention in the form of R&D programs and the various interfaces between civilian and military R&D. Unless some international oversight regime is created, continued West European involvement in U.S., NATO, and West European high-tech military programs poses the risk of distortion of nonmilitary technological and economic-political priorities. Present military R&D policies are likely to have an adverse effect on the future of international trade in high technology and on the cooperation efforts of major powers and large firms in West-West and East-West relations. A failure to set up an international regime of constraints on the military dimension of dual-use R&D could hamper West European efforts to use advances in high technology to make macroeconomic adjustments, unify the Common Market, and increase West European competitiveness in nonmilitary markets.

The irony here is that an immense potential lies beyond the military arena. New technological infrastructures in telecommunications, transport, data sharing, and research networks could extend across the European continent to create rich and varied patterns of cooperation in Western Europe and in East-West relations in many areas of political and economic activity. But such expansion will require arms control and disarmament measures in order to remove inhibiting military factors. The objective would have to be to create a global environment in which economic and technological development can freely unfold into the next century without the security, proliferation, and economic risks linked to militarization.

This objective raises the question of what specific measures could be useful in constraining the military dimension of R&D. In this context, Marek Thee has written:

> One measure is budgetary restrictions for military R & D; these would require the solution of the long-standing problem discussed in the United Nations: the standardization of military budgets so as to arrive at an agreed system to measure, compare and verify proposed limitations of military expenditure. Another measure would aim at the establishment of national and international technological assessment institutions for continuous monitoring and evaluation of the course of technological innovation, particularly in the military domain, so as to develop early warning systems on the work on new weapon systems. Finally, it is imperative to activate moral and ethical restraints against the race to oblivion in R & D.[79]

In a similar vein, the European Parliament has formulated a set of social and economic criteria to evaluate West European technology projects. They are phrased in the form of the following questions:[80]

- Do [the projects] enhance Western Europe's industrial competitiveness?
- Do they create jobs and stimulate wealth?
- Are they "environment-friendly" and do they actively promote the protection of the environment?
- Do they further [European] Community objectives in the medical sphere as regards safety and the fight against hunger and poverty in the world? . . .
- Do they take into account the need to conserve energy or to further the [EC's] energy objectives?

The following questions might be added:

- Do the projects promote a deepening of East-West economic détente and make possible a further relaxation of military tensions?
- Can they contribute to economic recovery and at the same time to arms control and demilitarization of technology development?
- Can they remove restrictions that are blocking a freer flow of goods, information, and people across West-West, East-West, and North-South divides without prejudicing the security of small or large states?

Notes

1. John Marcum, "High Technology and the Economy," *OECD Observer*, No. 131, November 1984, p. 4, quoted in Bruce L.R. Smith, "A New 'Technology Gap' in Europe?" *SAIS Review*, Vol. 6, No. 1, Winter/Spring 1986, pp. 219–236. See also in this context the more detailed analysis in Margaret Sharp and Claire Shearman, *European Technological Collaboration* (London: Routledge and Kegan Paul and the Royal Institute of International Affairs, 1987), pp. 5ff.

2. European Communities, Economic and Social Consultative Assembly, Economic and Social Committee, *Europe and the New Technologies, R&D, Industry, Social Aspects* (Brussels: European Communities, 1986) p. 1; Sharp and Shearman, op. cit., pp. 6ff.

3. European Communities, ibid.

4. Sharp and Shearman, op. cit., pp. 2–3, 17ff. See also in this context Rob van Tulder and Gerd Junne, *European Multinationals and Core Technologies* (New York: Wiley, 1988) Chapter 7; Walter Zegveld and Christien Enzing, *SDI and Industrial Technology Policy: Threat or Opportunity?* (New York: St. Martin's, 1987).

5. André Danzin, "ESPRIT et les vulnérabilitiés de la Communauté européene," *Défense nationale*, Vol. 41, No. 2, February 1985, pp. 7–32.

6. The introduction of new technologies necessary to produce new jobs will also destroy employment and generate mounting structural unempioyment. West European long-term unemployment is estimated at 10 million; Giles Merritt, "Social Policy Rethink," *European Affairs*, Vol. 2, No. 1, Spring 1988, pp. 88–94. Although it is expected that new technologies will have a long-term positive effect on job creation, it is predicted that technological innovation will not significantly expand the job market until well into the 1990s. In earlier periods of major economic shifts, jobs lost through rationalization were offset by new employment in the tertiary sector; this is no longer the case today. According to one estimate, for example, the introduction of new technologies will affect 40 percent to 50 percent of all jobs, thus producing a large drop in employment during the coming years and creating an increasing pool of structurally unemployed. (European Communities, op.cit., p. 64). The other side of the technological revolution is the job-creating effects of capital investment, particularly in information technologies (Dieter Kimbel, "Information, Technology: Increasingly the Engine of OECD Economies," *OECD Observer*, No. 107, August-September

1987, pp. 17–20). Under current conditions, the growth of European economies would have to be above average to substantially reduce current trends of increasing unemployment. European Communities, op. cit. pp. 64–66.

7. Pierre Dussauge, *L'industrie française de l'armement* (Paris: Economica, 1985), p. 121. A West German example of the problems of the military-civilian symbiosis and trade in the context of the industrial strategy of major firms is the case of Daimler Benz and its takeover of MBB, West Germany's largest arms firm. See in this context "Mercedes: "Im Kern treffen," *Der Spiegel*, Vol. 41, No. 47, November 21, 1987; "Die neue deutsche Rüstungsmacht," *Der Spiegel*, Vol. 42, No. 31, August 1, 1988.

8. Dussauge, ibid.

9. Ibid.

10. Ibid., pp. 121f.

11. Ibid. p. 122.

12. Ibid.

13. Ibid.

14. Ibid., p. 123.

15. Ibid. Idle capacity in the French defense industry stemming from falling exports is a particularly serious problem because of the high dependency of this sector on export sales. According to Dussauge, "If France suddenly ceased all its arms exports, 40% of French military industrial capacity would be idled." Ibid., p. 126. A drop in sales would "affect the volume of sales to the French Department of Defense. Entire sectors of the French arms industry would be put at risk." Ibid.

16. Ibid., p. 123.

17. Ibid., p. 122.

18. Ibid., pp. 123f.

19. Hans-Hilger Haunschild, "Zivile Forschungsförderung und Perspektiven der Technologieentwicklung" *Wehrtechnik*, Vol. 18, No. 7, 1986, pp. 34–36.

20. Ibid.

21. Konrad Seitz, "SDI—Die technologische Herausforderung für Europa," *Europa-Archiv*, Vol. 40, No. 13, 1985, pp. 381–390.

22. "Die Industrie drängt sich nicht nach SDI," *Frankfurter Allgemeine Zeitung*, April 25, 1985. In 1980 the prestigious Association of German Industry, which during the 1950s had subscribed to the notion of spin-off, emphatically rejected the link between defense R&D programs and the civilian economy, pointing out that research designed to meet military-related goals results in significantly less spin-off than does basic research. Although the association changed its mind in the mid-1980s and urged the Kohl government to embrace SDI, considerable skepticism remained. See in this context Rainer Rilling, "Welchen Zivilen Nutzen hat SDI," *Blätter für deutsche und internationale Politik*, Vol. 30, No. 5, May 1985, pp. 561–577. Zegveld and Enzing criticize SDI as an example of oversimplified "technology-push" innovation. They point out that despite the growing acceptance of more complex and interactive models of innovation, most governments continue to adhere to the simple premise that a larger amount of R&D can equate with more innovation. Zegveld and Enzing, op. cit., pp. 115–117.

23. *Frankfurter Allgemeine Zeitung*, June 11, 1985.

24. The analysis of civilian and military R&D in this section assumes UNESCO's broad definition of R&D:

Any creative systematic activity undertaken in order to increase the stock of knowledge, including knowlege of man, culture and society, and the use of this knowledge to devise new applications. It includes fundamental research (i.e. experimental or theoretical work undertaken with no immediate practical purpose in mind), applied research in such fields as agriculture, medicine, industrial chemistry, etc. (i.e. research directed primarily towards a special practical aim or objective), and experimental development work leading to new devices, products or processes.

UNESCO Statistical Yearbook 1985, p. V-1. Marek Thee in his study of military R&D written for the United Nations defines military R&D as follows: "By 'military R&D' we subsume mission-oriented R&D activity comprising basic and applied research, including development, testing and experimental production of new weapons and weapon systems. It further includes the improvement and modernization of existing weapons and weapon systems." Marek Thee, "Science and Technology for War and Peace," *Bulletin of Peace Proposals*, Vol. 19, No. 3–4, 1988, pp. 261–292. Thee points out that on the basis of data from 1980, there has been a steep rise in the number of scientists and engineers engaged in R&D: "From 1970 to 1980 this increase amounted to 44%. At the same time, world expenditure on R&D multiplied 3.5 times in current dollars and 2.5 times above the rate of inflation." Ibid. On some of the problems of defining military R&D and distinguishing it from civilian R&D, see Rainer Rilling, "Military R&D in the Federal Republic of Germany," *Bulletin of Peace Proposals*, Vol. 19, No. 3-4, 1988, pp. 317–342.

25. Jean-François Delpech, "New Technologies, the United States and Europe: Implications for Western Security and Economic Growth," *Atlantic Community Quarterly*, Vol. 25, No. 1, Spring 1987, pp. 47–63.

26. Ibid.

27. Ibid.

28. Marek Thee, "The Race in Military Technology and Arms Control" (Paper delivered at the 11th General Conference of the International Peace Research Association, University of Sussex, April 13–18, 1986). Thee's description should also be placed before the backdrop of high expenditures on military R&D. In his report on military R&D, Thee analyzes these as a percentage of all governmental outlays for R&D, civilian R&D included, and as a percentage of gross domestic expenditure on R&D: "In 1981–84, on the average, the US devoted to military R&D 60% of government R&D outlays on all R&D, and 28% of gross domestic expenditure on R&D. The respective figures for the UK are 50% and 27%, and for France 38% and 23%. A number of other countries involved in military production—from Sweden and Australia to Greece, FRG, Italy, Norway and Canada—have also followed the above trend, though at a lower level." Thee, 1988, op. cit.

29. Thee, "The Race," op. cit. See also Thee, *Military Technology, Military Strategy and the Arms Race* (London: Croom Helm, 1986), Chapter 6.

30. Analysis of the relationship of military to nonmilitary R&D is difficult because of the absence of systematic data and the complex interplay of the two. The Stockholm Peace Research Institute estimated in 1987 that world spending on military R&D is "roughly a quarter of world spending on all R&D and in 1986 was approximately US $85–100 billion a year in current prices." "Military Research and Development," in *SIPRI Yearbook 1987*, Chapter 6, as cited in Thee 1988, op. cit. In terms of the increase in R&D labor, the

institute estimated that "of the world's four million R&D scientists and engineers, probably over three-quarters of a million are engaged in military R&D. If support people are included, there are probably at least one and a half million people in the world working in military R&D." Ibid.

31. Phillippe Lemaitre, "Le Programme Eureka doit proposer un champ d'application civil plus large que le projet stratégique de M. Reagan," *Le Monde*, May 8, 1985; see also John Fenske, "France and the Strategic Defense Initiative: Speeding Up or Putting on the Brakes," *International Affairs*, Vol. 62, No. 2, Spring 1986, pp. 231–246.

32. Michael Lucas, "SDI and Europe," *World Policy Journal*, Vol. 3, No. 2, Spring 1986, pp. 219–249. On diminishing fears of SDI among West European industrialists, see Guy de Jonquieres, "Back to Basics," *Financial Times*, July 23, 1987. On European collaboration in the form of increased mergers, see Guy de Jonquieres, "Hard in Practice but Unavoidable," *Financial Times*, October 5, 1987.

33. Jacques Isnard, "The EUREKA Project and the Strategic Defense Initiative," *International Defense Review*, Vol. 18, No. 6, 1985, p. 858. See also in this context Pierre-Henri Laurent, "Eureka, or the Technological Renaissance of Europe," *Washington Quarterly*, Vol. 10, No. 1, Winter 1987, pp. 53–66.

34. Isnard, ibid.

35. Ibid.

36. Ibid.

37. See in this context Chapter 3.

38. Lemaitre, op. cit.

39. "Les multi-composants d'une Europe chercheuse," interview avec Yves Stourzé, *Libération*, July 17, 1985. France's foreign minister at that time, Roland Dumas, commented on the challenge of SDI for Western Europe as follows: "The challenge for Europe is in the first place technological. The military challenge will come later and perhaps in a form which one cannot determine in advance and unilaterally. This is the philosophy of the project known in France as EUREKA;" M. Dumas: "le défis pour l'Europe est d'abord technologique," *Le Monde*, April 25, 1985.

40. Stourzé, ibid.

41. Ibid.

42. See Chapter 3.

43. Commission of the European Communities, *First Report on the State of Science and Technology in Europe*, November 29, 1988 (hereafter *First Report*), pp. 64, 66.

44. Ibid.

45. Ibid.

46. See in this context "Rabita—eine Giftgasfabrik made in Germany," and also "Deutsche bauen Tankflugzeuge für Libyen," *Der Spiegel*, Vol. 43, No. 2, January 16, 1989.

47. Ibid.

48. *First Report*, op. cit., p. 80.

49. Ibid., p. 83.

50. Ibid., p. 85.

51. Ibid.

52. Ibid., p. 6.

53. Ibid.

54. Ibid.

55. Ibid., p. 55.

56. Ibid., p. 57.

57. Ibid.

58. Ibid., p. 58.

59. Ibid., p. 84.

60. Ibid.

61. European Communities, op. cit., pp. 132f; for a list of EUREKA projects, see ibid., p. 133; European Parliament, Committee on Energy, Research, and Technology, *Draft Report on the Proposal to Establish a European Coordinating Agency (EUREKA) and on Community Participation in Star Wars Research* (Rapporteur: Glyn Ford), February 28, 1986, p. 25. The five areas of research in the initial EUREKA proposal were Euromatique (advanced computer hardware and software); Eurobot (factory automation, agricultural and security robots, high-power industrial lasers); Eurocom (data-processing networks, digital switches, wideband communication between data processing and office automation systems, broadband transmission); Eurobiot (biotechnology); and Euromat (new materials, turbines, high-speed transportation systems).

62. European Communities, ibid. For a French view of EUREKA with a discussion of its European context, see Laurent, op. cit.

63. See in this context Ulrich Briefs, "EUREKA schafft mehr neue Probleme, als es vorhandene löst," in Johannes Becker, Beate Wagner, and Klaus Peter Weiner, eds., *EUREKA, Westeuropäische Technologiepolitik im Spannungsfeld wirtschafts- und sicherheitspolitischer Interessen* (Marburg: Arbeitskreis Marburger Wissenschaftler für Friedens- und Abrüstungsforschung, 1987), pp. 20–25; Roland Schneider, "Technologische versus soziale Integration," in Becker et al., ibid., pp. 26–30.

64. European Parliament, op. cit., p. 25; Pascal Boniface and François Heisbourg, *Les puces, les hommes et la bombe: L'Europe face aux nouveaux défis technologiques et militaires* (Paris: Hachette, 1986), p. 262.

65. European Parliament, op. cit., p. 25.

66. Boniface and Heisbourg, op. cit., p. 291.

67. *First Report*, op. cit., p. 81.

68. Ibid., p. 90.

69. Ibid., pp. 90f.

70. Ibid.

71. Ibid.

72. European Communities, op. cit., p. 93.

73. Sharp and Shearman, op. cit., p. 51. It should be noted that in 1986 there were countertendencies to "Europeanizing" R&D programs. Pressure on the part of Britain, France, and West Germany, for example, resulted in the reduction of the EC's funding budget proposal for framework programmes in 1986 from 10.3 billion ECUs to 7.7 billion. West European firms began to adopt a more selective policy concerning which areas of high tech they wanted to pursue. They also became more open to joint ventures with U.S. and Japanese firms and more reluctant to cede too much influence over their respective R&D resources to Brussels and thus also, via the European Community, to competing firms. Another important factor has been a diminution of West European fears of SDI as a military or civilian R&D program threatening Western Europe's economic future. See Sharp and Shearman, op. cit., in their concluding remarks on the costs and benefits of European collaboration, pp. 84–104.

74. Smith, op. cit.

75. European Communities, op. cit., p. 94.

76. Ibid., pp. 94f.

77. See Chapter 8.

78. Important in this context is IBM's relationship to the European Community. See Sharp and Shearman, op. cit., Chapter 4, in particular pp. 79–83; also p. 94.

79. Thee, "The Race," op. cit.

80. European Parliament, op. cit., p. 9.

U.S. Technology Export Controls and the Economic-Security Dilemma

The technological revolution in Western Europe and the interplay there of military and civilian R&D were discussed in Chapter 7 as yet another aspect of the political watershed for the Western Alliance in which the postwar and the post-containment models of security are competing as policy alternatives. That the R&D of new technologies could lead either to a spiral of continued and more dangerous arms racing or contribute to a new era of détente based on disarmament and East-West cooperation tends to confirm the overarching hypothesis of this book—that the Western Alliance is in the throes of a historic but uncertain and difficult shift in its definition and organization of security policy. In order to deepen the demonstration of this hypothesis, I will show in this chapter how this policy watershed is also reflected in the intensifying West-West debate on Western export security controls related to the Coordinating Committee on Multilateral Export Controls, better known as COCOM.

The views of Western Europe and the United States have markedly diverged on the question of the proper role of exports of high technology to the East. The central question at issue is whether such exports should be (a) withheld in order to gain technological-military and technological-economic leverage over the Soviet Union and its allies—a view embodied in the U.S. concept of "competitive strategies," or (b) used as an instrument to lower East-West security-related mistrust and tension; promote economic reform and recovery in the East; and deepen cooperation that benefits both Eastern and Western economies. This second view corresponds to the general policy climate and direction of West European economies today, particularly that of the Federal Republic.

This chapter suggests that the economic-political factors discussed in Chapters 6 and 7 are rapidly eroding the foundations of the postwar export security system—a process being driven by a number of factors, including the accelerating growth of East-West cooperation and economic intercourse. Because the benefits for both the United States and Western Europe are becoming more tangible, these factors put into question the COCOM regime and the model of security that underpins it.

The main argument presented here is based on what will be referred to as the U.S. "economic-security dilemma." It can be summed up as follows: On the one hand, U.S. security export policy hurts U.S. economic interests. On the other hand, U.S. security policy based on increasing U.S. military-technological advantage, forbids radically reducing export security restrictions. In this view, boosting exports to emerging Eastern markets, to reduce the trade deficit and increase competitiveness could seriously prejudice U.S. military security by enhancing Soviet technological and military capabilities. The U.S. policy of competitive strategies means restricting the transfer of high-tech, particularly dual-use, exports to emerging Eastern markets.

This chapter suggests that the United States in order to overcome its economic-security dilemma must move resolutely with its European allies and the Soviet Union in the direction of the post-containment model of security. Because West European economies favor more open high-tech export policies, a too-slow U.S. adjustment could produce increasing friction within the Western Alliance and a further weakening of the U.S. position in the international economy.

This chapter briefly describes COCOM policy and other instruments of the U.S. export control apparatus. This is followed by an analysis of current U.S. military-technological strategy and its links to security export controls. Changes in the international economy are also taken up followed by a concluding discussion of West European criticism of the U.S. approach to East-West trade.

U.S. Executive and Legislative Export Controls

Using technological superiority to achieve military-political and economic leverage over the Soviet Union is linked to the arms race, the dominant framework of the U.S-Soviet relationship since the end of World War II. COCOM, created in 1949, must be viewed as an economic corollary to the U.S. policy of political and military containment of the Soviet Union. During the postwar era, direct U.S.-Soviet economic competition and cooperation have played an insignificant role, for the most part foreclosed by the East-West arms race, the formation of a bloc-against-bloc international system, and the autarkic character of the Soviet economy under Stalin. Multilaterally withholding advanced technology from the Soviet Union through COCOM became a central element of U.S. policy. The United States and its allies abandoned the wartime strategy of being prepared to outproduce potential adversaries in favor of relying on (1) superior military technology to offset the numerical advantage in troops and certain classes of weapons of the Warsaw Pact; and (2) withholding Western technology from the Soviet Union through an elaborate system of restrictive mechanisms.

Restriction of Military Items

The Arms Export Control Act (AEC) of 1976 empowers the president to restrict the production and export of defense goods and services.[1] The State Department implements the act through the International Traffic in Arms Regulations (ITAR), which is based on the U.S Munitions List compiled by the Department of Defense (DOD).[2] Once items are placed on this list, an export license from the State Department becomes mandatory.[3] The DOD, in its role as adviser to the Office of Munitions Control (OMC) in the State Department can also veto decisions concerning the 22 categories of items on the Munitions List.[4]

ITAR defines a defense article as any item specifically designated on the U.S. Munitions List. Armored vehicles, military aircraft, space electronics, and encoding devices are just a few examples of the classes of goods subject to trade restrictions. "Defense service" is defined by ITAR as "the furnishing of assistance, including training, to foreign persons in the design, engineering, development, production, processing, manufacture, use, operation, overhaul, repair, maintenance, modification, or reconstruction of defense articles."[5] Category 18 covers the special domain of "technological data," which include information on the design, production, and reproduction of items on the Munitions List. The term "export" is very broadly defined and includes technical data in oral, visual, or written form. The AEC further specifies "export" to apply to data that leave the United States by post or other means of transport, to technical information made public by a U.S. citizen abroad (for example, at a conference or discussion), and even to technical data communicated in the United States to a foreign visitor.[6] This covers, for example, even cases in which information would be informally communicated to foreign students attending U.S. universities.[7]

Restriction of Dual-Use Items

The Export Administration Act (EAA) of 1979, as subsequently amended, empowers the U.S. government to restrict the export of commercial goods and services for reasons pertaining to national security, foreign policy, and protection of the economy against export of scarce resources.[8] The EAA's definition of export goods also includes "technical data" and applies to dual-use technologies that can be used for civilian as well as military purposes. These are contained in the Commodity Control List (CCL) and the Military Critical Technologies List (MCTL), which are compiled by the Pentagon for the Commerce Department, the administrator of the EAA.[9] In 1979 the MCTL became an important policy instrument and major source of transatlantic controversy stemming partly from the problems of interpreting and applying this highly complex statute. The International Trade Administration of the Department of Commerce administers controls over U.S. exports and over reexports of U.S.-origin commodities. The Export Administration Regulations (EAR) contains the U.S. Control List, which specifies the characteristics of each commodity subject to control. The list contains 240 entries divided into 10 categories: metal-working machinery; chemical and petroleum equipment; electrical and power-generating equipment; general industrial equipment; transportation equipment; electronics and precision equipment; metals, minerals, and their manufactures; chemicals, metalloids, petroleum products; rubber and rubber products; and miscellaneous.[10]

Particularly troublesome for foreign firms and governments has been the applicability of the EAA to foreign firms in the United States and abroad. The U.S. gas-pipeline embargo against the Soviet Union in 1982 was based on the EAA's extraterritorial authority. Foreign firms were prohibited from reexporting equipment containing U.S. technology not approved for reexport by the Commerce Department. As a result of reexporting rotary blades and technical data for the production of turbines and compressors in the USSR, the firms AEG-Kanis of the Federal Republic, John Brown of Great Britain, Nuovo Pignone of Italy, and Dresser of France were prohibited by the U.S. government from receiving U.S. goods.[11]

The Coordinating Committee for Multilateral Export Controls (COCOM), made up of NATO countries, less Iceland and Japan, was formed for the purpose of controlling the flow of sensitive technology to the Soviet Union.[12] The COCOM restrictions comprise three distinct lists. The International Munitions List and the International Atomic Energy List, covering military goods and atomic energy, are the least controversial among COCOM member states, which fully accept the principle of not exporting military goods to the Soviet Union and other socialist countries. The International Industrial List contains industrial and dual-use goods, including turbines, machine tools, and electronic devices such as aircraft radar and computers. This third list is in turn broken down into three categories: goods whose export is prohibited (International List 1); goods whose export is limited in number (International List 2); and goods whose export is monitored and must be registered with COCOM (International List 3).[13] The main sources of dispute between the United States and other COCOM member states are the approximately 10 different classes of goods on International List 1, which are also contained in the larger U.S. Commodity Control List.[14]

Although the COCOM lists are classified, COCOM member states have their own export control lists that are more or less identical with important sections of the COCOM registries.[15] With the growing criticism of the COCOM in Western Europe, Japan, and Australia,[16] there has been greater public discussion of COCOM and increasing evidence of diminishing adherence of foreign governments to a strict enforcement of COCOM rules.[17]

An important legal characteristic of the U.S. export control apparatus is that the Export Administration Act of 1969 specifically exempted from judicial review penal decisions made against violators of the export regulations. While the Export Administration Act of 1979 modified this provision by allowing some review of penalties, the 1985 amendments gave the secretary of commerce final authority in such disputes.[18] U.S. laws now provide for limited judicial review of export regulations or individual licensing decisions.[19]

The International Emergency Powers Act (IEPA) of 1977 empowers the president to directly intervene in an extraordinary manner to restrict foreign economic relations of U.S. firms and commercial agents.[20] The invoking of the IEPA allows the president to act in crisis situations with the justification of national security, U.S. foreign policy, or simply U.S. economic interests. The emergency decrees issued under the IEPA are valid for a period of one year.

The various classification laws of the United States by which the federal government can declare scientific and technical data (including, for example, patent applications) and access to equipment or goods "classified" are also an important set of instruments to restrict exports and technology transfer.[21] Important in this respect are also restrictions on U.S. subsidiaries of foreign firms under the regime of Industrial Security Regulations, which are expressly designed to prevent access to classifed data.

As a result of the Pentagon's increasing influence in university research programs financed by the federal government, the publication, communication, and transfer of scientific data stemming from such projects became subject during the Reagan administration to tighter restrictions than formerly.[22] These have been applied to civilian dual-use data as well as to strictly military technological data.

The Jackson-Vanik Amendment to the Trade Act of 1974 conditioned the awarding of Most-Favored-Nation status on communist countries' liberalizing their emigration policies. MFN status is essentially the nondiscriminatory trading arrangement that the United States has with most of its trading partners. The amendment was designed to exercise leverage on Soviet emigration and human rights policy, although there is little evidence that it has had this effect.[23] The Stevenson Amendment to the Trade Act of 1974 sets a limit of $300 million on credits from the Export-Import Bank to the Soviet Union.[24]

Partly as a result of U.S. pressure, COCOM accepted in 1984 a new list of dual-use technologies to be withheld from sale to COMECON countries.[25] The list included high-tech goods such as robots and robotic technology, large floating docks, electronic-grade silicon, and a wide range of new metals. The more rigorous COCOM controls were in part designed to restrict export of large computers, dual-use mobile computers, and a variety of software. In addition, the United States urged COCOM at that time to set up an informal group of military advisers for improving its operations. The proposals met with criticism from West European governments.

The Export Administration Amendments Act of 1985 was in part a response to domestic and Western Alliance criticism of U.S. export control policy. The measures adopted were an attempt to simplify and raise the efficiency of U.S. administrative procedures. These included

1. A reorganization of the Office of Export Administration (OEA) with the aim of introducing more efficient administrative and technical procedures for implementing export licensing regulations and for consulting with other government agencies
2. The establishment of the China Team Center to deal specifically with the problem of expediting the large increase in export licenses to the People's Republic
3. An upgrading of the Foreign Availability Division to expedite the issuing of export licenses for products generally available in international markets and to improve enforcement of administrative and criminal sanctions against perpetrators of illegal transfers of controlled goods.[26]

These changes, although welcomed in the United States and abroad, have not succeeded in satisfying either U.S. or West European critics who argue that the COCOM system requires a more thorough overhaul.

During the COCOM negotiations in January 1988, the demand of West European governments for a 40 percent reduction of industrial items regulated by COCOM was rejected by the Reagan administration.[27] Despite the rising pressure from U.S. allies for a drastic revision of COCOM, the meeting ended with simply an updating of about 25 percent of controlled dual-use items. Restrictions were lifted on articles such as personal computers not considered state-of-the-art and on other goods whose sale to COMECON could no longer be controlled because of their international availability and/or whose presence in the East is not construed to be a compromise of Western military security.

At the January meeting, a consensus was reached on the general principle of "higher fences around fewer goods"—meaning the list of restricted items should be further reduced and the still overly complex and inefficient export licensing procedure simplified.[28] According to the rationale of the revision, the pruning of the COCOM list of superfluous items without military significance would allow U.S. allies to more rigorously enforce COCOM restrictions for the remaining more sensitive goods and would go some distance toward meeting West European demands for a more open trading and export security regime.[29]

The ongoing review procedures and piecemeal decontrol of dual-use items did not quiet the criticism of West European and U.S. firms that produce the high-tech commodities and services in increasing demand throughout Eastern Europe and the Soviet Union.[30] William Verity, Jr., an industrial executive whose appointment as secretary of commerce during the Reagan administration was a concession to proponents of reducing restrictions, tried to pursue a more liberal course.[31] He played an important role in easing restrictions and in the liberalization of U.S. COCOM policy contained in the Omnibus Trade and Competitiveness Act of 1988 (discussed later in this chapter). Despite changes in COCOM as a result of U.S. moves, the basic premises underpinning U.S. export policy have remained intact and firmly rooted in U.S. security policy.

U.S. Military Doctrine and Technology Policy

Competitive Strategies

Under the Reagan administration, Secretary of Defense Frank Carlucci emphasized the importance of "competitive strategies" in U.S. military policy. This doctrine, in the words of Pentagon strategist Jon Englund, "holds that, in casting its force posture, technological strategy and procurement policies, the United States (and the Western Alliance more broadly) should hew to clear and explicit criteria of capitalizing on relative advantages and areas of strength, while exploiting the disadvantages and weaknesses of the Soviet Bloc."[32]

As this description implies, the doctrine of competitive strategies is designed to weaken and contain the Soviet Union by placing it under greater military and economic pressure. This approach to Moscow and its allies assumes that Soviet military expansionism and Soviet numerical superiority in troops and certain classes of weapons require this type of military-technological competition in order for the West to maintain its security. Another version of competitive strategies is that of Senator Sam Nunn, who has called for "technological leapfrogging" in the development of new high-tech conventional weapons,[33] which would have the effect of making Soviet weapon stocks obsolete and forcing the Soviets into investing more in military R&D and procurement.

The doctrine of competitive strategies can be viewed as a softened version of the earlier policy of "economic and technical war" promoted during the early phases of the Reagan administration by Secretary of Defense Caspar Weinberger. The rationale for this policy was reiterated in the official assessment of technology flows to the Soviet Union published in 1985 by the U.S. Department of Defense (DOD) and supervised by Assistant Secretary of Defense Richard Perle. The study makes extensive use of a CIA report of

1982 to emphasize that "stopping the Soviet's extensive acquisition of military-related Western technology . . . is one of the most complex and urgent issues facing the Free World today."[34]

In order to accomplish this goal, the DOD report recommended more stringent technology export security relations. Nevertheless, in its assessment of the pros and cons of such a policy, the study raised a number of problems resulting from U.S. Soviet policy and its effects on West-West military and nonmilitary trade. These concerns included competitive military-commercial pressures on the United States to expand its exports of advanced technology:

> Not only has competition in the commercial sector increased, there has also been greater pressure to export military technology to our allies and then in turn compete with these allies for sales of military equipment to third-world countries. In prior years, the U.S. could simply sell second-generation (or older) equipment to other countries and reserve the most modern systems for our forces. This option, however, is changing.[35]

The study also pointed out that the Export Administration Act (EAA) of 1979 reflected these pressures and called for weighing the pros and cons of curbing dual-use exports not only "in the larger national policies" but also in "each export case decision."[36] On the one hand, policy must take account of the need to "encourage trade and remain competitive in world markets."[37] On the other hand, this must be weighed against the need to "restrict the flow of military critical technologies to proscribed nations to enhance our national security."[38] The study failed to address the more fundamental question of whether this tension is manageable or irreconcilable and likely to become increasingly so. In its policy prescriptions, the DOD report, adhering to what was to become the policy line of the first Reagan administration, argued strongly in favor of a more extensive and stringently enforced regime of export controls and insisted that this would be compatible with U.S. economic interests and responsibilities vis-à-vis U.S. allies.

The close interrelationship between U.S. military planning and the high-technology export security regime during the early phases of the Reagan administration is also reflected in the Pentagon "defense guidance" document of 1982. Though classified, this 125-page, five-year planning directive was summarized and selectively quoted in a background piece by Richard Halloran, the defense correspondent of the *New York Times*.[39]

The Pentagon statement emphasizes the role of "economic and technical war" as a major policy instrument of the administration:

> In peacetime competition with the Soviet Union, the West's trade policies would put as much pressure as possible on a Soviet economy

already burdened with military spending. . . . As a peacetime complement to military strategy, the guidance document asserts that the United States and its allies should, in effect, declare economic and technical war on the Soviet Union.[40]

In a further paragraph, the author of the *Times* piece adds that

Reducing Soviet access to technology from the United States and other non-Communist countries has long been among Mr. Weinberger's keenest objectives and the Pentagon plan reflects that. It also reflects an intention to execute a technical strategy designed to erode Soviet economic strength. That strategy, the plan says, should focus "investment in weapon systems that render the accumulated Soviet equipment stocks obsolescent."[41]

Economic Sanctions as an Instrument of Foreign Policy

In addition to the export controls to erode Soviet military strength, the Reagan administration in its recommendations for amending the Export Administration Act of 1979 argued in favor of extending the president's power to use economic sanctions to achieve foreign policy goals.[42]

The experience of the unsuccessful U.S. grain embargo of 1980–1981 against the Soviet Union and the gas pipeline sanctions of 1982, however, put into relief the failure of U.S. attempts to use export sanctions to achieve economic and political goals. The grain embargo had to be withdrawn because of the protest of U.S. farmers.[43] The pipeline embargo, while depriving U.S. companies of lucrative contracts and playing havoc with assiduously cultivated business relationships, failed in the end even to delay the completion of the Soviet project. In addition, West European governments criticized the Reagan administration's policy of using economic sanctions to achieve foreign policy goals as being a violation of internationally accepted rules of conduct.[44]

The conflict with West European governments as a result of the sanctions against Western European companies underlined the striking differences in transatlantic attitudes toward export controls in general. Hanns-Dieter Jacobsen, in summing up these differences, emphasizes the West European view of economic relations with the East as an important instrument for fostering political stabilization:

In contrast to the U.S. administration, West European governments have proved to be much more cautious with regard to the use of economic sanctions as an instrument of foreign policy. If necessary, they were prepared, as for example in the case of the Federal Republic of Germany, to offer economic inducements to encourage politically desirable conduct on the part of communist countries. . . . As a general principle, even if with certain nuances, West European countries see economic relations as a means of stabilizing East-West relations. Economic relations are alternatively treated separately from political relations, and by no means used as an instrument to punish or discipline the USSR or other Eastern countries.[45]

COCOM Policy on the Defensive

With the thaw in U.S.-Soviet relations, the dramatic shift in the direction of disarmament with the INF Treaty, the progress in the START negotiations, and the boom in East-West détente initiatives in Europe, the Reagan policy toward the Soviet Union had significantly changed. Nevertheless, the basic philosophy of military-technological competition—and thus the linkage between high-tech trade and military policy—remained essentially intact. Administration policy on export controls was reiterated by Secretary of Defense Frank Carlucci in Tokyo in June 1988:

> The Soviet Union has the world's largest military-industrial complex. They produce approximately one half of the weapons produced in the world. What is the West's advantage? How do we deal with this? We deal with it through our superiority in technology.
>
> Overall, we estimate we probably have a ten-year lead on the Soviet Union in technology. In some areas such as computers, communications, command and control, we may be even further ahead. But if we ever lose that lead, we are in serious trouble—given the Soviet emphasis on quantity—and the Soviets now realize it. Part of Gorbachev's "perestroika" is to build up the Soviet Union's technological capabilities. Traditionally, they have done that by getting technology from the West—either through open sources, or by stealing it, or getting it through third countries.
>
> It is vital for our collective security that we seek to strengthen COCOM, not relax it. It is not an outdated organization. . . . Now we can modify some of the COCOM procedures. We can simplify some of the lower tier items—the less sophisticated items. We need to keep this process under continuing review. But we need to prevent our technology from flowing into the Soviet military machine.[46]

Carlucci implied that as long as the NATO–Warsaw Pact arms race continues in its present form, the antagonism will remain between promoting a free flow of high-tech exports produced in the West and protecting U.S. and Western security interests through technology export controls. Yet Carlucci's statement also reflected the readiness of the Reagan administration to streamline the COCOM reviewing process and to remove items from the COCOM list that were internationally available in markets not controlled by COCOM.

These changes reflected a relatively greater sensitivity to U.S. business interests and to the demands of West European governments for a more drastic pruning of COCOM. They were a response to the growing political pressures from allies to make the COCOM list less restrictive in the light of the deepening perception of a diminishing Soviet military threat and confidence in Gorbachev's stated program of disarmament, political reforms, and restructuring of the Soviet economy.[47] These pressures were linked to a cautious optimism in Western Europe that the disarmament process could bring about significant Soviet military reductions and in the process create a political climate more favorable to a normalization of East-West economic relations.[48]

West European optimism begs the question whether this normalization is compatible with a security model based on maintaining a significant technological edge over the Soviet Union in order to compensate for the Soviet's quantitative superiority in numbers of troops and certain classes of weapons.[49] The United States defends technology export controls as an instrument to prevent the Soviet Union from closing the East-West technology gap. This means blocking Soviet acquisition of Western advanced military technology or dual-use technology. According to the more hard-line Western position, the Soviets should also be denied nonmilitary high technology, because it can be used to advance the economy and thereby free resources for developing the Soviet military machine.[50]

The National Academy Critique of U.S. Policy

The major high-level study by the U.S. National Academy of Sciences (NAS) is a detailed examination of the Reagan administration's restrictive policy on high-tech exports.[51] It carefully elucidates the antagonism between maintaining multilateral and bilateral export controls on the one hand and the dangers of such a policy for the future of U.S. export performance and relations with its allies on the other. In its recommendations for policy reform, the study attempts to find a practical mean between these two poles of economic openness and security-related restrictiveness. The study suggests, however, that the two cannot be satisfactorily reconciled: At best, the benefits of controls, measured by their effectiveness in preventing dual-use technology from falling into the hands of the Warsaw Pact, must be "weighed against their costs in terms of the domestic economy and relations with allies and friendly trading partners."[52] Although "there is evidence that controls do slow Soviet acquisition efforts and increase the price of the items they acquire,"[53] thus justifying their continuation, there are also extensive problems linked to the U.S. export security regime. These, according to the authors, include (1) loss of U.S. market share in West-West and East-West trade; (2) reduced investment in R&D that U.S. producers of goods and technologies may forgo as a result of reduced revenue from lost sales and market share; (3) reduced present and future sales of U.S. products in the U.S market; (4) a lower growth rate and reduced innovation with "resulting adverse effects on both the commercial and military sectors;" and (5) friction among the Western allies "that may interfere with their successful collaboration on weapons development, production, and standardization."[54]

The NAS panel takes exception to the Pentagon's claim that Western technology has contributed significantly to Soviet R&D programs and has resulted in large cost savings for Moscow's military buildup. The study argues that the DOD has not turned up a solid body of evidence to justify its defense of export restrictions. Its conclusions and methodology are, according to the NAS panel, "unconvincing."[55]

Yet the authors do concede that certain items of process control or manufacturing hardware known as "keystone equipment" can provide the Soviet Union with substantial leverage. Even if only a few items are obtained, keystone equipment can facilitate the production of quantities of other equipment. For example, particular types of precision ballbearing grinders that the Soviets legally acquired in the past contributed significantly to their missile program, according to the DOD 1985 study. The National Academy panel points out in this context that by "standards of Western productivity the Soviets are generally weak in automated manufacturing techniques."[56] Already in 1976 the Bucy Report recommended for this reason that the emphasis of U.S. national security policy should be on constraining the flow of essential technologies and manufacturing equipment rather than on restricting end products of the manufacturing process.[57] The National Academy concludes that the Soviets continue to lag behind the West, despite their extensive efforts to close the gap. Although the United States should not facilitate Soviet access to militarily critical technology, the NAS panel considers it "unlikely that an influx of Western technology will enable the Soviet Union to reduce the current gap substantially—as long as the West continues its own rapid pace of innovation."[58]

In sum, the NAS study criticizes U.S. technology controls for their ineffectiveness in achieving their intended results; and their tendency to weaken both the domestic U.S. economy and relations with U.S. allies.

The Economic-Security Dilemma

Although the NAS panel acknowledges that a comprehensive cost/benefit analysis of U.S. economic losses as a result of export security controls is not feasible because of the lack of data and the complexity of the control system, it nevertheless provides rough estimates of U.S. losses. According to the panel's conservative calculation, the United States in 1985 suffered short-term economic losses of $9.3 billion and a reduction in U.S. employment of 188,000 jobs.[59] However, if one were "to calculate the overall impact on the aggregate U.S. economy of the value of lost export sales and the reduced research and development, the associated loss for the U.S. gross national product would be $17.1 billion."[60]

U.S. economic losses stemming from high-tech export controls may have increased during the Reagan administration. This is suggested by the fact that the U.S. trade surplus in high-technology products declined from $26 billion in 1980 to $7 billion in 1985, despite the emphasis of the administration on high-tech R&D in the context of its military buildup.[61]

The fear of potential Soviet military use of Western technology and know-how is the most widely accepted and least questioned justification for security export control regimes. This fact raises the question of possible avenues of policymaking that could mitigate the economic-security dilemma. But the choices remain difficult if considered within the status quo framework: restructure the control system to improve economic performance and thereby endanger U.S. security or risk continuing high-tech export decline to protect security.

The second facet of the economic-security dilemma are the limits to U.S. efforts to convince its COCOM and non-COCOM trading partners to cooperate multilaterally in denying the Soviet Union and other COMECON economies dual-use technology. This factor will take on greater importance because new technologies tend to be increasingly of the dual-use type and can be expected to play a central role in East-West economic cooperation in the coming years.

The National Academy panel's recommendations for dealing with the problems of U.S. controls call for a combination of reinforcing the multilateral consensus on the need for COCOM and more flexible adjustment to economic and political trends on the other:

> As a general policy the United States should strive to achieve clarity, simplicity, and consistency in its national security export control procedures, as well as in the multilateral CoCom structure, and broader consensus on the need for national security export controls among the Free World nations that use and produce dual use technology. To achieve this goal, the United States should develop policies and procedures that emphasize efficiency and effectiveness over total comprehensiveness.[62]

The report also states: "Over the long term, U.S. national security export control policies also should remain flexible to political and economic changes in the world situation."[63] But the authors fail to deal with the longer-term problems of the economic-security dilemma, the worsening of which is suggested by the growing importance and rapid commercialization of new technology.[64] Increasing availability of high-tech products will tend to erode export security restrictions. A number of different factors will play a role here, some of which are richly documented by the NAS panel:

• Economic competition of high-tech firms in the West and Far East eager to sell their products to the Soviet Union and other COMECON countries.[65]

• Trade and other economic links between East and West, particularly between Eastern and Western Europe, will tend to increase as they did throughout the Reagan era, despite possible U.S. measures to slow this trend.[66]

• The Soviet Union and the COMECON economies have adopted policies to accelerate their international economic integration.[67]

• Most Western governments are not satisfied with U.S. export control policy, particularly its affects on their exports of dual-use technology whose military value for the Soviet Union is often a matter of interpretation.[68]

• West European allies generally reject the policy of economic and technical war against the Soviet Union. They are more inclined to increase trade and other forms of direct and indirect economic cooperation with COMECON economies, as reflected in the 1988 agreement between the EC and COMECON and the marked increase in East-West joint ventures.[69]

• A severe further economic decline in COMECON nations could result in political instability. Preventing a new "technological division" of Europe that would result from withholding dual-use technology from Eastern Europe has become an important factor in overcoming the deepening economic crisis.[70]

• Trade with COMECON countries has helped to promote reform in the socialist world, lower East-West tensions, and encourage arms control.[71]

The NAS panel's recommendation to strengthen COCOM through more effective enforcement of restrictions is not fully consistent with its call to adjust COCOM to new economic and political realities.

The emphasis on stricter enforcement of current controls can be linked to the postwar model of security and competitive strategies. The panel's other emphasis on adjustment to the changing international environment reflects the post-containment notion of security, which forswears zero-sum military-economic competition in favor of East-West economic cooperation as the more effective instrument to promote disarmament and support political and economic reforms that can expedite the integration of Eastern nations into the international community. The NAS recommendations can perhaps be justified with the argument that although Western policies are in the process of shifting, the system of East-West arms racing is nevertheless still in place and therefore (1) security controls on both military and dual-use technology are necessary and justified; and (2) a policy of flexible adjustment allows for change in COCOM as East-West trust and détente deepen. But this interpretation begs the question of how to go beyond simply "muddling through" between two security paradigms that have fundamentally antagonistic implications for West-West and East-West relations and that therefore cannot be the basis of a stable consensus within the Western

Alliance. New mechanisms and approaches to overcome the "double-paradigm crisis" of Western policy and East-West relations must be found. The following policy research themes, which were not taken up in the NAS study,[72] would be relevant in this context:

1. The fundamental antagonism between the U.S. policy of competitive strategies and reforming COCOM to allow for greater East-West economic interaction
2. The link of U.S technology R&D policy with U.S. military doctrine
3. Whether the postwar paradigm of security in the form of the current East-West arms race can be economically and politically maintained as the basis of U.S. or Western security in the coming decades; and similarly, whether military-technological competition in its present form, which impels the Soviets to use Western technology for its military effort, must remain the basis of U.S. policy
4. Whether the United States and the Soviet Union could cooperatively set up within the framework of the disarmament process an export-import regime that could verifiably eliminate the military use of imported Western technology
5. Whether alternative approaches based on common security–type models linking economic cooperation and nonmilitary forms of competition with the disarmament process might be appropriate to explore as a possible policy road toward a new East-West relationship

The call for easing controls and undertaking flexible adjustment to international economic trends clearly implies the broadening of existing avenues of East-West trade and cooperation. The rest of this chapter will attempt to show how international trends appear to be moving in this direction and thus toward an intensifying "creative collision" between the two paradigms and cultures of security. These dynamics are reflected in the areas discussed in the remaining sections of this chapter: (a) the changing conditions of the international economy and the position of the United States in it; (b) the expanding role of cooperation as an instrument of enhancing security; (c) West-West differences over COCOM; (d) intensifying transatlantic competition for Eastern markets; (e) the U.S. Omnibus Trade Legislation of 1988 and West European recommendations for reforming COCOM.

COCOM and the Changing International Economy

The new conditions in which U.S. foreign economic policy operates were described in a study by the President's Commission on Industrial Competitiveness:

Although the United States was once fairly immune from the vicissitudes of the economies and the economic policies of other governments, today the American economy is sensitive to changes in the international marketplace as it has never been before. Disruption caused by external factors such as macroeconomic changes or government decisions to impose trade embargoes, for example, have a much more significant impact than they did in the past.[73]

The new involvement of the United States in the world economy has a number of significant implications for U.S. policymaking:

As our involvement in the global economy has deepened, so too has the importance of economic, political, social, defense and foreign policy relationships. Balanced and effective public policies on trade and investment are critical, since they define the fundamental economic environment in which U.S. firms operate, often making the difference between success and failure.[74]

The political scientist Richard Ellings describes the changing geopolitical position of the United States in the international system as follows:

The international system has [been] transformed since 1945 from a condition of U.S. dominance to one of greater equality and complexity. This process has not been an even one. Economically, the world has become multipolar, with the U.S. contributing between one-fifth and one-fourth of the world product compared with about one-half at the war's end. The U.S. has recently been plagued with the transfer of industrial production overseas and serious balance of trade deficits. . . . At the same time, the political map of the world has increased in complexity as the number of decisionmaking centers, i.e., states, has more than tripled due to decolonization. This diffusion in the array of decisionmaking centers in combination with reduced superiority has greatly complicated the pursuit of global foreign policy by American leaders.[75]

The transformed economic and international environment today compared with what existed during most of the postwar period is also emphasized by the NAS study, which stresses the following general points:

1. The diffusion of technology has markedly accelerated and has become globalized, in part as a result of the practice by multinational corporations of locating research and production facilities around the world.[76]
2. As the market for dual-use products has significantly grown, the ability of the military establishments to restrict new high-tech systems for purely military use has diminished. Rapid technological advances as a result

of heavy investment in R&D are "tending to push commercial development of technology ahead of military development—a reversal of the pattern established after World War II."[77] The result is an increased availability of dual-use products embodying technology more advanced than that found in weapons systems.[78]

3. Because the United States is the single largest international trader, with exports of $360 billion in 1985, the U.S. economy has become more sensitive to patterns in international trade than formerly. Trade policies directed against the Soviet Union that also diminish West-West trade can damage the U.S. economy by reducing sales of U.S. high-tech products and creating an environment that discourages U.S. export.[79]

4. Faced with stiff competition in almost every high-technology sector, the United States is losing its dominant position in advanced technology. The global competition the United States confronts stems both from developed and newly industrialized countries.[80]

Changing international conditions have reduced the effectiveness of U.S. economic controls. As Ellings points out:

> On the one hand, as the U.S. structural advantage declined, its political and economic leverage declined. Its bargaining vis-a-vis many countries eroded and thus in a bilateral sense embargoes typically were less powerful. Second and relatedly, it lost leverage to secure degrees of multilateral cooperation that were once within its capacity.[81]

The U.S. loss of monopolies in leading technologies also affect the ability of the United States and COCOM to control trade flows. In this context Hanns-Dieter Jacobsen has written:

> The USSR doubtless exploits technological advances in the West as completely and profitably as it can for its own military expansion. It is doubtful, however, that substantially tighter U.S. and CoCom export controls could prevent the USSR and other East European countries from obtaining the technologies, that they not only want but could also absorb given their relatively limited high-tech capacity, from elsewhere in the West. After all, other technologically advanced, but neutral, countries such as Sweden, Austria and Switzerland belong to the West. There are in addition the newly-industrializing countries such as the ASEAN states.[82]

Jacobsen's comment implies that an economic and a military-technological containment policy as practiced by the United States since the first decades of the postwar period against the Soviet Union can no longer be effective in today's highly internationalized economy. A second implication, and one that can be also drawn from the NAS study, is that the international availability and rapid diffusion of dual-use technology, makes it more difficult and economically questionable for the United States to attempt to achieve a technological "quantum jump" in military capabilities that could provide an undisputed, absolute defensive or offensive superiority—goals that have been ascribed to SDI and the restrictive military-technological policies of the Reagan administration.[83]

Many high-tech systems formerly restricted by COCOM were predestined to become "technological commodities," so-called to denote their wide availability in international markets and their disqualification as controllable items. In 1984, personal computers, microchips found in children's toys,[84] and other electronic goods that were judged by the United States to be of potential military value were restricted, to the ire of West European governments. These goods have since been recognized as technological commodities and therefore eliminated from the COCOM list.[85]

The removal of restrictions on these products was based on the COCOM criterion of foreign availability and not on their potential for military applications. The increasingly invoked yardstick of availability reflects the difficulty of maintaining restrictions on dual-use technology developed and diffused in the commercial sector.

Economic Cooperation and East-West Security

West German Foreign Minister Genscher has emphasized the link between growing global interdependence and the need for a common security approach with the Soviet Union:

> If the internal development in the Soviet Union improves that country's ability to engage in the broadest possible cooperation with the West, the West for its part must encourage such development through its actions and reactions.
>
> In a world dependent on cooperation, this is also in the interest of the West. Here, too, interdependence prevails. . . . In order to overcome the backwardness of the economy, Mr. Gorbachev also needs a new foreign policy, a policy which creates stability in external relations. The cost of an expansionist foreign policy is to be reduced, the arms-burden lightened, and economic, technological and financial cooperation with the West developed. Détente and cooperation in relations with the West are of central importance to the success of Mr. Gorbachev's internal reform policy. That is why he says that coexistence is not only the absence of war but a way of living together for states with differing political systems, a way which allows for mutually beneficial cooperation and mutual assistance in the solution of global problems. Security, he says, is not only a military but also a political responsibility. The security of one side cannot be achieved at the other side's expense. Joint security is necessary.[86]

In a related context, Heinrich Vogel has written the following on the advantages of strong economic competition with the East:

> In a world of peaceful competition, strong competitors are preferred to weak ones, not least because of their being more predictable in sharing certain vital economic interests. Every step in the direction of developing the competitiveness of Eastern economies on a global scale, therefore, is in the longterm economic and political interest of partners in the West and in the South.[87]

West-West Collisions over COCOM

Advanced computer hardware and software, sophisticated numerically controlled machine tools, and other high-technology goods are examples of critical technologies whose export to the East has been sharply opposed by the United States.[88] For Western Europe, however, these items represent a vital part of its growing inventory of exports to Eastern Europe and the Soviet Union. Many are indispensable to the growth of the European Common Market as part of an evolving European East-West economic entity, whose existence is a result of the weakening of East-West economic-political barriers over the past two decades.

In commenting on West European dependence on developing Eastern markets, Dr. Horst Ehmke, the Social Democratic floor leader in the Bundestag and an expert on East-West relations, explains why the Reagan administration's policies became so controversial:

> The alliance will need to establish a better consensus around future goals if detente is not to create friction and misunderstandings within the alliance. The question of technology transfer is of particular note, both because East-West trade is likely to increase in future years and because of the political problems this issue has caused for alliance relations in the past. Although the United States has begun to relax some of its technology transfer restrictions, this question remains a politically divisive one. The European economies, whose international competitiveness depends on access to large homogeneous markets, are extremely dependent on exports to Eastern Europe and the Soviet Union. The overly restrictive policy pursued by the Reagan administration within the Coordinating Committee for Multilateral Export Controls (COCOM), which tried to prevent transfer of virtually every technology that could have military application, and the other measures it has taken to restrain East-West trade, conflict with Europe's economic interests.[89]

Ehmke's position is by no means restricted to the Social Democratic Party, but is shared in essential respects by the conservative-liberal Bonn government as well as powerful West German industrial interests affected by U.S. restrictions.

In 1985 *Newsweek* anecdotally summed up West European dissatisfaction with U.S. policy on technology trade controls:

> As lately as July 1985 British Liberal M.P. Paddy Ashdown argued in the House of Commons that "unwarranted American claims of extraterritorial jurisdiction" are turning Britain into a "technological satellite of the United States." Martin Bangeman, West Germany's economic minister, said recently that his government "will not tolerate" further American restrictions on its trade policy, while Etienne Davignon, until recently the European Community's commissioner for industry, warned that gathering disputes over high-technology transfer will dwarf previous Euro-American conflicts over steel and agriculture.[90]

These observations suggest that West European polities will be less likely in the future to accept U.S. export-related restrictions at the expense of their well-being and economic future, especially as pan-European East-West cooperation tends to deepen.[91]

The trend of increasing East-West cooperation is reflected in the fact that U.S. and COCOM restrictions have been losing their teeth as allies and nonallies alike increasingly consider them as a form of unfair protectionism. As a result, many non-U.S. companies have "de-Americanized" some of their products to avoid having them restricted by U.S. controls. British Aerospace, for example, informed Hewlett-Packard of the United States that although it is at the top of the list of companies that produce desirable technology, the fact that it is a U.S. firm puts it at the bottom of the list of desirable partners.[92] Many West German companies making deals with East European and Soviet partners are taking special care to insulate their products and services from COCOM by removing U.S. technologies and components from product lines pegged for Eastern markets.

COCOM and Transatlantic Competition

The military-security justification for the COCOM list of dual-use goods is losing credibility among West European governments and business interests. The suspicion is widespread, particularly in West Germany, that the United States is using the COCOM restrictions as an instrument of economic competition against West European firms interested in entering Eastern markets.

It has been pointed out, for example, that the United States has exported significant amounts of military and sophisticated dual-use high technology to the People's Republic of China, while at the same time using COCOM to block non-U.S. firms from such deals. U.S. military exports to China have included

- $98 million of equipment for the modernization of Chinese production of artillery ammunition
- A contract for 24 Black Hawk S-70 helicopters
- A $550-million contract in April 1986 for radar and sophisticated missile guidance systems to make the Chinese interceptor tactical aircraft, the F-8, all-weather-capable
- A contract for the coproduction of antisubmarine torpedoes
- Assorted other systems, including an improved antitank missile system[93]

These transactions were not subject to consultation within COCOM. Yet in the summer of 1988, the West German firm Siemens experienced considerable difficulties in exporting sophisticated telecommunications equipment to China as a result of U.S. action.[94]

West European governments and firms point to such interventions as examples of U.S. unilateralism and policy inconsistency. They make no secret of their suspicion that security considerations are often put aside for economic competitive reasons. Following the Toshiba affair in which the United States declared punitive sanctions against Japan for allowing the export of military technology to the Soviet Union, the United States announced major export deals of advanced passenger aircraft to Poland and Romania. Washington defended its apparent and arbitrary shift of policy to the U.S. public by putting forth the argument that the move was necessary in order to defend the United States against competition from the West European aircraft manufacturer Airbus. West Europeans tend to view such arguments as further evidence of the increasing inconsistency, if not hypocrisy, in Washington's export control behavior. Thus *Der Spiegel* commented as follows:

> Security reservations disappear when the price is right. For years there were no permits issued for the sale of civilian jets to the East. Then, last June, the European Airbus consortium sold three such aircraft to East Germany. This was possible only because Boeing at that time was negotiating a similar deal with Poland and Romania. In the end Washington could not refuse the Airbus manufacturers what it obviously wants to grant Boeing.[95]

The "Toshiba affair" in 1987—in which Japanese, Norwegian, and French companies were caught violating COCOM restrictions on high-tech exports to the Soviet Union—reflects how allied support for COCOM and U.S. controls is eroding and suggests that this process is likely to accelerate in the coming years. Here it is also noteworthy, as mentioned in Chapter 7, that U.S. multinational giants have been organizing joint ventures with West European and Japanese firms in order to better position themselves to gain more efficient entry into communist economies.[96] Such cooperative moves are likely to further complicate the enforcement of COCOM rules and are examples of how technological advances and the intensified competition to translate them into markets are colliding with existing national, regional, and intersystemic barriers. Factors such as the high cost of R&D, increased risk of investment in new technologies, and the need to combine a wide range of scientific and market resources are promoting new forms and a significantly faster pace of collaborative activity. From this perspective, traditional postwar political and military structures, including the militarized division of Europe, are viewed as protectionist anachronisms of the cold war era holding back pent-up economic forces.

There has also been growing concern in West European policy circles about bans on the flow of technological and scientific information from the United States to West European firms and research institutions. Information from U.S. data bases has been withheld from West European partners with the justification of the security involved.[97] As the West German expert Henrik Bischoff points out, information withheld has included

> data collected by NASA weather satellites. The "Fermilab" data bank of the US nuclear research centre, for instance, has been closed for Europeans under the pretext that European "hackers" had illegally entered the data network. United States information practices also include the banning of West Europeans from scientific conferences on hightechnology subjects in the United States as well as restricting the access of Europeans to information to be derived in future from the "Columbus" space station.[98]

Such incidents are interpreted in West Germany as an attempt at competitive expansion of U.S. control of international high-tech data flows and prevention of East-West cooperation:

> COCOM serves the United States as an instrument to maintain its technological lead on a world-wide basis by preventing the export of hightech data. The policy of withholding technology from the East on the basis of COCOM is not only aimed at weakening the East European economies, but also at undermining efforts towards an East-West-European co-operation. The ban on the transfer of microelectronic components to Eastern Europe, for instance, obstructs the data flow between East and West Europe. As a general principle, leading United States data banks give access to West Europeans only if they commit themselves to restrict the flow of information to Eastern Europe.[99]

U.S. Legislation and the Transatlantic Debate on COCOM

The Omnibus Trade and Competitiveness Act of 1988 is an important contribution to liberalizing the U.S. export security control system. The law streamlines licensing requirements; reduces the control list; provides limited judicial review for civil penalties related to violations of U.S. export security laws; clarifies and expands the procedures for decontrolling commodities on the basis of foreign availability; and somewhat reduces the role of the Pentagon in export security policymaking.[100]

The legislation's significant modifications of U.S. COCOM policy will tend to reduce transatlantic disputes in a number of areas, but the changes do not deal with the more fundamental West European and Japanese criticism of COCOM. The final conference bill that was approved watered down the original House version by rejecting a number of its proposals, including the proposed mandate to shorten the COCOM list by 40 percent.[101] In addition, the law contains provisions for linking U.S.-Soviet trade relations to the implementation of workers' rights and provides the U.S. executive with discretionary powers to block U.S.-Soviet business transactions.[102] Although these clauses pertain to U.S. trade policy, they could, if invoked, become a source of transatlantic friction.

Although the provisions of the Omnibus Trade Act must be viewed as an important step in the ongoing reform process of COCOM and toward ameliorating the deepening policy crisis that it seeks to address, the law is unlikely to prevent further disputes between the United States and other COCOM members. By liberalizing certain aspects of the COCOM regime, the legislation will indeed have the effect of encouraging greater East-West economic interaction, including trade, joint ventures, and scientific and ecological cooperation. But such cooperation will only raise the basic problems of the remaining COCOM restrictions on dual-use goods and services to a new level, especially as the quality of East-West cooperation is enhanced, as is likely to occur in the coming years. In this context, the interpretation of what can be construed as militarily useful high technology—dual-use commodities—will continue to be at issue. Similarly, dual-use items such as nuclear goods and services could become the subject of debate as a result of the 1988 Soviet–West German contracts involving West German nuclear export firms. Because these contracts include projects to improve the safety systems of Soviet nuclear power plants, they are considered a form of ecological protection with obvious benefits for East and West, especially in the light of the Chernobyl nuclear accident. Nevertheless, these activities or similar future projects may be put into question by COCOM's rules pertaining to the militarily sensitive area of nuclear energy.

The potential conflicts between the United States and Western Europe on COCOM policy raise the question of its more radical reform. The following proposals from West European policy research circles provide a rough overview of West European thinking on modifying COCOM.

The removal of the cloak of secrecy that surrounds COCOM. The classification rules and regulations that permeate all of COCOM's activities are viewed as an anachronistic holdover of the cold war. According to one West European study, which reflects a growing climate of opinion, the management of COCOM should be subject to open parliamentary debate in the different COCOM member states.[103] This reform, according to proponents, would have the advantage of building a stronger consensus on the basis of a more democratic, minimal control regime, which would make for a more effective enforcement system and benefit West European states by integrating the United States into a more multilateral and open regime. It would also offer Western Europe greater protection against U.S. unilateralism, such as the U.S. practice of issuing an inordinate number of "exceptional" licenses to U.S. firms based on considerations of economic competition rather than on security criteria. The fact that U.S. companies have been the principal recipients of exceptional export licenses under COCOM is a major source of allied irritation.[104]

Self-regulation by corporations. Since corporations want to protect their most advanced technology, it is argued they would tend to refrain from exporting it to the Soviet Unon for obvious commercial reasons under a less strict COCOM regime. Free-market principles of self-restriction, according to proponents, would be a simpler and more effective approach for moving toward a minimal COCOM regime than is the existing system.[105]

Normalization of East-West economic relations. West European critics consider a reform of COCOM in the context of gradually normalizing the West's commercial relations with COMECON countries. A minimal COCOM regime, managed more democratically by all COCOM members, would allow the Soviet Union and East European economies to move toward more open commercial relations with the West. The prospect and gradual realization of such normalization would function as a political incentive for greater openness and democratic reform of Eastern societies and would generate greater East-West trust and confidence.[106]

Conclusions

The West European recommendations about COCOM reflect its growing erosion, which has become increasingly evident in the following areas: (a) the violation and lax enforcement of COCOM rules; (b) officially agreed reductions of the COCOM lists; (c) increasing irritation of U.S. trading partners with COCOM restrictions they view as arbitrary; (d) the rapid pace of new technology development and the weakening of barriers to East-West technology exchange; (e) the ongoing efforts by the United States to streamline its export licensing procedure; and (f) the increased readiness of the U.S. government to issue exceptional licenses to U.S. firms negotiating commercial high-tech deals with the Soviet Union and other COMECON nations.

The U.S. policy of competitive strategies is an important example of the lack of consensus between the United States and Western Europe in their political, economic, and military approach to the Soviet Union. Although West European governments, particularly the Federal Republic, officially accept COCOM restrictions, they reject the notion of using foreign policy and foreign economic policy as an instrument to intentionally weaken the Soviet economy and place the Soviet military apparatus under heightened pressure. They do not view competitive strategies as a means of increasing East-West security but, on the contrary, as a source of tension that could reinforce instead of overcome the division of Europe. As long as this fundamental difference in U.S. and West European policy persists, it will continue to generate transatlantic friction and hinder the construction of a stable consensus in the Western Alliance on the future of East-West political, economic, and military relations.

It is likely that the United States will increase its export dealings with COMECON governments and nongovernment entities. An important aim of the Omnibus Trade and Competitiveness Act is to expand U.S. export activity. To be effective as an export economy, the United States must promote high-tech as well as low-tech goods. The sales of Boeing aircraft to Poland and Romania are good examples of the type of highly sophisticated goods and services that are indispensable for the United States to export if it is to sustain its position as a leading economic power in the post-containment international economy. But the continuation of the U.S. strategy of competitive strategies collides with the increasing liberalization of COCOM and growing trade with the Eastern bloc to produce a policy mix based on the two diametrically opposed models of security. This competition reflects the uneven shift of the United States and Western Europe from the postwar paradigm of security based on arms racing and military-technological competition with the Soviet Union to a post-containment security paradigm based on disarmament, détente, and expanded East-West cooperation.

The transatlantic debate within COCOM exemplifies the uneven shift from the postwar security model to a new security order. A more resolute move on the part of the United States in the direction of common security could provide a solution to the U.S. economic-security dilemma. It would make possible a reforging of Western and Eastern security according to the notion that intensified cooperation can promote higher and more effective forms of security than can present arrangements. This proposition is becoming an increasingly explicit West European and Soviet rationale for current moves in the direction of deepening economic, political, cultural, and ecological cooperation between the two social systems.

While it is likely the COCOM lists will be further reduced under the pressure of Western export interests and West European governments, a more radical transformation of COCOM is difficult to foresee without more comprehensive changes in U.S. foreign and economic policy in phase with further major advances in East-West disarmament. This is because the policy of export security controls, like U.S. NATO policy, is a logical extension of the postwar competitive arms race and is domestically rooted in the Military Keynesian structure of the U.S. economy. If these links suggest the formidable nature of meaningful policy change, they also imply (a) that liberalization and a long-term plan for replacing COCOM by a regime of East-West economic cooperation and demilitarization of trade could be used as a fulcrum to accelerate disarmament; and (b) that the disarmament process could be used as a fulcrum to replace COCOM.

Part 3 of this analysis will show how the uneven decline of the postwar order and its challenge for the Western Alliance is taking the form of the diminishing of the Soviet military threat; the expansion of East-West détente; and the evolution of the CSCE as a pan-European forum in which the postwar and the post-containment models of East-West relations are finding one of their most politically promising and creative points of collision.

Notes

1. National Academy of Sciences, Committee on Science, Engineering, and Public Policy, *Balancing the National Interest: U.S. National Security Export Controls and Global Economic Competition* (Washington, D.C.: National Academy Press, 1987), hereafter NAS, p. 80.

2. Ibid., p. 8.

3. United States Code, para. 2751, also cited in Werner Hein, *Beschränkung des internationalen Technologietransfers durch die USA: Auswirkung auf die deutschen Unternehmen* (Studie im Auftrag des Bundesministerium fuer Forschung und Technologie, mimeo, Washington, D.C., 1984), p. 11; on the relationship between the Commerce Department and Department of Defense in the administration of export control licensing, see U.S. General Accounting Office, *Export Licensing: Commerce-Defense Review of Applications to Certain Free World Nations* (NSIAD-86-169); for a bibliography on this theme, see NAS, op. cit., pp. 307f.

4. NAS, op. cit., p. 80.

5. 10 C.F.R. 120.8, as cited in NAS, p. 80.

6. NAS, op. cit., p. 87. On U.S. policy of controlling unclassified information, see Stephen B. Gould, "Secrecy: Its Role in National Scientific and Technical Information Policy," *Library Trends* Vol. 35, No. 1, Summer 1986, pp. 61–81.

7. See in this context the discussion of a number of cases of conflict

between U.S. universities and U.S. export control authorities in Hein, op. cit., pp. 73ff. An excellent source on such conflicts is David Dickson, *The New Politics of Science* (New York: Pantheon, 1984), pp. 152ff; on the control of scientific information, see also Dorothy Nelkin, *Science as Intellectual Property: Who Controls Scientific Research?* (New York: Macmillan, 1984).

8. NAS, op. cit., pp. 80f. See also Hein, op. cit., pp. 121f; Hanns-D Jacobsen, "U.S. Export Control and Export Administration Legislation," in Reinhard Rode and Hanns-Dieter Jacobsen, eds., *Economic Warfare or Détente* (Boulder and London: Westview, 1985), pp. 213–235; on the major provisions of the 1979 Export Administration Act, see U.S. Congress, Office of Technology Assessment, *Technology and East-West Trade: An Update* (Washington, D.C.: General Printing Office, 1983).

9. NAS, op. cit., p. 90.

10. Ibid., p. 81.

11. Hein, op. cit., pp. 20–21. For case studies on the problem of reexport to Eastern Europe and the Soviet Union, see U.S. General Accounting Office, *Details of Certain Controversial Export Licensing Decisions Involving Soviet Bloc Countries* (Washington, D.C.: General Printing Office, 1983).

12. COCOM is not anchored in a formal treaty but is an informal coordinating arrangement based on consensus of COCOM members. The implementation of COCOM restrictions is at the discretion of COCOM member states. The communist nations to which COCOM restrictions apply are Warsaw Pact countries plus Albania, China, Kampuchea, Mongolia, North Korea and Vietnam. Although Cuba is not included in COCOM controls, it is subject to a general U.S. trade embargo. See Philip Hanson, *Western Economic Statecraft in East-West Relations*, Chatham House Paper 40 (London: Routledge and Kegan Paul, 1988), p. 27. On the history of U.S. export control policy, see Gunnar Adler-Karlsson, *Western Economic Warfare 1947–1967* (Stockholm: Almquist and Wiksell, 1968); Gary Bertsch, *East-West Strategic Trade: COCOM and the Atlantic Alliance*, Atlantic Papers No. 49 (Paris: Atlantic Institute of International Affairs, 1983).

13. Reinhard Rode, *Wieviel Exportkontrolle? COCOM auf dem Prüfstand*, HSFK-Report (Peace Research Institute Frankfurt), June 1988.

14. Ibid., p. 11.

15. Ibid.

16. Chris Sherwell, "Australia Concerned at Western Controls on Military Technology," *Financial Times*, August 17, 1988; on the positions of Western governments, see Rode and Jacobsen, op. cit. See also in this context Ellen Frost and Angela Stent, "NATO's Troubles with East-West Trade," *International Security*, Vol. 6, No. 8, Summer 1983, pp. 179–200. See also Jan Feldman, "Trade Policy and Foreign Policy," *Washington Quarterly*, Vol. 8., No. 1, Winter 1985, pp. 10–21. Feldman describes the negotiation process in 1984 as "characterized by trench warfare and endless infighting. . . . While the July meeting demonstrates that compromise can be achieved, the key concern remains how to keep COCOM from doing more harm to its members and the alliance than to the Soviets." See also in this context Frost and Stent, op. cit.; Bertsch, op. cit.

17. An example in this context is the German government. See Anton-Andreas Guha, "Geheimdienst ließ illegalen Export zu," *Frankfurter Rundschau*, August 15, 1987.

18. NAS, op. cit., pp. 107f., fn. 7.

19. Ibid. The Omnibus Trade and Competitiveness Act of 1988 modified

previous legislation by introducing a limited form of judicial review. See the section in this chapter on this legislation.

20. On the difficulties the United States has faced in its efforts to implement its restrictive policies, see NAS, op. cit., Chapter 5, pp. 103–135.

21. NAS, op. cit., p. 91.

22. Dickson, op. cit., Chapter 2; see also in this context the discussion of the changing relationship of the Department of Defense to academia in Rosy Nimroody, *Star Wars: The Economic Fallout* (Cambridge, Mass.: Ballinger, 1988), Chapter 6, pp. 77–92.

23. On the passage of the Jackson-Vanik Amendment, see Raymond Garthoff, *Détente and Confrontation* (Washington: Brookings Institution, 1985), pp. 453–463. For a critique of Jackson-Vanik, see Sarah C. Carey, "A New Look at MFN and the Jackson-Vanik Amendment," in Margaret Chapman, ed., *Forum on U.S.-Soviet Trade Relations* (Washington, D.C., American Committee on U.S.-Soviet Relations, 1987), pp. 117–120.

24. On the political context of the Stevenson Amendment, see Daniel Yergin, "Politics and Soviet-American Trade: The Three Questions," *Foreign Affairs*, Vol. 55, No. 3, April 1977, pp. 517–538.

25. Scott Sullivan, "High-Tech Soviet Spies," *Newsweek*, November 11, 1985.

26. *Implementation of the Export Administration Amendments Act of 1985*, Hearings, Subcommittee on International Economic Policy and Trade of the Committee on Foreign Affairs, House of Representatives (Washington, D.C.: Government Printing Office, 1988), pp. 70–82ff.

27. Rode, op. cit. See also in this context *Summary Description of Conference Agreement on Export Control Provisions of Omnibus Trade Bill*, Washington, D.C., 1988, p. 813.

28. The criticism of U.S. export security controls by U.S. trading partners is summed up in the NAS study as follows: "U.S. national security controls are not generally perceived as rational, credible, and predictable by many of the nations and commercial interests whose active participation is required for an effective system." NAS, op. cit., pp. 15f.

29. Ibid; see also on this issue Rode, op. cit.

30. See in this context James Giffen, "Opportunities for Expansion of U.S.-Soviet Trade and Economic Relations," in Chapman, op. cit., pp. 35–39; John Murphy, "Soviet Energy Development: Opportunities for U.S. Business," in Chapman, ibid., pp. 73–82.

31. Clyde Farnsworth, "West is Easing Policy on Sales to Soviet Bloc," *New York Times*, February 15, 1988.

32. Jon Englund, "The Doctrine of 'Competitive Strategies', *Strategic Review*, Vol. 15, No. 3, Summer 1987, pp. 63–73; Hanson, op. cit., pp. 35ff.

33. Senator Sam Nunn, "The American/Soviet Disarmament Negotiations and Their Consequences for NATO" (Speech to Wehrkunde Conference), February 7, 1988.

34. Office of the Undersecretary of Defense for Policy, *Assessing the Effect of Technology Transfer on U.S./Western Security*, February 1985 (Washington, D.C.: Government Printing Office, 1985) pp. 1–3.

35. Ibid.

36. Ibid.

37. Ibid.

38. Ibid.

39. Richard Halloran, "Pentagon Draws Up First Strategy for Fighting a Long Nuclear War," *New York Times*, May 30, 1982.

40. Ibid.

41. Ibid.

42. See in this context "Prepared Statement of Lionel Olmer," Undersecretary for International Trade Administration, Before the Subcommittee on International Economic Policy and Trade, Committee on Foreign Affairs, House of Representatives, April 5, 1983. For a discussion of Olmer's statement, see Hanns-Dieter Jacobsen, "U.S. Export Control and Export Administration Legislation, in Jacobsen, op. cit., pp. 213–231.

43. Jacobsen, ibid.

44. Ibid. For a discussion of different roles of East-West trade, see Herbert Wulf, "East-West Trade as a Source of Tension," *Journal of Peace Research*, Vol. 19, No. 4, 1982, pp. 301–322.

45. Jacobsen, ibid., p. 219.

46. "Carlucci Wants High–Technology Controls Strengthened," *U.S. Policy Information and Texts*, June 6, 1988.

47. Andrew Nagorski, "A New Page in Relations Between the East and Bonn," *Newsweek*, January 25, 1988.

48. Heinrich Vogel, "Wirtschaft und Sicherheit in den Ost-West Beziehungen," *Europäische Rundschau*, Vol. 16, No. 3, Summer 1988, pp. 31–42. Interviews with West German experts.

49. Carlucci, op. cit.

50. See Englund, op. cit.; Office of the Undersecretary of Defense for Policy, op. cit.

51. NAS, op. cit.

52. Ibid., p. 8

53. Ibid., p. 9.

54. Ibid.

55. The NAS panel also cites a number of factors to back up its claim that the Pentagon overestimates Soviet gains. These include, for example,

the inevitable problems in putting a product or technology into effective use. The Soviets may attempt to reverse-engineer a product—that is, use an item obtained in the West as a basis for producing the technology themselves for military systems. The panel believes that this strategy is generally unproductive for many types of items (such as high-density semiconductor devices) because often the ability to copy a technology depends more on technological infrastructure and the capability of the manufacturing process than on the observable features of a particular device.

NAS, ibid., p. 47.

56. Ibid. On the Soviet ability to absorb technology from the West, see Morris Bornstein, *East-West Technology Transfer: The Transfer of Western Technology to the USSR* (Paris: OECD, 1985). See also in this context, Seymour Goodman, "The Impact of U.S. Export Controls on the Soviet Computer Industry" in Gordon Smith, ed., *The Politics of East-West Trade* (Boulder: Westview, 1984), pp. 109–127.

57. NAS, ibid.

58. Ibid., p. 49; *An Analysis of Export Control of U.S. Technology—A DoD Perspective: A Report of the Science Board Task Force on Export of U.S.*

Technology ("Bucy Report") (Washington, D.C.: Government Printing Office, 1976).

59. NAS, ibid., "Calculation of Economic Costs," Appendix D, p. 266.

Components of the Estimated Economic Impact of Export Controls in 1985 (in billions of dollars)

Component	Impact[a]
Administrative cost to firms	0.5
Lost West-West export sales	5.9
Lost West-East export sales	1.4
Reduced research and development spending	0.5
Value of licenses denied	0.5
Lost profits on export and foreign sales	0.5
Total	9.3

Source: National Academy of Sciences, *Balancing the National Interest* (Washington, D.C.: National Academy Press, 1987), Table D-3, Appendix D, p. 266.

[a]Employment loss of 188,000 jobs

60. Ibid., pp. 266–275.

61. Department of Commerce, *1986 U.S. Industrial Outlook: Prospects for Over 350 Manufacturing and Service Industries* (Washington, D.C., January 1986).

62. NAS, op. cit., p. 4. For the full range of recommendations, see NAS, op. cit., pp. 167–177.

63. Ibid., p. 173.

64. Hanns-Dieter Jacobsen, Heinrich Machowski, and Klaus Schröder, "Politische und ökonomische Rahmenbedingungen der Ost-West-Wirtschaftsbeziehungen," *Aussenpolitik*, Vol. 39, No. 2, 1988, pp. 138–150.

65. Ibid.; Henrik Bischof, "Der Stand von Wissenschaft und Technologie im Ost-West-Zusammenhang" (Speech before the Atlantic Assembly meeting in Hamburg, November 1988, mimeo).

66. See in this context Axel Lebahn, "Politische und wirtschaftliche Auswirkungen der Perestrojka auf die Sowjetunion sowie auf ihre Beziehungen zu Osteuropa und zum Westen," *Aussenpolitik*, Vol. 39, No. 2, 1988, pp. 107–124. On increased flows of technology from East to West, see Bischof, ibid.; John Kiser, "Technology Transfer from East to West," in Chapman, op. cit., pp. 149–155.

67. See in this context Mathias Schmitt, *Das Ostgeschäft von morgen* (Baden-Baden: Nomos, 1988), pp. 107–112ff.

68. Jacobsen, in Rode, op. cit.; Vogel, op. cit. See also "Panel Foreign Fact-Finding Mission Reports," Appendix B in NAS, op. cit., pp. 183–220.

69. Kiser, op. cit.; Kiser, "Tapping Eastern Bloc Technology," *Harvard Business Review*, Vol. 60, No. 2, March–April 1982, pp. 85–93; Schmitt, op. cit.

70. Hans-Dietrich Genscher, "New Approaches to East-West Security Cooperation" (Speech at the meeting of the Institute for East-West Security Studies, Potsdam, June 11, 1988), in *Statements and Speeches*, Vol 11, No. 10, June 13, 1988.

71. Ibid.; Vogel, op. cit. On the concepts of common security and security partnership see the essays in Egon Bahr and Dieter S. Lutz, eds.,

Gemeinsame Sicherheit Idee und Konzept (Baden-Baden: Nomos, 1986). See also in this context Peter Schlotter, "Reflections on European Security 2000," *Bulletin of Peace Proposals*, Vol. 15, No. 1, pp. 3–11.

72. This view has been clearly formulated by West German Foreign Minister Hans-Dietrich Genscher. See in this context the interview with Genscher in *Deutsche Wirtschaft*, April 4, 1988.

73. President's Commission on Industrial Competitiveness, *Global Competition: The New Reality* (Washington, D.C.: Government Printing Office, 1985), Vol. 2, p. 174.

74. Ibid.

75. Richard Ellings, *Embargoes and World Power: Lessons from American Foreign Policy* (Boulder and London: Westview, 1985), pp. 147–148; an early important study of U.S. economic embargo policies during the postwar era is Adler-Karlsson, op. cit.

76. NAS, op. cit., p. 6.

77. Ibid.

78. Ibid.

79. Ibid., pp. 6f.

80. Ibid., p. 9.

81. Ellings, op. cit., p. 148.

82. Jacobsen 1985, op. cit.

83. See in this context Heinrich Vogel, "Außenwirtschaft als Indikator und Instrument der neuen Politik in der UdSSR," *Osteuropa*, Vol. 38, No. 7, 1988, pp. 532–536. On the economic and technological dimensions of SDI, see Nimroody, op. cit., pp. 119–144.

84. Sullivan, op. cit.

85. Ibid.

86. Hans-Dietrich Genscher, "Towards a Strategy for Progress," in Bill Bradley et al., *Implications of Soviet New Thinking* (New York: Institute for East-West Security Studies, 1987), pp. 33–47.

87. Heinrich Vogel, "Wirtschaft und Sicherheit," op. cit.

88. NAS, Appendix B, op. cit.

89. Horst Ehmke, "A Second Phase of Détente," *World Policy Journal*, Vol. 4, No. 3, Summer 1987, pp. 363–382.

90. Sullivan, op. cit.

91. See in this context Michael Lucas, "The United States and Post-INF Europe, *World Policy Journal*, Vol. 5, No. 2, Spring 1988, pp. 183–233.

92. David Buchan and Peter Montagnon, "Backing Reluctantly into the Limelight," *Financial Times*, December 8, 1987.

93. Rode, op. cit., see also Appendix B in NAS, op. cit.

94. David Marsh, "Cocom Row Blocks W. German Exports," *Financial Times*, July 27, 1988.

95. "Cocom: Ein Relikt des Kalten Krieges" *Der Spiegel*, Vol. 43, No. 34, August 22, 1988.

96. See in this context Margaret Sharp and Claire Shearman, *European Technological Collaboration* (London: Royal Institute of International Affairs and Routledge and Kegan Paul, 1987), Chapter 5.

97. Henrik Bischof, "COCOM Politics and the Data Flow Between East and West," Kurzpapier, Friedrich Ebert Stiftung, February 1988.

98. Ibid.

99. Ibid.

100. The Omnibus Trade and Competitiveness Act of 1988, Summary of Conference Agreement, April 19, 1988, pp. 20f.

101. Summary Description of the Conference Agreement on the Export Control Provisions of the Trade Bill, op. cit., p. 813.

102. Relevant provisions in this context include the following: (1) The United States is authorized to block state trading regimes (such as the Soviet Union) from joining the General Agreement on Tariffs and Trade (GATT) unless they first agree to trade on a free-market basis; (2) the United States can retaliate on the basis of Section 301 of the 1974 Trade Act if workers' rights are denied, which is considered an unfair trading practice. Workers' rights include the right to association; the right to organize and bargain collectively; freedom from forced labor; a minimum working age for children; and standards for minimum wages, working hours, and occupational safety and health. Retaliation is not mandatory, but is at the discretion of the U.S. trade representative, who has the authority to decide unfair trade cases. The law also authorizes the president to suspend or halt the merger, acquisition, or takeover of a U.S. firm if he considers the move a threat to national security. For a useful short summary of these provisions, see "Implications of Trade Law on East-West Trade," *CSCE Digest*, August-September 1988, p. 5.

103. Rode, op. cit.

104. Ibid.

105. Ibid.

106. Ibid.

PART 3

The Challenge of Détente and Pan-Europeanization for the Future of the Western Alliance

The Reforging of Soviet Policy and Diverging Western Perceptions of the Soviet Union

Chapter 8 demonstrated that although the postwar model of military-technological competition and arms racing still remains the basis of U.S. policy, there are indelible signs of its erosion and an uneven, contradictory shift to an approach of deepening economic relations with the Soviet Union and other COMECON nations. This chapter takes up Soviet military, economic, and foreign policy and Western assessments of the meaning of Soviet reforms and "new thinking" for the future of Western policy.

The chapter begins with a discussion of the revision of Soviet military doctrine under Gorbachev and how the new doctrine is linked to Soviet foreign policy and economic perestroika. I will show that the general aim of Soviet economic policy is to transform the Soviet status quo economic-political structure into a more open, internationally integrated system and that as this process advances, it will expose the Soviet state to domestic and international pressures to further shrink the military sector in order to make the economy more competitive in the domestic and international markets. I will argue that the success of this venture will depend on the development of stabilizing relations between East and West.

The last part of the chapter examines Western analyses of Soviet development. Three viewpoints are presented: a U.S. common security interpretation; a British Atlanticist perspective; and the official West German view.

The Shift in Soviet Military Doctrine

The decline of the postwar paradigm of security is reflected on the military-strategic level in the effects of contemporary arms racing on the stability of the strategy of deterrence. These are summed up by the Soviet researcher Alexei Arbatov in his account of the Warsaw Pact's shift from a military doctrine focused on the requirements of waging nuclear war to one of war prevention:

The aim of "preventing war" was not mentioned in the former general definitions of a military doctrine. . . . The latter was characterized as a system of views on the essence, aims and nature of a possible war, and on the preparation for and methods of waging it. The prevention of war and an attack of a possible enemy was becoming a sort of "byproduct" of the all-around strengthening of the defense capability, the main task of which was to increase the potential of waging war should one be forced on the socialist countries. The prevention of war was mainly considered as belonging to the sphere of foreign policy and it was thought that the greater the might of the armed forces the more reliable was the country's security.[1]

Arbatov describes the immanent factors in the technological arms race that quantitively and qualitatively undermined the security of East and West as a result of the enlargement and technological refinement of their respective military arsenals. The evolution of deterrence resulted not in achieving the official goal of greater stability in the East-West balance of terror but in producing greater instability. This uneasy state became an important factor that led to a fundamental reevaluation of military policy in the Soviet Union, which Arbatov explains as follows:

The new approach reflected the reality that in addition to foreign policy and diplomacy, military doctrine, strategy and military buildup seriously influence the probability of war by the inexorable law of "feed-back." While the strengthening of the defense capability does to a certain limit serve the purpose of preventing war . . . because it deprives a potential aggressor of any hope to achieve success by launching a first strike, once that limit is exceeded, the enhancement of the military potential, especially with well-pronounced offensive characteristics, begins to increase the threat of war no matter how peaceful the foreign policy intentions and the diplomatic and propaganda activity of a state might appear to be. If the military potential exceeds limits of reasonable sufficiency for defense, it will inevitably be perceived by other countries as a sign of aggressive intentions, outweighing any political obligations and statements. Such a situation causes distrust and suspicion, and generates political tension in relations between states, which, in some unforeseen crisis, could turn into an uncontrollable military conflict. This intensifies the arms race, which has itself been a strong source of tension. Political will and government decisions in a crisis situation can become hostages to military plans aimed at seizing the initiative and destroying the enemy.[2]

The unceasing buildup of military arsenals also "obstructs disarmament negotiations—the primary means of diminishing the threat of war in our time—and dooms them to lagging behind the process of piling up and perfecting military arsenals in a period of rapid scientific and technological progress."[3] The difference between conventional and nuclear instability has also become blurred by the danger of escalation:

> Finally, it was understood that there could also be no victor in a large-scale conventional war between the main alliances of states, because the losing side, unable to reconcile itself to defeat considering the enormous political stakes involved, would undoubtedly use nuclear weapons with all the ensuing consequences. This is not to mention that a conventional war would have a tremendous geographic scope and would also entail huge destructive consequences.[4]

Arbatov also stresses the difficulties of actually shifting military doctrine and force structures after the Soviet Union had officially adopted a defensive posture as a policy goal:

> Recognition of the unattainability of "victory" and the existence of the previously mentioned "feed-back" effect goes against the long-standing traditions of the art of war and military buildup. It will not be easy to adapt them to other tasks and aims from the established principles of seizing the initiative, concentrating power and acting resolutely in order to destroy the enemy and score victory as quickly as possible. But the new realities of the nuclear-space-age, unprecedented in history, demand precisely such a course.[5]

Common, or Mutual, Security

In his analysis of the new Soviet thinking on military strategy and doctrine, Michael MccGwire of the Brookings Institution focuses on the Soviet attempt to redefine national security in terms of common or "mutual security":

> At the center of the new thinking lies the question of national security. The Soviets claim that the traditional approach is outmoded, that a state that unilaterally seeks to improve its security will automatically increase the insecurity of the other, and that reliance on military might will actually reduce security by increasing the danger of war. National security, the Soviets now say, can only be achieved by cooperating with other nations to provide mutual security. Guaranteeing national security has "become above all a political task and not a military one." While stressing the need for equal security, the Soviets have moved beyond the idea of parity to talk of sufficiency. They acknowledge the need for asymmetrical reductions in arms and for levels that preclude the possibility of surprise attack or general offensive operations. Some quarters are promoting nonoffensive means of defense.[6]

In a similar vein, Robert Legvold, director of the New York Harriman Institute, discusses the Soviet notion of "military sufficiency" applied to conventional war.[7] He cites a key article written in 1987 on this subject by A. Kokoshin and V. Larionov, who point out that

> "Conventional military forces must be lowered to a level of reasonable sufficiency, that is, to a level essential for solving only defensive tasks." Operational doctrine, they say, should be genuinely defensive, which in turn requires adjustments in the "numbers, structures, armaments and deployments of forces, in troop training and military exercises, and in military planning." To move in this direction, they bluntly note, "certain changes will have to occur in the way military professionals think." They will have to "reconsider a number of widely held postulates of military theory and practice," including above all else the notion that "only an all-out offensive leads to victory."[8]

Links to Foreign Policy

Legvold describes the Soviet effort to translate the new military thinking on reasonable sufficiency and non-offensive defense into foreign policy:

> Even Soviet officials have seemed eager to give Gorbachev's formulas a push forward. In September 1987 before the U.N. General Assembly, Foreign Minister Eduard Shevardnadze strongly endorsed the need to move toward military doctrines of "an exclusively defensive character," and added the notion that all sides should "adopt the principles of non-offensive defense." A month later, the head of the Foreign Ministry's arms control department, Victor Karpov, repeated Gorbachev's exhortation to reduce military force on both sides to a level where neither could move offensively against the other. He then went on to suggest that this might be accomplished by "scrapping nuclear weapons and by reducing the most dangerous types of arms, which could include tanks, tactical aircraft, and strike helicopters."[9]

The objectives stated are closely linked to what Soviet Foreign Minister Eduard Shevardnadze has called the "economizing" of Soviet foreign policy.[10] This process entails the restructuring of foreign policy, military doctrine, and economic policy. In emphasizing that changing one of these presupposes simultaneously changing the other two, Shevardnadze lists the following Soviet goals:[11]

1. Reducing of the financial burden of foreign policy programs
2. Increasing economic activity with capitalist economies to draw Western technology, management know-how, and capital and consumer goods to the Soviet Union

3. Reducing military rivalry and confrontation with the West in order to drastically curtail military expenditures
4. Lowering international tension to enable the Soviet leadership to more effectively focus its attention on domestic concerns

The implementation of the above goals must confront deeply entrenched, conservative forces in Soviet society.[12] This resistance is reflected, for example, in the debate in the party on the future role of class struggle, liberation struggles, and on the definition of coexistence in Soviet policy. Gorbachev's fundamental revision of the doctrine of class struggle in international relations was summarized by Shevardnadze as follows:

> Coexistence, which is founded on such principles as non-aggression, respect for sovereignty and national independence, non-interference in internal affairs, etc., cannot be equated with class struggle. The struggle of two opposing systems is no longer the tendency that defines the contemporary era. At the contemporary stage what is important is the ability to increase material benefits as quickly as possible on the basis of advanced sciences and to distribute them justly, and to restore and protect the resources necessary for the survival of mankind.[13]

The repudiation of the military-political systemic conflict, however, has been criticized by Soviet Politburo member Yegor Ligachev, a leading conservative proponent of perestroika within the Soviet bureaucracy who has stubbornly defended the traditional role of international class struggle:[14] "We proceed from the class nature of international relations. Any other framing of the issue only confuses Soviet people and our friends abroad. Active involvement in resolving the common problems of mankind does not mean any artificial slowing of the social and national-liberation struggle."[15]

Ligachev's statement reflects the persistence of postwar thinking in the Soviet foreign policy debate, even if Soviet hardliners, such as Ligachev, do accept a much reduced level of military confrontation with the West and the avoidance of large-scale military interventions, such as Afghanistan.

The Soviet Economic Reforms and the Opening to the West

The three general goals of the Gorbachev economic reform program are to shift the Soviet economy to intensified growth (*intensifikatsiya*), accelerated growth (*uskorenize*), and modernization of the technological base of industry (*perestroika*).[16] Hans-Hermann Höhmann has summed up the Soviet domestic economic reforms as follows:

> The main objectives of the *"radical economic reform,"* which took

effect following the resolutions of the plenary session in June 1987 and after the passage of the state enterprise law at the subsequent meeting of the Supreme Soviet, can be described as follows. The reform aims to *alter the status of the enterprise* in the overall economy by expanding self-planning, self-financing, and self-management mechanisms. It aims to introduce *changes in the enterprises' "functional environment"* (e.g., planning, the supply of capital goods, price formation, and the credit and finance system) by establishing a control over enterprise activity through indicative or indirect economic policy instruments (e.g. orientation indicators, taxes, norms, and margins), however, also by means of state commissions bearing obligatory contract fulfillment. And, finally, it also aims to implement changes in the "institutional environment" of the enterprises (e.g. in the structure and function of those ministries managing the economy).[17]

These goals are to be accomplished through domestic reforms linked to the integration of the Soviet Union in the international economy. In this context, a strategy of establishing joint ventures with Western firms has been adopted to attract investment capital, technology, and managerial know-how.[18]

The joint ventures, it is hoped, will have a transsectoral catalyzing effect by grafting Western production methods onto the Soviet economy and creating an environment conducive to the growth of market forces.

Sherr has emphasized the broad effects of the Soviet joint venture strategy on legal and financial institutions:

The need of Soviet officials to respond to Western demands in the context of joint venture negotiations accelerates the process of drafting and implementing corporate and financial law in the USSR. The process of "legalizing" Soviet society is a necessary adjunct to the effort to introduce throughout the Soviet economy wholesale contracting and pricing, self-accounting, and "socialist competition." Joint ventures support and accelerate this process because the demands are clear and unceasing from external sources (as opposed to the mixed signals being generated within the Soviet economy) and because Soviet reformers may be seizing on joint ventures (as well as cooperatives) as tools for goading the system into action.[19]

The economic reforms will expose the Soviet economy increasingly to international competition, which is expected to promote market-type mechanisms and allow the reduction of the role of the state in managing the economy.[20] External obligations, norms, standards, and patterns of behavior characteristic of the international economy are also to help nurture the development of a private market sector (firms, management, sections of the work force, and consumers) which will have a vested interest in the deepening of the reform process. The Soviet economic reforms and follow-up policy measures designed to realize the above vision include:[21]

1. The Ministry of Foreign Trade's monopoly of external trade relations has been abrogated and the property law revised to permit foreign ownership and stimulate entrepreneurship.
2. There have been measures to recentralize control in certain key economic sectors while decisionmaking regarding other sectors less important to the center have been decentralized. The newly created State Foreign Economic Commission has been mandated to coordinate interministerial foreign trade operations and improve infrastructures and incentives related to trade. According to Ed Hewett, the aim of these measures is "to retain monopoly of foreign trade, but to streamline the system in order to enhance incentives for Soviet enterprises to export manufactured goods."[22]
3. Other ministries and enterprises have been granted the right to import and export on their own.
4. Linked to (3), there have been efforts to promote new products and to extend the control of enterprise associations over the research, development, design, and marketing cycles of new products.
5. With the advice and cooperation of Western banks and corporations, the Soviets have created political, juridical, and financial structures to facilitate foreign investment and other commercial activity.
6. Negotiations have produced some 1000 joint ventures with foreign firms; these projects (some of which are discussed in more detail in Chapter 10) are in various stages of completion.
7. A campaign has been launched to increase the Soviet Union's role in international economic organizations. Important here are Soviet formal requests for membership in the General Agreement on Tariffs and Trade (GATT) and the International Monetary Fund (IMF).[23] A future membership in GATT would not only pressure Western nations to remove tariff and nontariff barriers blocking imports of Soviet goods but would also encourage the Soviet Union to remove—or keep to a declining minimum—its import barriers.[24] Soviet planners and emerging private-sector forces would be encouraged to find the right degree of openness to best promote the growth of the Soviet economy.

The New Soviet Financial Policy

Until 1988 Moscow generally held its credits from Western banks to a minimum, despite its international financial rating as a reliable borrower.[25] This policy was designed to avoid financial dependency on the West and corresponded to Soviet autarky characteristic of the pre-Gorbachev era. The Gorbachev leadership reversed this policy with its decision to negotiate relatively large Western credits. In January 1988 the Soviet Union borrowed 100 million Swiss francs and in July 500 million DM in Western capital markets.[26] In May the Deutsche Bank lent $1.8 billion to the Soviet Union for the purchase of West German capital and consumer goods. This was followed in October by the Soviet Union's signing agreements for Western loans amounting to $9 billion.[27] The Federal Republic provided $3 billion and France and Japan $2 billion each, with the remainder coming from British, Italian, and Austrian banks.

These credits were arranged in order to underwrite imports of Western goods, alleviate the bottlenecks resulting from restructuring, and to link the Soviet Union financially and commercially more closely with the West. Other important factors in the shift in financial policy include the fall in world prices for raw materials, the weakening of the U.S. dollar, and the considerable costs of the Soviet reform program.[28]

Nonmilitary Forms of Security as a Tool of Economic Recovery

Another important dimension of Soviet reform efforts is the attempt to link cooperative economic development projects and ecological protection with East-West disarmament. An example of this linkage was the comprehensive disarmament and development plan for Northern Europe and the Arctic zone outlined in Gorbachev's 1987 speech in Murmansk. The main features of the proposal were[29]

1. A nuclear weapon–free zone in Northern Europe
2. Consultation between the Warsaw Pact and NATO on restricting naval activity off the coast of Northern Europe and limiting naval and air force activities in the Baltic, North, Norwegian, and Greenland seas
3. Peaceful cooperation between East and West in developing the resources of the Nordic and the Arctic zone
4. A scientific study of the Arctic that would be organized and coordinated by a conference of subarctic states
5. A comprehensive plan for protecting the environment of the Nordic zone
6. The opening up of shipping and travel routes from Europe to the Far East and the Pacific Ocean through the Arctic with the help of Soviet ice-breaking vessels

The Murmansk proposals illustrate the adoption by the Soviet leadership of policy aims corresponding to the post-containment model of security in which disarmament is explicitly linked to East-West détente and deepened economic, ecological, and scientific cooperation.

Economic conversion from military to civilian production. The international economic integration of the Soviet Union, it should be pointed out, would be difficult to realize on the scale necessary to make a difference in Soviet development without a major adjustment of military spending, strategy, and doctrine. This need to refocus is linked to a number of different factors, including the oft-cited drain of military production on the Soviet economy. According to Sovietologist John Tedstrom:

> Soviet economic decay and stagnation has made the trade-off between investment for growth, consumption, and defense more painful now than perhaps at any other time in the post War era. While there is little hard evidence to turn to, much of what we see in the Soviet press and economic and defense literature speaks to this problem in rather clear terms. The way in which the allocation of resources between investment, consumption, and defense at the macro-economic level has changed in the last two to three five-year plans is also telling. Specifically, there is a good deal of evidence—though no proof—that since the late 1970s growth in investment has taken place at the expense of increments in the defense budget.[30]

Soviet restructuring efforts are aimed at scaling down military production. One of the attempted ways of accomplishing this is the conversion of military R&D and weapons manufacturing plants to civilian production facilities. As Tedstrom explains:

> The defense industries are being called on in increasingly strong terms to do more for the civilian economy. Examples of this are plentiful, but most recently the 1989 plan called on the defense industries significantly to boost their contributions to the consumer goods sectors and light industry. The plan states that (in reference to the stagnation in light industry) "The ministries of the defense complex have attached the best design talents and 108 new enterprises to the solution of this problem." Shortly thereafter, an interview with Lev Ryabev, the Minister of Medium Machine-Building (Minsredmash), was published in *Izvestia*. Ryabev's message was that his ministry is already doing a good deal for the civilian economy—largely at its own expense—and that even more increases are planned, all the way to the year 2000. For example, several hundred types of machinery for the dairy processing industry are going to be built by Minsredmash, which is the USSR's primary producer of nuclear weapons. Most of his ministry's contributions will be in the form of machinery for the light and agricultural industries and in "complex" consumer goods such as video equipment and computers.[31]

The demilitarizing logic of the Soviet economic reforms. Economic-political opening to the West and the far-reaching changes in military doctrine and force structures are central components of the Soviet reform process, as the statements of Arbatov and Shevardnadze previously cited suggest.

The barriers to Soviet cooperation with the West are both internal and external. The autarkic structures and the "siege mentality" of the Soviet Union dating back to postrevolutionary Russia have been reinforced by Western postwar policies of military-technological competition, economic embargoes, and military-political containment.[32] These have precluded a large-scale economic opening to the West and still remain formidable obstacles to Soviet reform.

Soviet autarky has also been linked to the state's monopoly over the administration of the economy,[33] including in the state's former total control over investment, distribution of resources, foreign trade, and other levers of macroeconomic management.[34] The central organs of the state had the authority to set key priorities and to allocate disproportionately large amounts of investment resources to heavy industry and the military sector. In the context of the absolute and relative amounts of Soviet military spending, two factors are important to keep in mind:

1. The Soviet economy has a considerably less developed industrial and technological base than the United States. This weakness limits Soviet ability to satisfy the demands of a disproportionately large military sector and at the same time keep up with developing consumer demands, especially if these are measured according to Western standards.

2. The pre-Gorbachev era was characterized by the absence of an officially sanctioned consumer market sphere underpinned by democratic institutions. In Western democracies, the market and the ballot box—along with a "culture of consumption"—provide the consumer with comparatively powerful instruments to express economic and political preference. These affect, in varying degrees, the types of products produced and the direction of competition and influence the formulation of macro- and microeconomic policy.

With the above in mind, the likely effects of perestroika, democratization, and glasnost on the military sector can be summed up as follows: With the introduction of some market mechanisms under Gorbachev and the shrinking of the state's monopoly over investment and distribution of available resources, the Soviet military sector will be forced to compete with new market-oriented forces on both the demand and supply sides of the economy. These new forces include (a) economic ministries and agencies managing the nonmilitary public sector, (b) the embryonic market sector, and (c) government agencies and administrative organs set up to provide support for the private sector. Resources that formerly went into military production (with corresponding military-civilian trade-offs) will in the future tend to be regulated to a greater degree by market forces.

The degree of decentralization of economic management resulting from the devolvement of economic initiative and policymaking to firms and to demand forces—including Soviet consumers now politically enfranchised—will tend to increase if the Soviet Union can successfully sustain its reform course. If this proves to be the case, the result will tend at the same time to reduce the power of the military-industrial sphere to command resources and to function as a highly privileged de facto macroeconomic regulator and large absorber of Soviet industrial and technological capital and technical-scientific labor.[35]

The trend in this direction is clearly discernible from the nature of the reforms already discussed. But the degree to which these reforms will have their desired effect and what their lead times will be remain unclear, given their complexity, the additional problems their implementation is raising, and the forces within the Soviet bureaucracy who want to slow this process.[36]

It should be added that more concrete analysis of the Soviet restructuring will be possible only as the reform process unfolds and systematic data are published on military production and on the Soviet economy as a whole. Part of the task of Soviet perestroika is to set up an appropriate system of statistics that would make it possible, for example, to compare Soviet with Western military budgets—hitherto impossible except in a highly speculative and scientifically inaccurate manner. The publication of systematic data represents a significant challenge to the autarkic structure of the Soviet economy and can be considered also an indispensable step for the deepening of the reform process as a whole.

The inherently international nature of the Soviet reforms strongly suggests that their success will depend to a significant degree on responses of Western economic actors—firms, governments, banks, foreign publics, and international organizations. An important factor in this context is the degree to which the West is willing to adopt common East-West arms control policies and enter into disarmament treaties that could provide the Soviet reform leadership with the assurance and confidence to further reduce the Soviet military sector. The reform leadership in this context must deal with (a) the challenge of continuing arms racing in the West and (b) the internal political tensions that could arise between pro-defense interest groups and the embryonic market-oriented private sector with its interest in reducing the macroeconomic drain of social resources by the Soviet military-industrial sphere. Given this constellation of rivaling interest groups, cooperation from the West on economic and security issues could have the effect, for example, of weakening the pro-military conservative elements in the Soviet hierarchy and deflating the traditional arguments used by the military to maintain large military budgets.

The partial transformation of the Soviet economy from a totally state-managed entity to a mixed economy of a new socialist type (a state sector and a small but growing private sector) certainly does not exclude future military production and fluctuations of military outlays. Yet it places Soviet military production and the military budget in a qualitatively new domestic and East-West context, the demilitarizing dynamics of which could promote East-West disarmament that in turn could gain sustenance from the Soviet economic and political reforms.

However, there is a counterargument to this interpretation of Soviet reforms based on the postwar model of security, which holds that economic restructuring and opening to the West will provide the Soviet military with greater opportunity to use civilian dual-use technology produced domestically and in the West for its military-industrial sphere.[37] This argument in the abstract has merit, but it neglects the enormous pent-up pressures from nonmilitary sectors for consumer goods and the necessity of rapid advancement of the nonmilitary economy. The military sector cannot contribute very much to this process except as it shrinks, whether by being progressively reduced or by shifting to civilian production, as Tedstrom notes some military factories are doing.

It is also evident from the foregoing analysis that the different dimensions of the Soviet reform program form an interconnected whole. All have to be realized to some extent, or the program could unravel. A reversion to intensive military production with Western technology, for example, would certainly result in a powerful international backlash triggering the withdrawal of Western capital and forcing cutbacks in nonmilitary sectors. This regression could in turn unleash a backlash from Soviet consumers, market-oriented firms, and other social categories and interest groups whose political clout will tend to increase now that many of the basic political and economic reforms are formally in place. The fact that failure to shrink the military sector could thus result in the failure of the Soviet leadership's economic strategy as a whole is not taken into serious account by Western analysts who are dismissive of new Soviet military thinking in arguing that Western technology will unavoidably result in strengthening the Soviet military apparatus.

Western Perceptions of Soviet Strategy

Soviet "new thinking" on military strategy and doctrine has catalyzed a debate in Western policy circles whether it would be in the interest of the West to cooperate with the Soviets in ways that would accelerate (or in other ways facilitate) the implementation of perestroika, glasnost, and the new Soviet military doctrine.[38] This debate revolves around questions such as (1) What are the goals of the Soviet reforms? (2) What are the likely results of the restructuring efforts in the Soviet Union's foreign policy vis-à-vis the West? (3) What are the chances the Soviets will succeed? (4) How should the West respond, whether the objective is to prevent the Soviets from altering the postwar East-West relationship or to cooperate with the Gorbachev leadership to achieve a new set of common goals?

In Michael MccGwire's view, Gorbachev has promoted the military doctrine of nonoffensive defense because he sees it as being in the Soviet Union's national interests. The range of potential benefits, according to MccGwire, includes reducing the defense burden, checking the technological arms race, and enabling a new type of relationship with the West Europeans. He goes on to make the point that

> because a new security regime in Europe is in Soviet interests does not mean that it is against Western interests. Eschewing a zero-sum approach to East-West relations remains a sound policy, even though it is now being advocated by the Soviet Union.[39]

Moreover,

> At this stage the West is not required to do anything very difficult or dangerous. Essentially, we are asked to sit down with the Warsaw Pact and discuss how to work out a new mutual security regime for Europe involving greatly reduced force levels and major constraints on their structure and posture.[40]

In contrast to MccGwire's positive evaluation, the British historian Professor Michael Howard, a staunch Atlanticist, proposes four models to understand the development in the Soviet Union and its possible outcomes and meaning for the NATO alliance. Model A assumes a disintegrating Soviet Union, unable to hold together under populist and nationalist pressure. This process, Howard asserts, "if assisted by Western propaganda and pressures," could plausibly lead "to circumstances in which the Soviet leadership might initiate a nuclear war."[41] Therefore, he concludes, "superficially attractive as such a model may appear in some quarters," it is one the West would "do well to avoid."[42] Model B is that of a Soviet Union

> which feels itself neither under external pressure nor under any obligation to export a creed of revolutionary socialism which it has itself long-since abandoned as counter-productive. It has co-operated in arms reductions and transferred massive resources to the civilian sector. It has scaled down its troops in Eastern Europe to defensive cadres and is managing political diversity in that region with reasonable skill.[43]

Howard considers Model B improbable and also argues that were it to be realized in the Soviet Union, it would bring forth a regime that would require the West's acceptance of continued Soviet hegemony in Eastern Europe and a Soviet Union that would fall short of Western standards of human rights.

Howard's preferred Model C is what he calls "status quo plus," in which the Soviet Union would be "still economically weak but slowly strengthening itself, still keeping up its end in a crippling arms race . . . still maintaining its menacing forces in Eastern Europe, still trying to embarrass the West by exploiting the forces of revolutionary socialism in the Third World, and still feeding its own people with a diet of mendacious propaganda."[44]

Howard's Model D, in contrast, consists of a "triumphalist Soviet Union, which, however grave its internal problems, has achieved so great a measure of escalation dominance in nuclear weapons and superiority in conventional forces that it can blackmail Western Europe into submission and force the United States into a subordinate role in the international system."[45] Howard concludes that Western "governments and their advisers are likely to prefer the familiar dangers and disadvantages of Model C, not so much because of the uncertainties of Model B but because of their fear that what might ultimately develop is Model D."[46] This means for Howard that the West should

> from fear of Model D, remain within the known parameters, take no risks, continue to maintain and improve our existing level of defense (including strategic defences), work cautiously at the margins for incremental confidence-building measures of arms control and in general proceed on the assumption that no fundamental changes are occurring in the Soviet Union, none can be expected, and even if they did, they would make no difference.[47]

Howard offers the following rather cynical justification for his preference for Model C:

> With all its drawbacks it provides a credible framework for security: the risks involved in pursuing it are less than those attached to the bolder course; and above all it divides the Alliance least . . . We must conduct a skillful delaying action in the certain knowledge that we have powerful allies in the enemy camp. We must block Gorbachev's radical proposals, or counter them with demands for radical troop cuts and redeployment of Soviet armed forces which, however attractive to Gorbachev himself, will be quite unacceptable to his military leadership and their political allies. Together with them, sooner or later, we can wear the man down and frustrate his disturbing designs: after that it may be another generation before a Soviet leader emerges with the energy to try again. All that is required is patience and the negotiating skills at which the Alliance is now so adept.[48]

But Howard goes on in somewhat contradictory fashion to point out the dilemma that the Model C strategy entails:

> Few political leaders, however, would be prepared to accept the limited objectives implied in such a programme as being truly adequate for the Alliance, and even fewer would be prepared frankly to inform their publics that is what they intend to do. Option B, a benign relationship with the Soviet Union, is our declared objective, whatever difficulties we may confront in pursuing it. A policy of confrontation may remain inevitable in the short run, but many Europeans will find it unacceptable for the long. Immobilism, however skillfully pursued, will eventually impose an intolerable strain on our relationships. Unless we can look beyond immediate necessities to ultimate objectives and adjust our policies accordingly, the prospects before the Alliance in the twenty-first century will be bleak. The Gorbachev challenge calls for critical self-examination as well as a convincing response.[49]

The West German Response to Soviet Reforms

Whereas the United States has remained officially cool to Soviet reform intentions, the Federal Republic has adopted an active policy of encouragement and readiness to enter into agreements with Moscow with far-reaching economic, political, and security-related aims. Foreign Minister Genscher, in stark contrast to the skepticism of Howard and official NATO circles, has urged the West to support the Soviet reform process.[50]

Genscher has emphasized and officially embraced the link in Soviet policy between changing economic conditions and the need for a common— he calls it "joint"—security approach in East-West relations.

West German Chancellor Kohl, in describing his government's policy, emphasizes the links between the Soviet program to change its security relations and Moscow's economic opening to the West:

> A Soviet Union which really is opening domestically and in its foreign affairs would also be a more predictable security partner than an isolationist Soviet Union confronted with economic decline. To that extent, long-term stable cooperation with the Soviet Union is also in our political and economic interests.[51]

According to Kohl and Genscher, in addition to the military-political considerations for changing security policy, Gorbachev is faced with compelling economic reasons for reshaping Soviet force structures, military strategy, and foreign policy.[52]

Soviet Policy and "Splitting the Alliance"

Soviet moves to reshape its security approach have been interpreted in NATO and U.S. official circles as an attempt by Moscow to divide the United States from its NATO allies and bring about a withdrawal of the United States from Western Europe.[53] This interpretation follows from the assumption of the postwar model of security of military-political confrontation between the United States and the Soviet Union for influence and control over Europe. The U.S. Sovietologist Jerry Hough of Duke University disagrees with this conventional view and argues that Moscow has an important stake in the United States remaining in Western Europe:

> Many assume, mistakenly, that splitting NATO is Mr. Gorbachev's ultimate policy aim. Yet, the continuation of NATO under American leadership is in Moscow's best interests. . . . The Kremlin's major goals in Western Europe are, first, to prevent conflicts within the region that might draw America and the Soviet Union into war, and second, to prevent nuclear proliferation to West Germany.
>
> An independent Germany would eventually demand nuclear equality with France and Britain. Moreover, Japan, when confronted with a splintered NATO, might begin to rearm, mounting a costly challenge to Soviet power in the Far East. Thus, Moscow has a major stake in maintaining the military status quo.[54]

The Soviet analyst Alexander Bovin has similarly stressed the importance of a U.S. presence in Western Europe:

> I will not be revealing any secrets if I say that Soviet policy takes into account the differences of views between Western Europe and the United States. But it does so by no means in order to squeeze the United States out of Europe and gain political control of the continent which it so longs for, in the opinion of "perspicacious" analysts in the West. Our objective is much more modest. We would like to utilize Western Europe's potential to make good, via the transatlantic channel, the obvious shortage of common sense in the incumbent U.S. administration . . . Since Western Europe and the United States are allies, and in our opinion the elements of common sense in European politics are stronger, we are attempting to get Western Europe to influence the United States in order to make American policy more sober, reflecting a moderate quality to a greater extent. To a certain extent the Europeans are doing this, but in my view they could do more.[55]

Bovin's statement suggests that a U.S. withdrawal from Western Europe would not correspond to the model of cooperation that the Soviet leadership has made the main thrust of its foreign policy.

Consequences of Soviet Reforms for the West

Because Soviet reform depends on integration of the Soviet Union into the international economy and hence membership in international organizations, the pace and long-term success of Soviet restructuring will depend not only on internal political factors but also on the results of East-West cooperation and the West's response to Soviet reforms. West German Foreign Minister Genscher takes the view that the West is not a neutral bystander in the Soviet reform process and has much to lose if it were to fail. In stark contrast to the Atlanticist stance of Professor Howard previously discussed, the official West German position on this point is the most outspoken among U.S. allies and leading capitalist powers:

> In the West, people ask whether the Soviet Union might not become strong as a result of economic cooperation. Of course, economic cooperation can take place only if it benefits both sides. The question is this: Does economic cooperation make the Soviet Union on the whole more predictable and more able to cooperate? And we must also decide whether enormous differences in economic performance and in people's living standards tend to increase or decrease tension. Those differences in productivity and living standards which have their roots in the socialist system cannot be eliminated by us; that has to be done by the Soviet leadership. The question of how far this aim will be achievable must be answered in Moscow. But in an interdependent world it is in our own interests not to heighten these destabilizing differences by refusing to cooperate. We must not compound the political and ideological division with economic and technological divisions.[56]

Genscher also criticizes the view that the Soviet Union is seeking to gain time and will revert to the traditional policies of the pre-Gorbachev era:

> In the West, people are asking whether the Soviet Union merely seeks to win breathing space. This theory is refuted by the fact that *glasnost* and, even more so, *perestroika*, the reshaping of the economy and society, are processes which will take many years, probably even decades. By then, however, the world and the Soviet Union within that world will have altered to such an extent that it is almost impossible to imagine Moscow returning to its policy of the pre-Gorbachev era as if nothing had happened.[57]

In contrast to Atlanticist skeptics and nay-sayers, Genscher urges Western allies not to be bound by traditional anti-Soviet attitudes. He emphasizes the historic opportunity that Gorbachev has opened up and Bonn's determination not to be fettered by obsolete postwar attitudes:

A Soviet Union which seeks a comprehensive and lasting improvement in East-West relations will find the West to be a constructive and responsible partner. The Western attitude must depend on our interests concerning the development we desire. If today, after decades of East-West confrontation, a turning point is attainable, it would be a mistake of historic dimensions if the West were to miss this opportunity. We look soberly at the facts, but we will not allow ourselves to be shackled by outdated thinking and deep-seated antipathies. Whoever takes the worst-case scenario as the sole basis of his action, including his action via-à-vis the Soviet Union, becomes a political deadweight.[58]

Conclusions

The Soviet Union is no longer attempting to seek economic and political security by holding its ties to the West to a minimum—and thereby avoiding dependency—as it has done in the past. Moscow is now opening to the West in an effort to construct historic new conditions for détente and more intensive economic and political cooperation deemed mutually beneficial for East and West. This fresh approach is evident in its changed military doctrine (with its emphasis on war prevention, reasonable sufficiency, and common security), in its internationalist foreign policy, and in its new domestic and external economic strategy.

The economic, political, and security-related dimensions of Soviet restructuring correspond in their logic and consistency to the post-containment model of security. The Soviet military and economic reform process, Soviet foreign policy, perestroika, and glasnost aim at constructing a security architecture in which disarmament, common security, and détente would become mutually reinforcing elements in a comprehensive approach.

The analysis in this chapter suggests that the general principles of the post-containment model of security underpin the Soviet leadership's approach to international development in the coming decades. The Soviet Union is attempting to use the post-containment model

- As a set of presuppositions for forging the domestic and international dimensions of its reform strategy
- As a comprehensive and unified set of overarching policy aims
- As a normative model for global development

The elements of the post-containment model of security are discernible in the Soviet efforts to overcome the legacy of the postwar era based on East-West arms racing, economic autarky that generally closed off far-reaching forms of détente and East-West cooperation, and the state's overwhelmingly dominant position within the Soviet economic and political system. A centrally important feature of the Soviet reform process is the interrelationship between economic restructuring and demilitarization of foreign policy.

The thrust of the Soviet domestic and international economic strategy entails placing the Soviet economy in a field of political, economic, and international organizational forces that will tend to modify radically the highly centralized bureaucracy within the state and the central position of the military sector in the Soviet economy. This process is aimed at making the Soviet economy into a socialist type of mixed economy that would become increasingly compatible with its more market-regulated, international economic environment.

The military sector, as a result, will have to compete for capital and labor resources in an environment in which firms, managers, consumers, and the East-West partners in joint ventures would begin to function politically as a significant pressure group demanding resources to meet their particular production and consumption needs. These forces are linked to the emerging market sector and the greater political enfranchisement of the approximately 320 million Soviet consumers.

In addition to compelling economic reasons for the Gorbachev leadership's strong commitment to a reform course, there are equally compelling political reasons. Important among these is that the Kremlin leadership has tied its political survival to its policy of far-reaching change. As a number of Soviet experts have warned—and as also suggested by Michael Howard's models of the future of the Soviet Union—the danger exists that if perestroika and opening to the West on a demilitarizing economic and political basis fail, it could lead to a remilitarization of Soviet policy, an end of the Gorbachev era, and the closing of channels of cooperation that have been tenuously opened up since he came to power.[59] This retrenching would at the very least significantly heighten political-military tensions throughout Europe and globally.

Professor Howard's models reflect the paradox and dilemma of the Atlanticist defense of preserving the NATO status quo based on the postwar security model. On the one hand, the events in the Soviet Union are significant enough that NATO cannot remain indifferent to them, as Howard suggests. Yet he feels NATO's response should perhaps be to preserve the status quo by doing what it can in the way of wearing Gorbachev down in order to stop the Soviet reform process from having the effect of altering the postwar basis of the East-West conflict. But in pursuing this spoiling strategy, Western governments, in Howard's view, would run the risk of catalyzing legitimacy crises, given the strong public sympathy and support in the West for Gorbachev's overall program.

The risk of domestic political opposition to Howard's proposed response to Gorbachev recalls the debate in West Germany over Pershing II and cruise missiles (see Chapter 1) in which NATO officialdom, the West German government, Washington, and the steel-helmet wing, misjudged the degree of popular and elite rejection of the U.S. systems. Given public desire for disarmament, a similar scenario could repeat itself if political pressure builds for follow-up agreements to the INF treaty. It should also be recalled that the Western demand for large reductions of Soviet missiles in the form of the zero solution was, to the surprise of the West, accepted by the Soviets. Against this backdrop, Howard's proposal of making radical demands on Gorbachev to make large reductions in order to counter the Gorbachev military reforms could produce an effect opposite than intended because (1) large Soviet reductions are among the most important aims of Gorbachev's reform program and (2) such demands from NATO, combined with serious responses to them from the Soviets, could further legitimize disarmament in the West. The NATO campaign for large Soviet reductions could awaken additional expectations and lead to demands from West European publics for NATO (a) to reciprocate with quantitatively or qualitatively equivalent reductions and (b) for NATO, together with the Soviets, to shift to nonmilitary forms of security to replace the status quo NATO–Warsaw Pact conflict. This public pressure could either result in concessions on the part of NATO or a more stubbornly obstructionist stance. A NATO attempt to forestall change by efforts to implement Howard's Model C of wearing Gorbachev down could also have the unwanted result of complicating West-West relations, as disagreement within the alliance deepens over Western policy toward the Soviet Union.

Calling for Western passivity or obstructionist tactics toward Soviet reforms would also encounter opposition from the Federal Republic, which emphatically rejects this position. Official West German support of common security and East-West economic cooperation reflects the deepening polarization within NATO between Atlanticists, who have called for a veiled anti-Gorbachev campaign in order to preserve the status quo of East-West relations and NATO, and the pro-détente forces. The West German government is actively engaged in supporting Soviet reforms and opposes the idea of preserving the status quo of NATO. Genscher has called for a new approach to East-West relations in Europe. These appeals are also linked to such notions as the "common European house" (discussed briefly in Chapter 10) and the work of the CSCE (the main topic of Chapter 11).

In the West German view, in contrast to Howard's Atlanticist view, a failure of efforts to modernize the Soviet economy and transform Soviet security policy would lead to a worsening of the already serious economic crisis in the East. Affected in turn would be the future of West European economic adjustment, political cooperation with the East, the expansion of the Common Market, and the international competitiveness of West European industries in the years to come. The sizable credits granted the Soviet Union by British, French, and other West European banks suggest that the Atlanticist obstructionist view is unrealistic and inconsistent.

Alexander Bovin's view that the Soviet Union is not opposed to the

U.S. military presence in Europe leads to the following conclusions when considered against the backdrop of the two security models discussed in this book and the foregoing analysis of the new Soviet military and political strategy:

1. If U.S. policy were to be reforged according to the post-containment model of security based on disarmament and cooperation, the Soviets, acting on the premises of their present policy, would not have an interest in the United States decoupling from Western Europe.

2. If Western Europe were to move expeditiously in the direction of a common security policy, while the United States rejected such a move and attempted to obstruct European détente, a lessening of U.S. influence in Western Europe might be welcomed by the Soviets. But this would be at best a damage-limiting outcome, because it would reflect and promote a general worsening of West-West and West-East relations and therefore would not serve Soviet restructuring interests or correspond to the Soviet aim of placing East-West relations on a new, cooperative basis.

3. A cooperative model of security in East and West based on the withdrawal of U.S. troop contingents from central Europe does not necessarily mean the United States would reduce its involvement in Europe. A withdrawal of U.S. troops roughly in tandem with a withdrawal of Soviet troops from Eastern Europe could, on the contrary, open the door to a new, more intense demilitarizing involvement of the United States and the Soviet Union in Europe without lessening the security of either. This point will be discussed in more detail in Chapter 11 in the context of the CSCE.

The fact that the Federal Republic and the Soviet Union share the same view concerning the need for a shift to the principles of the post-containment model of security is a potent demonstration of support for this shift as necessary for East and West to solve their respective and shared policy dilemmas. Yet there remains substantial opposition within the government and military bureaucracy in both countries and throughout both military alliances to such a move. This complexly polarized constellation between East and West—and in both East and West—reflects the nature of this transition as a historic interface between two eras and two antagonistic policy models, both of which cannot be maintained simultaneously over the long term. If the United States, for example, adopts a generally passive or negative position toward Soviet reform, while West Germany and other European governments pursue a policy of active support and cooperation with Moscow, the problems of a serious political-economic divergence of U.S. from West European policies will tend to grow correspondingly.

This chapter has shown that the evolution of East-West relations in the wake of the INF Treaty has been variously interpreted with the assumptions of both the postwar and the post-containment models of security. The competition between these two models in the West is reflected in the sharply diverging views of the reform process in the Soviet Union and its meaning for the future of NATO.

The interpretations that assume the postwar model of security tend to view the new East-West détente in the zero-sum terms of Soviet gains in military and political strength versus U.S. losses. In this perspective, Soviet gains would include achieving greater access to Western dual-use technology to upgrade the Soviet military arsenal; splitting the Atlantic Alliance; and increasing Soviet global influence.

The interpretations of the post-INF environment based on the assumptions of the post-containment model of security project a very different picture of possible positive-sum outcomes. In this perspective, East-West security would not be diminished by greater and more open East-West relations but qualitatively increased. Enhanced political and economic cooperation and disarmament would give both systems mutually vested interests in structures of nonmilitary security in which military-political forms of security can be progressively reduced. Military competition in such an environment could be harmoniously phased out as a regulatory mechanism of the East-West conflict as arms racing and military-technological competition revealed themselves to be increasingly incompatible with the normalization of cooperative economic and political relations. The next chapter explores this view of East-West relations in the context of current developments of East-West détente.

Notes

1. Alexei Arbatov, "Military Doctrines," in USSR Academy of Sciences and the Institute of World Economy and International Relations, *Disarmament and Security, 1987 Yearbook* (Moscow: Novosti, 1988), pp. 201–224.
2. Ibid.
3. Ibid.
4. Ibid.
5. Ibid.
6. Michael MccGwire, "Rethinking War: The Soviets and European Security," *Brookings Review*, Vol. 6, No. 2, Spring 1988, pp. 3–12; see also in this context Bernard Trainor, "Soviet Arms Doctrine in Flux: An Emphasis on the Defense," *New York Times*, March 7, 1988.
7. Robert Legvold, "Gorbachev's New Approach to Conventional Arms Control," *Forum* (Harriman Institute), Vol. 1, No. 1, January 1988. The quoted material is taken from A. Kokoshin and V. Larionov, "Kurskaya bitva v svete sovremennoi oboronitelnoi doktriny," *MEMO*, No. 8, August 1987, p. 32–40. Legvold points out that Kokoshin is a deputy director of the Institute for the Study of the USA and Canada and that General Larionov had a substantial role

in drafting the Sokolovsky volumes on military strategy in the 1960s. Gorbachev has described the Soviet notion of strategic sufficiency as follows: "It is our feeling that armaments must be lowered to a level of reasonable sufficiency, that is, to a level essential for defence only. It is time to make the necessary amendments in the strategic concepts of both military alliances for defensive purposes." Mikhail Gorbachev, *Perestroika: New Thinking for Our Country and the World* (Moscow, 1987), as cited in Arbatov, op. cit.

8. Legvold, ibid.

9. Legvold, ibid. The statement from Shevardnadze is cited from *Pravda*, September 25, 1987, p. 4. The Karpov statement is from Victor Karpov, *TASS*, October 12, 1987.

10. Eduard Shevardnadze, "An Unconditional Requirement—Turn to Fix the Economy" (Speech given July 4, 1987), reprinted in Foreign Broadcast Information Service (FBIS), *Daily Report*, Soviet Union, p. 49, as cited in Alan Sherr, "The Links Between Soviet Foreign Policy and Domestic Economic Policy" (Paper at the Conference on "Superpower Commerce: Economic Relations with the USSR and U.S. National Interests," Center for Foreign Policy Development, Brown University, December 2, 1988, hereafter CFPD Conference). For an overview of Soviet economic reform measures, see the special issue on this subject of *Soviet Economy*, Vol. 3, No. 4, October–December 1987, in particular, Abel Aganbegyan, "Basic Directions of Perestroyka," pp. 277–297, and Leonard Abalkin, "The New Model of Economic Management," pp. 298–313. These are transcriptions of oral presentations with roundtable discussions in which Soviet experts from the Brookings Institution also participated.

11. Shevardnadze, in Sherr, ibid.

12. Sherr, ibid.

13. Eduard Shevardnadze, paraphrased in *Izvestia*, July 27, 1988, p. 4., as cited in John Quigley, "The New Soviet Perception of the U.S.-U.S.S.R. Rivalry" (Paper delivered at CFPD Conference).

14. Ligachev's position has been summarized by Roy Medvedev, a dissident historian, as follows:

> On his own Ligachev represents the union of the old and the new.
> . . . He is opposed to corruption, alcoholism and parasitism.
> However, he believes in order imposed by the party by dint of
> declarations and wants to keep the country under the CPSU's close
> control—especially the press and television, which he believes
> should broadcast only political programs. It is clear that many
> conservatives and the entire apparatus have a natural defender in him.

La Republica, July 3–4, 1988, cited in Patrick Cockburn, "Misreading the Obstacles to Reform," *World Policy Journal*, Vol. 6, No. 1, Winter 1988–89, pp. 81–106.

15. E. K. Ligachev, "For What Needs to be Done" (Speech at the Gor'kii Region organization), *Pravda*, August 6, 1988; Bill Keller, "Gorbachev Deputy Criticizes Policy," *New York Times*, August 7, 1988, as cited in Quigley, op. cit.

16. Axel Lebahn, "Politische und wirtschaftliche Auswirkungen der Perestrojka auf die Sowjetunion sowie auf ihre Beziehungen zu Osteuropa und zum Westen," *Aussenpolitik*, Vol. 39, No. 2, pp. 107–124; Sherr, op. cit.

17. Hans-Hermann Höhmann, *Economics and Politics in "Perestroika":
Developments, Interdependencies, Western Perceptions*, Report of the
Bundesinstitut für ostwissenschaftliche und internationale Studien, No. 21,
1988, p. 41.
18. Lebahn, op. cit.
19. Alan Sherr, *Socialist-Capitalist Joint Ventures in the USSR: Law and
Practice* (Briefing Paper No. 1, Center for Foreign Policy Development, May
1988), p. 7.
20. Ibid.
21. Ed Hewett, "The Foreign Economic Factor in *Perestroika*," *Forum*,
Vol. 1, No. 8, August 1988; Steven Rosefielde, "The New Soviet Trade
Mechanism: East-West Trade Expansion Possibilities Under Perestroika" (Paper
delivered at CFPD Conference).
22. Hewett, ibid.
23. Ibid. Although not accepted by either organization, the Soviet Union
did receive limited representation at the meeting of the Pacific Economic
Cooperation Council (PECC) in Ottawa in 1986 and Osaka in 1988. The
Soviets also announced in 1987 that they had joined the Common Fund for
Commodities, which is sponsored by the United Nations Conference on Trade
and Development (UNCTAD) to create funds for stabilizing prices of key
commodities.
24. Ibid. Hewett describes the importance of the Soviet demarche to join
GATT as follows:

GATT is an agreement among market economies to actively pursue
and protect liberal trade rules among themselves in order to promote
free trade. It has been a powerful force in the postwar reductions in
tariff barriers to trade, and an on-going venue for reductions of non-
tariff restrictions on imports (quantitative restrictions, unnecessary
quality requirements for imports, etc.). GATT membership will be
important to the USSR if and when it develops a capacity to export
manufactured goods competitive on world markets, since it will need
to eliminate many tariff and non-tariff barriers targeted specifically
on Soviet or East-Bloc products.

25. Bernard May, "Normalisierung der Beziehungen zwischen der EG und
dem RGW," *Aus Politik und Zeitgeschichte*, No. 3, 1989, pp. 44–54.
26. May, ibid.
27. Ibid.
28. Economic development under Gorbachev has produced increases
in output, but it has had little success in achieving the qualitative changes
to resolve the Soviet Union's major economic difficulties. Economic indicators
have been mixed. Although economic growth accelerated in 1986, it
was followed by a slowdown in 1987. "Die Perestrojka greift noch nicht,"
DIW Wochenbericht, No. 33, August 1988, pp. 425–433. In the first
nine months of 1988, output increased and national income rose at 4.7
percent over the same period in 1987. But because wages in many enterprises
rose faster than productivity, monetary income continued to exceed available
goods and services. Domestic output has not risen sufficiently to meet
demand, nor has a new price system been introduced. The dissatisfaction
of Soviet consumers over shortages, long lines, and the poor quality of

consumer goods remains unresolved and a serious problem for the Soviet leadership. At the same time, the government deficit has been growing, amounting to 70 billion rubles (about 8 percent of the gross national product) in 1987. Ibid. Exports and imports have also fallen, despite the fact that increasing exports is a major priority of Soviet economic restructuring. The expansion of oil and gas industries in the 1970s made the Soviet Union one of the world's largest oil exporters; gas and oil accounted for more than half of the Soviet Union's hard-currency earnings. The decline in the price of oil cost the Soviet state 40 billion rubles ($64 billion) in lost revenues between 1985 and 1988. Cockburn, op. cit. The loss of oil and gas revenues and the drop in the value of the dollar have not only reduced hard-currency earnings but have also severely cut into the benefits of the administrative reforms carried out during the 1980s. *DIW Wochenbericht* No. 33, op. cit.

29. Mikhail Gorbachev, "Speech at a Formal Meeting in Murmansk on October 1, 1987," in *Reprints from the Soviet Press*, Vol. 45, No. 9, November 15, 1987, pp. 5–35.

30. John Tedstrom, "Soviet Economic Restructuring and East-West Joint Ventures" (Paper delivered at CFPD conference). It should be pointed out that the Soviet program to shift resources out of defense into the civilian sector will not occur until the next five-year plan in 1991 because of fixed investment for arms production. Cockburn, op. cit.

31. Tedstrom, ibid.

32. Cockburn, op. cit.

33. Rosefielde, op. cit. As Hewett, op. cit., has noted:

Soviet enterprises can be confident that if they produce a product, no matter how low its quality and how high its price relative to the qualities and prices of similar products on world markets, Soviet customers will be forced to buy the product or go without. Central planning, as it has been implemented in the USSR, is institutionalized protectionism. It is equivalent, in a market economy, of placing prohibitively high tariffs on the importation of every foreign commodity which is also produced by domestic enterprises.

34. Hewett, ibid. Under the centralized trading system, the Ministry of Foreign Trade and its administrative subdivision, the specialized Foreign Trade Organizations, controlled international commerce. They determined the level and composition of trade; as Rosefielde points out, consumers were forbidden to participate.

35. On the distribution of economic inputs, Tedstrom points out: "In the broadest terms, there are three claimants to economic wealth: investment, consumption, and defense. The first two contribute to economic growth by, respectively, developing the industrial base and creating real labor incentives for consumers. In contrast, the third claimant tends to be a drag on economic growth. The choice of how much to devote to defense thus determines in part the growth strategy for the rest of the economy." John Tedstrom, "The Economics of Soviet Defense Spending," Radio Free Europe/Radio Liberty, September 5, 1988 (this is a revised version of Radio Liberty Supplement Vol. 36, No. 4, August 15, 1988).

36. Höhmann, op. cit.; Jerry Hough, "Gorbachev Consolidating Power,"

Problems of Communism, Vol. 36, No. 4, July-August 1987, pp. 21–43. The problems that the Soviet economic reforms are bringing in their wake are likely to include trade-offs between resources devoted to expanding exports on the one hand and satisfying consumer demand on the other. Rosefielde, op. cit., has pointed to microeconomic dislocations that would result from the absence of automatic price adjustment mechanisms and resulting supply bottlenecks.

37. Dov Zakheim, "Perestroika, Trade and U.S. National Security" (Paper presented at the CFPC Conference).

38. Joseph Nye and Whitney MacMillan, *How Should America Respond to Gorbachev's Challenge?* (Special Report, Institute for East-West Security Studies, New York, 1987); Harry Harding and Ed Hewett, "Reforms in China and the Soviet Union" (Roundtable), *Brookings Review*, Vol. 6, No. 2, Spring 1988, pp. 13–18; Thane Gustafson and Dawn Mann, "Gorbachev's Next Gamble," *Problems of Communism*, Vol. 36, No. 4, July-August 1987, pp. 1–20; Richard Tucker, "Where Is the Soviet Union Headed?" *World Policy Journal*, Vol. 36, No. 4, Spring 1987, pp. 179–206.

39. MccGwire, op. cit.

40. Ibid.

41. Michael Howard, "The Gorbachow Challenge and the Defence of the West," *Survival*, Vol. 30, No. 6, November/December 1988, pp. 483–492.

42. Ibid.

43. Ibid.

44. Ibid.

45. Ibid.

46. Ibid.

47. Ibid.

48. Ibid.

49. Ibid.

50. Hans-Dietrich Genscher, "Towards a Strategy for Progress," in Bill Bradley et al., *Implications of Soviet New Thinking* (New York: Institute for East-West Security Studies, 1987), pp. 33–47.

51. Helmut Kohl, "For a Comprehensive Defense Strategy" (Speech at the International Wehrkunde Conference, translation of Advanced Text, February 6, 1988), in *Statements and Speeches*, Vol. 11, No. 5, February 10, 1988.

52. Ibid.; Genscher, "Towards a Strategy," op. cit.

53. See in this context Robbin Laird, "Soviet Strategy Toward Western Europe: Implications for the Post-INF Environment" (Paper delivered at the Conference on "Domestic and Foreign Policy Objectives at the End of the Reagan Era" at the Friedrich Ebert Stiftung, Bonn, November 13–16, 1988). See also Robbin Laird, "The Soviet Union and the Western Alliance: Elements of an Anti-Coalition Strategy," in Robbin Laird, ed., *Soviet Foreign Policy Today* (New York: Academy of Political Science, 1987), pp. 106–118.

54. Jerry Hough, "The Europeanization of Gorbachev," *New York Times*, April 8, 1988.

55. FBIS, September 15, 1985, p. G-2; FBIS, July 1, 1986, p. AA-10; Bovin as cited in Laird 1988, op. cit.

56. Genscher, "Towards a Strategy," op. cit.

57. Ibid., p. 37–38.

58. Ibid., p. 44.

59. See Alexander Yanov, "Why We Should Root for Gorbachev," *New York Times*, April 19, 1988; Zdanek Mlynar, "Das einsame Rennen gegen die Uhr," *Die Zeit*, Vol. 42, No. 12, March 12-13, 1987.

CHAPTER 10

The New Détente

Although proceeding under diverse national conditions, the reform dynamics of perestroika, glasnost, and democratization are evident in different stages of development and rates of advancement in all countries of Eastern Europe. A severe political and economic crisis throughout Eastern Europe has led to reform efforts to demonopolize the role of the state in the management of the economy and to move beyond a one-party system. As in the Soviet Union, this reform transition is inseparable from a process of opening to the West and, as I suggest in this chapter, illustrates the political-economic dimension of the uneven movement away from the postwar order of security.

Several empirical examples of this shift in Europe indicate that cooperation between Eastern and Western actors is an essential component in the East European political reform process. The example of Poland will be used to show that the cooperative involvement of East and West has been important in the efforts to achieve the historic Polish reforms of April 1989. I will suggest that the "system-interdependent" aspect of such cooperation in Eastern Europe tends to create the conditions for positive-sum outcomes of interaction, which in turn create an environment in which political-military barriers can be more expeditiously dismantled.

I will also expand on a point made in earlier chapters—that the competition in Europe between policy approaches based on the postwar and the post-containment models of security is resulting in a clearly visible net trend in the direction of deepening East-West economic-political cooperation. The 1988 treaty between the European Community (EC) and the Council for Mutual Economic Assistance (COMECON) to normalize relations will be used as an example in this context.

The following additional examples will be briefly discussed to illustrate the trend of growing East-West cooperation: (1) the deepening economic and scientific cooperation between the two Germanies; (2) Franco-Soviet economic and technological collaboration; (3) Soviet-Western joint ventures; (4) the evolving West German economic-political partnership with the Soviet

Union; and (5) the West German Foreign Ministry's notion of the "common European house."

The Example of Poland

The Polish reform agreements of 1989, aptly referred to by the communist government at the time as a new "social contract," included the following measures:[1]

1. In the general elections of June 1989, the Polish Communist Party would compete for the first time with political opposition groups. These would include citizen initiatives and political clubs able to gather the minimum 5,000 signatures necessary to place their candidates on the ballot. The opposition elements were guaranteed 35 percent of the Sejm, the Polish Parliament, and were elected according to the principles of free elections. For the first time in postwar Poland, groups of all political persuasions ranging from left socialists to right anticommunists were able to put up candidates of their choice. The official Communist Party, the Polish Democratic Party, and the Peasants' Party were guaranteed 65 percent, or 460 seats, of the Sejm. Although these official groupings thus would remain the most powerful party bloc, the official communist sector of the government could no longer expect to win all decisions in the Sejm, not to mention all political debates. In this sense, the state's political monopoly has been significantly reduced. The defeat of the Communist Party in the elections set the stage in August 1989 for the appointment of Tadeusz Mazowiecki of Solidarity as the first noncommunist prime minister in Poland since 1947. This occurred following the decision of the Democratic Party and the Peasant's Party to support Solidarity in the Sejm in the debate on forming a new government. Their sudden desertion of the Communist Party gave the opposition a majority of 57 percent, making possible the first democratic coalition government in a Warsaw Pact state. It was decided that the government would be a grand coalition, with the Communists retaining only key cabinet posts such as defense, foreign policy, and internal affairs.

2. A new upper house, the Polish Senate, was set up and is composed of 98 members. The Sejm and the Senate together form the Polish National Assembly, which elects the Polish president.

3. The Polish trade union Solidarity and its sister organization, Solidarity-Agriculture, were legalized. Under the new arrangement, the official union, the OPZZ, set up in 1982 to replace Solidarity and with a membership of 7 million members, will compete with Solaridity for shop-floor control.

4. Approximately 30 new laws designed to radically restructure the Polish economy were passed. The reform, for which Hungary served as the

model, ended the total control of the Communist Party over the economy by incorporating elements of market competition.

5. Possession and exchange of foreign currency, formerly prohibited, were also approved.[2] It was expected that the new currency laws would result in investment of a considerable portion of the $12 billion in U.S. currency notes held in private hands by Poles, monies formerly inaccessible to the official Polish economy for the purpose of investment or for taxation. It was predicted at the time of the reforms that this currency measure could play a significant role in reducing the Polish foreign trade deficit and spurring investment of Poland's dollar wealth.

6. The wages of 85 percent of the work force were indexed to inflation. In return, the newly legalized Solidarity union accepted a limited right to strike and pledged to settle labor-management conflicts through negotiations. A commission was also set up composed of union and state representatives to formulate a price-and-incomes policy. It was also agreed that Solidarity would solicit the cooperation of Western governments and international organizations by encouraging them to contribute to the Polish recovery effort.

The 1989 reforms became possible in part as a result of the Soviet reforms and the tentative shift in East-West relations in the direction of disarmament and détente. These trends provided the Polish government and the opposition with the legitimizing conditions and a propitious international climate for their far-reaching reform process. This interpretation is suggested by the fact that many of the restructuring measures, although already blueprinted in the early 1980s, remained a dead letter until 1989.

To understand the events that led to the new "social contract," it is necessary to survey briefly the collapse of the Polish economy in the early 1980s and the withdrawal of support by the majority of the population from the Jaruzelski government.[3]

Ruinous Debt and the Economic Stalemate

Between 1972 and 1975, industrial production in Poland was growing at an average rate of 10 percent. Agricultural production and real wages were also increasing, though this growth was generated largely by untied international loans. Gross Polish debt grew from $1.6 billion to $8 billion during this same period, while the trade deficit grew from $0.2 billion to $3.3 billion.[4] A U.S. congressional study described the reasons for the failure to produce the export growth that had been expected to fuel the Polish economy as follows:

The export-oriented projects were not generating the anticipated results because of trouble in applying Western technology, choices of investment projects that proved unproductive, and the Western recession of 1974–75 which cut demand for Polish exports. Furthermore, increasing diversion of Western credits from capital investment, applications to raw materials and other goods contributed to the escalating trade imbalance.[5]

Poland's Foreign Trade Ministry estimated in 1986 that during the period 1971–1981 only one-third of financed investment was used for modernization and the rest went to meet domestic consumption.[6] Living standards rose sharply but at the cost of increasing inflation, as planners lost control of consumption outlays. Serious disequilibriums developed, with a wide gap between purchasing power and the value of goods available.[7]

In summarizing the results of poor Polish economic planning, Jean Boone and John Hardt of the Congressional Research Service (CRS) note that

Mistakes in policy decisions in Poland that allowed for too much investment in import-intensive projects, the neglect of agriculture, and lack of discipline imposed on credit, consumption and living standards all played a role in the mounting crisis. Instead of improving the feed grain conversion ratio for meat production, more corn was imported; instead of improving mining or energy efficiency, more inefficient coal mines were opened; instead of tying each new project financed by Polish localities to some central financial plan that would include realistic Western market research, new credit commitments were easily and independently made. As the Foreign Trade Ministry report notes, "the economic reforms—necessary to base investment and production decisions on economic criteria—were shelved."[8]

At the same time, dialogue between Solidarity and the government deteriorated. The ensuing economic-political collapse of the Polish economy following the declaration of martial law in December 1981 resulted in a drastic fall in output—25 percent between 1981 and 1982. A comprehensive economic reform program was put together and approved by the Sejm in order to reverse the massive rejection of the government by the majority of the population. Reforms included elements of decentralization, price flexibility, greater enterprise autonomy, and the support of private-sector activities in agriculture and the service sector. But the program failed to receive the political mass support necessary for its implementation.[9] Even in those areas where reform measures were able to be implemented, they were generally too weak to be effective.

The declaration of martial law also resulted in the decision of the United States to declare sanctions, while the West European countries, in a more restrained reaction, removed economic support necessary for the success of the government's reform package. Although the Communist Party experi-

enced a radical decline in membership in the 1980–1986 period, the opposi-
tional forces, in part supported by the Catholic Church, expanded. But this
growth was not sufficient to overcome the social and economic stalemate,
which was reinforced by the support both sides received from their respective
international allies: the Jaruzelski government from the pre-Gorbachev Soviet
leadership and Solidarity from major Western governments and elements of
the international financial community. The impasse was destined to continue
as long as efforts toward a more open dialogue and a normalization of
relations between Poland and the United States and the international financial
community were not forthcoming. Furthermore, the regime refused to agree
to the opposition's demands to surrender its total monopoly of political
power.

Between 1986 and 1988, some positive steps toward political
normalization were taken, including trade initiatives, an amnesty for political
prisoners, and the establishment of a national consultative council to enhance
social dialogue. In addition, the government was able to improve its dialogue
with the Church, the work force, and Solidarity—interaction that was
essential in paving the way to the 1989 agreements. A turning point occurred
as the different domestic and international actors in East and West involved in
the Polish political drama moved toward a consensus that reconciled key
Eastern and Western interests. Boone and Hardt have made the following
breakdown of the domestic and international principal actors in the Polish
drama:[10]

• *The Polish state* had to implement a new plan for achieving intensive
growth based on the reform of the economic mechanism and the creation of a
market sector. This was to be combined with expanding exports to the West,
improving Polish terms of trade, and boosting hard-currency earnings. These
measures were expected to lead to better management of Poland's external
debt. On the political level, "socialist pluralism" had to be expanded by
greater decentralization and democratization of the political process, including
more political rights for individuals and organizations.

• *The work force and the majority of Polish society* were not willing to
participate in a recovery scheme without prior satisfaction of their reform
demands by the government. The recovery plan proposed by the opposition
included wide-ranging measures for genuine participation of worker and other
popular organizations in economic policymaking and representation of the
opposition in the Sejm and other political bodies of Polish society. This
program called on the government to make major, indeed historic, political
concessions, including the recognition of representative democratic
organizations, the renunciation of absolute one-party rule, and the
introduction of market mechanisms into the economy.

• *The international financial community* had an interest in pursuing a
policy of managing Poland's external debt through promotion of growth and

improving Poland's repayment conditions. For Western banks and the International Monetary Fund (IMF), this presupposed Poland's acceptance of conditionality requirements on economic performance, which were made the basis for providing Western credits necessary for economic recovery. But the regime could not guarantee the conditionality requirements as long as it did not have the support of the work force.

• *The United States*, which had been active in renewing dialogue with the Polish government in the middle 1980s and supporting popular reform forces, had an interest in removing discriminatory measures against Poland and initiating a new stage of cooperative U.S.-Polish relations. It undertook steps in this direction by adopting the policy of "active reengagement," with which it was able to continue a dialogue with the government yet remain supportive of the opposition's broad program for reform.

• Finally, *the Soviet Union* continued to encourage structural reforms throughout Eastern Europe in part to create an environment more favorable to Soviet restructuring. In this context, a precondition for the Polish agreements of 1989 was the coming to power of Gorbachev in 1985 and his radical change in Soviet policy toward Eastern Europe. In his speech November 2, 1987, commemorating the seventieth anniversary of the Bolshevik Revolution, Gorbachev outlined the model of "socialist pluralism" as the basis of the Soviet Union's relations with Eastern Europe:

> Accumulated experience makes it possible to do a better job of building relations among socialist countries on generally recognized principles. These principles include unconditional and complete equality. They include the responsibility of the ruling Party for affairs in its state, and patriotic service to its people. They include concern for the common cause of socialism. They include respect for one another, a serious attitude towards what has been achieved and tested by one's friends, and voluntary, diversified co-operation. They include strict observance of all the principles of peaceful co-existence. The practice of socialist internationalism is grounded in these principles. . . . The world of socialism rises before us now in all its national and social variations. This is good and useful. We have become convinced that unity does not mean being identical or uniform. We have also become convinced that socialism does not and cannot have a model against which all are compared.[11]

Poland and East-West Realignment

The need for mutual input and flexible cooperation of the actors just described in the reforms of 1989 can be summed up as follows: Given the political gridlock of the Polish economy and the problem of debt, Poland needed additional credits from the IMF. But new credits for economic restructuring would have been difficult to obtain and risked being ineffective without the cooperation of the work force and population in a common effort to revitalize and stabilize the economy. Required, therefore, was a major compromise to end the de facto noncooperation of the work force vis-à-vis the government. Cooperation had not been forthcoming on the scale necessary to overcome the social stalemate, and it became clear that this was not going to change without unprecedented concessions on the part of the government to reduce the state's role—that is, introduce greater democratization and popular participation that would shrink the party's power in the running of the economy and in Polish society as a whole. These reforms were granted in March 1989. Similarly, the cooperation of the United States in its policy of active reengagement, including renewed support for IMF credits, was linked to acceptance by the Jaruzelski regime of political and human rights reforms.[12] Last, the implementation of reform was unlikely to be fully effective without the cooperation of the Soviet Union in an environment of glasnost, perestroika, and democratization. The United States and the Soviet Union out of their respective interests in Poland thus became economic-political partners in the Polish reform experiment because each had developed an important stake in its success.

Boone and Hardt, writing before the 1989 breakthrough, emphasized the watershed conditions that were operating in Poland and the role of East-West consensus in the reform process this way:

> What is clear about Poland's economic development is its past record—the poorest of any socialist economy in recent years. What is not clear, however, is the current policy commitment and what results it could achieve. *The uniqueness of Poland's dynamics suggests that the major actors can contribute to either gridlock or to fulfillment of a strategy for significant progress.* Therefore, the unique consensus among all key actors influencing Polish developments could take on considerable cumulative weight, if it results in a coordinated consensus policy that offers promise of improvement in Poland's economic prospects from the traps of indebtedness and stagnation.[13]

The nature of the "new social contract" of 1989 appears to confirm this analysis. As Poland moves beyond the phase of formal legalization and institutionalization of its reforms, their successful implementation will depend on the cooperation of the majority of Polish society, the dominant communist sectors of the government, the Soviet Union, Western Europe, and the United States. It will also depend on the future policies of the United States and the Soviet Union toward each other. The Polish reforms, like those in other East European countries, could be jeopardized or stillborn if the major global powers are unable to sustain and deepen their rapprochement. The example of Poland demonstrates that the transition from the postwar to the post-containment order based on détente and East-West economic interaction is necessarily linked to complex forms of East-West cooperation.

East-West Joint Ventures and Cooperation Initiatives

Agreements for trade and other collaborative projects in the fields of science and technology between East and West have markedly increased in the course of the new détente. Following are several examples of this trend.

The Two Germanies

The historic visit of East German Party Secretary Erich Honecker to West Germany in September 1987 was symptomatic of the accelerated pace of European détente.[14] Although the visit was marked by the expected airing of serious differences on a variety of issues, such as human rights and national sovereignty, this tension was overshadowed by the array of cooperation agreements signed in the course of Honecker's stay. These included an accord on reciprocal electricity deliveries and agreements to improve the Hanover-Berlin rail link; to examine border claims along the Elbe River; and to step up scientific cooperation in twenty-seven different projects ranging from physics and production technology to research on AIDS. It was announced that East Germany would become an associate member of the European research program EUREKA and that East German scholars and researchers would receive improved access to West German universities. Also agreed to were a number of joint projects aimed at reducing environmental damage along the common border, exchanging information on nuclear reactor safety, and improving radioactive waste disposal. Further steps were also announced to upgrade German-German travel, communication, and other forms of direct personal contacts.[15]

France and the Soviet Union

France's military-political support for U.S. and NATO military programs has not prevented it from taking up the Soviet Union's attractive offers for joint ventures and East-West scientific and technological cooperation. Barely ten months after the relevant Soviet legislation was passed, France was involved in twenty joint ventures with the Soviet Union.

Similarly, French-Soviet cooperation in space exploration has also expanded. In 1988 French and Soviet scientists conducted joint space photographic experiments in the framework of the Soviet-French Gamma and Granat projects.[16] The French Space Agency along with the U.S. National Aeronautics and Space Administration (NASA) took part in the Soviet-hosted Vega project to explore Venus and Halley's comet until the program's conclusion in 1986. The Soviet-French Vesta project, scheduled for 1994, will explore asteroids and comets.[17]

As already discussed in Chapter 9, the Soviet Union has registered 1000 joint ventures with East-West ownership and management.[18] These include the large $5–6 billion petrochemical project linking the Soviets with Montedison of Italy, Occidental Petroleum of the United States, and Marubeni of Japan.[19] There is a textile project with the Finnish firm Kati Miounti; a food-wrapping scheme with Volanpack of Hungary; a sawmill project with Taikuru Trading of Japan; a restaurant in Moscow with Thacker of India; a crane venture with Liebherr of Switzerland; and a shoe project with Salamander of West Germany.[20] The financial arrangements of Soviet joint ventures with Western companies vary: In some cases companies are permitted to transfer profits internationally and to maintain standard telephone, telefax, and telex links to the West. In other cases transfer of profits is not permitted. Although most of the 1000 joint ventures are still pending and may require lengthy negotiations to complete, the trend toward greater Soviet-Western economic cooperation on a profit-making basis is clearly evident.[21] The positive response of Western capital to the Soviet offers increased significantly when the Soviet Union eased its tax and export requirements. It was agreed that the 30-percent company tax would be first imposed after a two-year tax holiday.[22]

To facilitate joint ventures and other forms of economic interaction with the West, the Soviet Union is also in the process of reforming its banking system. Facilities have been created, for example, to provide credits, either in rubles or foreign currencies, for firms doing business with the West. The Soviet External Economy Bank and Gosbank have undertaken a major effort to coordinate with Western banks and to formulate common lending policies for firms involved in Soviet-Western joint ventures.[23] Examples include Soviet cooperation agreements with Crédit Lyonnais, Crédit Industriel et Commercial, and Eurobank for providing consultation and banking services for Soviet-French ventures set up in the Soviet Union.[24] According to Soviet banking authorities, protocols on cooperation with French, Finnish, Italian, and West German banks have been signed. These establish the basis for analyzing the performance rating and financial standing of prospective partners, developing financing schemes, and analyzing the lending and currency risks involved in export-import operations.[25]

Another area of intensified Soviet activity vis-à-vis the West has been space exploration for commercial and scientific purposes.[26] The Vega program previously mentioned involves scientists from nine countries and will launch two unmanned space stations. The goal, according to the Soviet Space Planning Commission, is to deploy in space an "astronomical window" to Mars.[27] This is the first step in a larger project to launch an international program to send men and women to Mars by 2020.[28] The Soviets have also emphasized their interest in foreign participation, pointing out that NASA has an agreement with its Soviet counterpart that will allow the United States to participate in the preparatory project to send robots to Mars to retrieve soil samples.[29]

COMECON

The policy watershed in Eastern Europe is inseparable from the two sides of the economic crisis in communist, state-managed economies. Eastern Europe, like the Soviet Union, is in the throes of deepening economic difficulties stemming from the decline of economic-political structures inherited from the pre-Gorbachev era that can no longer be militarily, economically, or politically sustained.[30] Their advanced decline and tendential collapse are reflected in the further deterioration of living standards; slow and stagnating growth rates; worsening terms of trade; intensifying problems in translating scientific and technological advances into internationally competitive products and systems; and in the reform movements that in different forms and stages of development exist in all East European countries. These tendencies have generated power struggles between political old guards still in power and the new democratic elite and popular groups that have been gaining influence and championing, in different degrees, experimental forms of perestroika, glasnost, and democratization. These reform efforts have in common the establishment of qualitatively closer ties to Western economies.

The economic problems of Eastern Europe and the Soviet Union are mirrored in the structural crisis of COMECON.[31] Unlike the European Community, COMECON is not a supranational organization with the authority to formulate collective policy. Coordination committees are its chief instrument for bilateral planning and policy recommendations. Individual COMECON members have not been willing to coordinate industrial, investment, or technology planning, which has placed severe limits on COMECON's ability to carry out the type of restructuring necessary for East European economies to overcome their severe economic and technological bottlenecks. The result is underutilization of potential economies of scale and poor coordination of available resources. Despite dissatisfaction within COMECON over the low quality of traded goods, inefficient distribution, and the high price for Soviet energy and raw materials, there is little indication that these problems can be easily overcome, given COMECON's present structures and the absence of the collective political will on the part of its members to construct a more cooperative system.[32] Little has resulted from Gorbachev's repeated calls at official party congresses and COMECON meetings for the construction of a "common socialist market" and the free convertibility of the ruble. Difficulties in this context include the opposition of the GDR and Romania to the introduction of a new pricing system that would be based to a greater degree on world market prices and would allow price fluctuation in accordance with supply and demand. Such a system, according to its proponents, could replace the present framework of bureaucratically set prices based on the transfer ruble, which is a major obstacle to integration of COMECON economies in the world market. Creating a "common socialist market" would also require a majority decision of COMECON members, but no such consensus exists.[33]

An important example of efforts to accelerate collective technological development in COMECON is the "Complex Program for Scientific and Technological Progess to the Year 2000." Created in 1985 partly as a social-ist response to the West European EUREKA program, the Complex Program 2000 is designed to promote the development of new technologies and inno-vations to modernize COMECON economies; to accelerate the innovation process from basic research to development and commercialization of new products and systems; and to transform COMECON into a "technological community."[34] Industry is to be restructured, productivity raised, high-value exports promoted, and military parity vis-à-vis the West strengthened. The 93 individual programs cover the areas of computer technology, automation of industry, nuclear energy, new materials, and biotechnology.

The problems that the Complex Program must overcome to be successful overlap with those of COMECON previously discussed. They also include the fact that R&D in COMECON is highly inefficient in translating research results into developed systems;[35] the quality of products is low; and there is an absence of the administrative organs needed for an effective coordination of R&D policy.

The problems of COMECON and those of the Complex Program strongly suggest that solving the economic and technological bottlenecks existing in Eastern Europe will depend on the degree to which East-West cooperation can be qualitatively intensified. Proponents of cooperation say it could provide Eastern economies with Western managerial and technological skills and innovations and introduce a competitive élan between West-East joint ventures located in the East and indigenous state-supported or private firms. This arrangement would replicate the Soviet East-West joint venture strategy discussed in Chapter 9 and many of the reforms already developed in Hungary.

Prospects of the Eastern Market

The Eastern reform programs are linked to the economic potential for Western firms of the emerging East European and Soviet market with its roughly 400 million consumers. The prospect for new outlets for Western exporters is reflected, for example, in the fact that although the Federal Republic is the largest Western trading partner of the Soviet Union, its Osthandel (West European trade with COMECON's European members and the Soviet Union) amounts to approximately 2 percent of its total exports.[36]

West German exports to Switzerland alone amount to three times as much as those to the Soviet Union. West German Foreign Minister Genscher has underlined the benefits of greater East-West economic activity, pointing out that the West, for its part, "would obtain access to a huge economic area, a huge market for its products, which, if mobilized, could stimulate the growth of the world economy as a whole."[37] Despite the slow development of the Soviet market since the beginning of the Soviet restructuring program, it is predicted that a boom will slowly materialize.[38] This prediction can be linked to the planned large reductions in the Soviet military budget that will first take effect in the 1990s and free resources for nonmilitary investment. The resulting reallocation of budgetary resources is likely to affect both the Soviet and Eastern European economies.

The COMECON Accord with the European Community

After several decades of unresolved disagreement, COMECON and the EC signed the historic "Common Agreement" in June 1988, thereby opening official diplomatic relations between the two bodies.[39] In addition, Hungary, Romania, and Czechoslovakia have also negotiated bilateral agreements with the European Community.[40]

The Common Agreement was the result of several phases of negotiations. During the COMECON-EC talks between 1978 and 1980, four areas of possible cooperation received special attention:[41] economic prognoses, statistics, norms and standards, and environmental protection. Economic cooperation was understood to include not only exchanging information and data but also exploring possibilities of harmonizing statistical and industrial norms and standards; improving the transsystem availability of statistics; and eliminating methodological and other research-related disparities in statistical analysis that have inhibited East-West trade.[42]

In 1979 the first meeting of East and West European official representatives responsible for environmental questions convened in Geneva in accordance with the Helsinki Final Act of 1975. The session concluded with the signing of a general statement on East-West transborder air pollution.[43] The accord provided a basis for East-West cooperation in monitoring the extent, sources, and geographical spread of migrant pollutants and laid the groundwork for future work on cooperative East-West norms that would limit the pollution of the atmosphere, waterways, and oceans.

Despite the importance of these advances, the political breakthrough that opened the way to a new era in European East-West economic relations had to await a changed Soviet policy regarding COMECON. In June 1985 Gorbachev reversed the traditional Soviet policy of hostility against the European Community and Soviet insistence on controlling the trading relations of East European economies with the West, thus opening the way to normalizing relations.[44] In elaborating the EC's position on the new

Soviet approach, an EC official pointed out: "It is not normal that 130 nations are accredited here and our closest European neighbors are a blank spot on our map."[45] The Federal Republic had been the strongest and most active supporter of normalization, but England and France, though less enthusiastic, also approved the move. The agreement gave the green light to official diplomatic and economic relations between the EC and COMECON as international organizations; it also encouraged official interaction at other levels—between states, between firms, and between chambers of commerce.[46] The treaty thus put into place a structural framework for commercial agreements in most areas of mutual economic interest.

The normalization of relations with the European Community may help COMECON states obtain much-needed Western capital, technology, and labor skills needed to overcome serious shortages and worsening debt problems. Added to the structural problems of the economy have been the fall in oil prices and the drop in the exchange value of the dollar.[47] Because of lower Soviet hard-currency earnings from oil and gas exports and the dollar's weakening, the Soviet Union's ability to assist its COMECON partners has been significantly reduced. Here it is also relevant that lower Soviet hard-currency earnings have also increased the burden of Soviet debt service on foreign obligations.

The West German–Soviet Economic Partnership

The visit of West German Chancellor Helmut Kohl to Moscow in October 1988 marked a significant deepening of West German–Soviet cooperation. The agreements that were signed reflect the political and economic support of the Federal Republic for the Soviet reform process and for creating a strong, long-term West German–Soviet partnership.

Among the results of the Kohl visit were the following:[48]

- An agreement on cooperation on environmental protection
- The first Soviet–West German cultural cooperation agreement, covering initially the period 1988–1989
- An agreement to inform each other promptly when a nuclear accident occurs in a Soviet or West German nuclear power plant
- An agreement to ensure against conflict in international waters
- An agreement between the West German Ministry for Food, Agriculture, and Forests and the Soviet State Committee for the Agro-Industrial Complex to promote cooperation among corporations, companies, and organizations active in food production industries
- An agreement between the West German Ministry for Research and Technology and the Soviet Academy of Sciences concerning scientific-technical cooperation in the area of research into the peaceful uses of space

Also established was a political forum that would meet regularly. The West Germans will also actively participate in the modernization of Soviet manufacturing industries. Additional agreements either signed or negotiated included plans for building a major West German trade center in Moscow; a project to create a joint expert commission to work out a juridical framework for protection of long-term investments; an accord for on-the-job training in the Federal Republic for Soviet business managers, skilled workers, technicians, and other personnel; and an agreement to undertake a feasibility study for constructing a major industrial park in the Soviet Union that would be built with West German expertise and provide Soviet personnel with on-the-job training for operating the facility. The two governments also agreed to exchange cultural institutes and to consider the offer (since accepted) of the West German art collector Peter Ludwig to build a museum of modern art in Moscow. Extensive agreements were also made in the areas of scientific exchange programs; student and pupil exhanges; setting up an annual discussion group on information and communication and other technology issues; cooperation on humanitarian questions; the return from West Germany of the city archives of Reval/Tallien to their original Soviet places of origin; and finally, an agreement to work together in the fight against international terrorism and drug trafficking.[49]

A Common European House

The evolving West German–Soviet partnership reflected in these agreements is also linked to the assumption that the unification of the European Common Market will alter Western Europe's relationship to Eastern Europe and the Soviet Union. Genscher, for example, views the growth of the European Community in the larger framework opened up by the evolving Soviet and Eastern European rapprochement with the West.[50] He links the growth of the European Community to the construction of a "common European house," in which the replacement of military by nonmilitary forms of security will fundamentally reshape the East-West relationship:

> The manifold forms of cooperation will determine the architecture of the peaceful order in Europe, or as it also can be termed, the common European house. The ensuing interdependence will enhance mutual confidence and make for greater stability. This new order must not be characterized by fences, but by open doors, by freedom of movement for people, ideas and goods, as well as respect for human rights.
>
> One of the pillars of the European structure is and will remain the European Community oriented towards openness and cooperation. We know: Europe is more than the European Community. President Mitterrand put this so impressively in his historic speech in Aachen in 1987. As a result of increasing cooperation, of genuine détente and

disarmament, the military elements will lose significance in the West-East relationship, whereas others—political, economic, ecological and cultural cooperation—will gain in importance. Thanks to this development, West and East will derive fresh potential which can be used not for armament but for the advancement of their own societies and for cooperation with the developing countries.[51]

Conclusions

The Polish reforms of 1989 reflect the evolving, uneven transition from the postwar model of security based on East-West military-technological arms racing to the post-containment model of security based on détente and East-West cooperation. The Polish reforms are a particularly clear example of the mutual and interdependent interests of both the United States and the Soviet Union in the transformation of Poland into a "socialist market economy" and "socialist pluralist" political system. Eastern and Western participation was indispensable in the complex political process that led to the Polish reforms of 1989. This participation also demonstrates the highly vulnerable and tenuous character of the recovery process and the need for stability in East-West relations to buttress the Polish reforms and make them irreversible.

It is evident that East-West normalization of economic-political relations cannot be accomplished without moving more resolutely in the direction of the post-containment model of security. In this context, it is generally agreed that a failure of the Polish experiment, as Solidarity leaders and others have warned, could lead to a return to political instability, further economic deterioration, possible revocation of reforms, and a remilitarization of political rule.[52] This would result in a serious crisis not only for the future of Poland but also for the reform process throughout Eastern Europe. Poland has thus become a crucial test case for East European and Soviet reform and the ability of the West to participate in the Eastern recovery process.

Like the Polish reform process, the EC-COMECON treaty of 1988 reflects the West's expanding stake in the success of perestroika, glasnost, and democratization throughout Eastern Europe and the Soviet Union.

The 1988 agreements between the European Community and COMECON also illustrate the uneven, conflicting nature of the transition to a new paradigm of security. On the one hand, the states of the European Community and COMECON are militarily ranged against one another as "enemies" in NATO and the Warsaw Pact. On the other hand, the 1988 agreements have formally normalized economic relations, making the members of the two military alliances into prospective economic partners. This dynamic mismatch suggests that if economic relations continue to advance more rapidly than security relations—which will probably be the case—the call will grow louder for more expeditiously dismantling East-West military and political barriers and reaching agreement on common disarmament goals. The military standoff of NATO and the Warsaw Pact and the many restrictions on East-West cooperation that are linked to existing postwar military structures will tend to become increasingly impractical—if not serious obstacles to further normalization of East-West relations. Impediments exist, such as the many security export controls on dual-use high technology; as discussed in Chapter 8, such controls are designed to prevent exporting to COMECON many types of advanced technology that are in fact necessary for economic modernization. It should also be noted in this regard that the 1988 EC-COMECON treaty and the bilateral treaties between the EC and individual East European economies are aimed precisely at reducing such trade barriers. These accords could thus create an area of policy divergence between Western Europe and the United States.

It is evident that the evolution of economic relationships provides a fulcrum for demilitarizing East-West relations. The risks of military aggression of one side against the other can be reduced if both sides develop positive-sum, vested interests in maintaining and deepening economic intercourse and interpenetration. As mutual interests develop, a reversal of the process of reform would violate the interests of both sides. Broadened economic relationships also tend naturally to spill over into other areas of cooperation—cultural, scientific, ecological, technological—which in turn pave the way to deepening economic relationships.

The EC-COMECON agreement has legitimized a framework that will allow West European states to situate themselves along a more complex East-West axis linked to the dynamic process of political, economic, and military change in Eastern Europe and the Soviet Union. As discussed in this chapter, West Germany's foreign policy is strongly opposed to any moves that could result in a reassertion of East-West arms racing and strongly supports the notion of increasing security by replacing military-political barriers with economic and other forms of East-West cooperation. Although Genscher's position in this context has not been fully embraced by all sections of the cabinet, it enjoyed a majority popular consensus and became the prevailing position within the Kohl government. Genscher's foreign policy approach—determined in part by the Federal Republic's geographical position not merely between East and West but, if one includes West Berlin, in both East and West—can be described as an attempt to move beyond the traditional balance-of-power policies to an approach linked to the notion that large and small, Eastern and Western states can collectively construct the "common European house." This vision is of a Europe not threatened by either East or West because it will be anchored geographically and politically in both systems. At the same time, it will be in a position to forge its own greater relative autonomy in deciding its collective future. In such a configuration, Europe would be neither simply "between the blocs," nor a bloc unto itself, but a new kind of multistate formation—a complex cluster and transsystemic network of economic, political, and cultural relations that would promote a new order: greater East-West security policymaking based on fostering the model of common security, overcoming the division of Europe, and developing political-economic cooperation. Such a Europe is likely to create in the short and medium term its novel, albeit highly controversial, coherence within—and yet experimentally beyond—the status quo of the postwar bloc-to-bloc world.

Notes

1. "Reines Abenteuer," *Der Spiegel*, Vol. 43, No. 12, March 20, 1989; Christopher Bobinski, "Now Solidarity's Difficulties Begin," *Financial Times*, April 6, 1989.

2. *Der Spiegel*, ibid.

3. This section relies heavily on the analysis of the Polish reforms developed by Jean Boone and John Hardt. A short version is contained in "Poland's Reform, Renewal and Recovery," revised Paper (October 1988) presented at Conference on "New Dimensions of the Polish Economy," Wichita State University, Wichita, Kansas, October 1987. Their paper is based on the congressional report that they authored: U.S. Congress, *Poland's Renewal and U.S. Options: A Policy Reconnaissance* (Washington, D.C.: Government Printing Office, March 5, 1987).

4. U.S. Congress, ibid.

5. Ibid., p. 11.

6. Ibid.

7. Ibid.

8. Ibid. Boone and Hardt also point out that "at the same time, a policy of 'uncritical preference' for Poland by the West, including the United States, led to the proliferation of untied loans (loans not concerned with export projects) and an absence of external discipline on the escalation of debt." Ibid., p. 11.

9. Ibid., p. 14.

10. Ibid.

11. "October and Restructuring: The Revolution Continues," *Pravda*, November 3, 1987, as cited in Thomas Cynkin, "*Glasnost, Perestroika* and Eastern Europe," *Survival*, Vol. 30, No. 5, July/August 1988, pp. 310–331; Adam Michnik, "Polen steht vor der Wende," *Der Spiegel*, Vol. 42, No. 34, August 22, 1988.

12. Boone and Hardt, op. cit.; Michnik, ibid.

13. Ibid. (Author's emphasis.)

14. David Marsh, "East and West Germany to Improve Links," *Financial Times*, September 9, 1987.

15. Ibid.

16. Anatoly Reut, "Space Flight to Mars?" in "USSR: New Approach to Foreign Trade," *International Herald Tribune* (advertising section with articles on Soviet policy by Soviet scientists and journalists), November 7-8, 1987.

17. Ibid.

18. For an overview of Soviet joint ventures, see Alan Sherr, *Socialist-Capitalist Joint Ventures in the USSR: Law and Practice* (Briefing Paper No. 1,

Center for Foreign Policy Development, May 1988). "USSR: New Approach," op. cit.

19. Ian Davidson, "Europeans Leap at Soviet Opportunities," *Financial Times*, November 26, 1987.

20. Ibid.; Sherr, op. cit.

21. Sherr, op. cit.

22. Yuri Ponomaryov, "Banking Backs Joint Ventures," in "USSR: New Approach," op. cit.

23. Ibid.

24. Ibid.

25. Ibid.

26. On the Soviet space program, see Henrik Bischoff, *IST DER HIMMEL ROT?—Einige Aspekte der sowjetischen Weltraumforschung* (Research Report, Friedrich Ebert Stiftung, January 1988). On Soviet commercial space interests, see William Broad, "Sales Blitz by Soviets Seeks to Tap Global Market in Space Services," *New York Times*, September 6, 1987.

27. Anatoly Reut, op. cit.; Bischoff, ibid.

28. Reut, ibid.

29. Ibid.

30. On the economic trends in Eastern Europe, see "Economic Developments in Eastern Europe," *Intereconomics*, May/June 1988, pp. 138–144; Heinrich Machowski, "Der Comecon in einer Krise," *Neue Zürcher Zeitung*, July 6, 1988; Machowski, "Rat für gegenseitige Wirtschaftshilfe, Ziele, Formen und Probleme der Zusammenarbeit," in Ostkolleg der Bundeszentrale für politische Bildung, ed., *Rat für gegenseitige Wirtschaftshilfe: Strukturen und Probleme* (Bonn: Bundeszentral für politische Bildung, 1987), pp. 15–40.

31. The European members of COMECON are Albania, Bulgaria, Czechoslovakia, the German Democratic Republic, Poland, Romania, the Soviet Union, and Hungary. Other members of COMECON are Mongolia, Cuba, and Vietnam. Afghanistan, Ethiopia, the People's Republic of China, Laos, Mozambique, North Korea, and South Yemen have observer status.

32. Machowski, 1988, op. cit.

33. Ibid.

34. Henrik Bischoff, *Das "Eureka"-Projekt Osteuropas — Zur Entwicklung der Schlüsseltechnologien in den RGW-Staaten* (Research report of the Friedrich Ebert Stiftung, December 1986); Machowski, ibid.

35. Bischoff, op. cit., provides evidence that Eastern Europe and the Soviet Union are more advanced in science and technology than is generally portrayed in the West.

36. Jochen Bethkenhagen, "Eine Wiederbelebung des Osthandels liegt in beiderseitigem Interesse," *Beiträge zur Konfliktforschung*, Vol. 17, No. 4, April 1987, pp. 99–115. Osthandel is used here to refer to Western European trade with the following members of COMECON: Bulgaria, Hungary, Czechoslovakia, Romania, and the Soviet Union. The 2-percent figure of West German trade with Eastern Europe is used by Bethkenhagen and customarily by other West German analysts to make the argument that the Federal Republic is not "dependent" on Osthandel, with the implication being that such trade does not constitute a "security risk" for the West. Exports of West Germany to East Germany are left out of this calculation. If the GDR is included, then the figure is actually 5 percent.

37. Hans-Dietrich Genscher, "Taking Gorbachev at His Word" (Speech at the World Economic Forum, Davos, Switzerland, February 1, 1987), in

Statements and Speeches, Vol. 10, No. 3, German Information Center, New York, February 6, 1987.

38. Axel Lebahn, "Politische und wirtschaftliche Auswirkungen der Perestrojka auf die Sowjetunion sowie auf ihre Beziehungen zu Osteuropa und zum Westen," *Aussenpolitik*, Vol. 39, No. 2, pp. 107–124.

39. Bernhard May, "Normalisierung der Beziehungen zwischen der EG und dem RGW," *Aus Politik and Zeitgeschichte*, No. 3, January 13, 1989, pp. 44–54. See also in this context Hans-Joachim Seeler, "Die Beziehungen zwischen der Europäischen Gemeinschaft und dem Rat für Gegenseitige Wirtschaftshilfe," *Europa-Archiv*, Vol. 42, No. 7, 1987, pp. 191–198.

40. May, ibid.

41. Ibid.; Seeler, op. cit.

42. Ibid.

43. Ibid.

44. James Markham, "Comecon Edging Toward Trade Accord with EC," *International Herald Tribune*, December 3, 1987.

45. Markham, ibid.

46. May, op. cit.

47. Wilhelm Nölling, "Zwang zum Erfolg," *Die Zeit*, Vol. 43, No. 52, December 23, 1988; Stephen Fidler, "Eastern European Foreign Debt Is Rising, Says OECD," *Financial Times*, November 23, 1987; Clyde Farnsworth, "Weak Dollar, Fall in Oil Prices Put Strains on Soviet Economy," *International Herald Tribune*, December 4, 1987.

48. "Offizieller Besuch des Bundeskanzlers in der Sowjetunion, von October 24. bis 27. 1988," *Bulletin*, November 1, 1988.

49. Ibid.

50. Foreign Minister Hans-Dietrich Genscher, "World Cooperation: Encouraging Developments and New Challenges" (Speech to the United Nations General Assembly, New York, September 28, 1988), in *Statements and Speeches*, Vol. 11, No. 17, September 29, 1988.

51. Ibid.

52. "Reines Abenteuer," *Der Spiegel*, op. cit.; Michnik, op. cit.

CHAPTER 11

The CSCE and the Future of East-West Relations

The Conference on Security and Cooperation in Europe (CSCE), created in 1975 by the Helsinki Final Act, has become the single most important multilateral European forum and decisionmaking body for deepening East-West security and cooperation.[1] The CSCE's thirty-five members include West European nations, the European neutrals (Austria, Switzerland, Sweden, and Finland), the United States, Canada, the nations of Eastern Europe, and the Soviet Union. The CSCE was created to promote security in Europe by placing it in a larger context of East-West cooperation based on the overriding principle of nonviolent resolution of conflicts.[2]

How the CSCE Functions

The work of the CSCE is divided into three broad areas designated as "baskets." Basket 1 deals with security, confidence-building measures, and political détente based on the principle of peaceful settlement of disputes. Basket 2 covers cooperation in the areas of the economy, science, technology, and the protection of the environment.[3] Basket 3 concerns transnational contacts, including travel and emigration rights; the free movement of information; human rights; East-West cultural cooperation; and education projects such as academic exchanges, cooperative research, and foreign language teaching.[4]

The work of the CSCE is carried on by "follow-up" conferences that evaluate overall progress in all areas of past CSCE activity and organize expert meetings and forums, which are held in the different member countries. Table 11.1 provides an overview of past and future CSCE meetings, often referred to as the "CSCE process." Between 1989 and 1992, twelve CSCE meetings will be held, including an environmental meeting in Sofia, a cultural forum in Cracow, an economic conference in Bonn, and human rights conferences in Paris, Copenhagen, and Moscow. CSCE follow-up conferences monitor the implementation of the Helsinki Final Act, pass

Table 11.1 The CSCE Process

1.	Helsinki July 3–4, 1973 Foreign Ministers Meeting
2.	Geneva September–July 1975 CSCE Consultations
3.	Helsinki August 1975 Final Act
4.	Belgrade October 1977–March 1978 Follow-up Conference
5.	Montreux October–December 1978 Expert Conference on the Peaceful Resolution of Conflicts
6.	Valletta February–March 1979 Expert Meeting on Cooperation in the Mediterranean
7.	Hamburg February–March 1980 Science Forum
8.	Madrid November 1980–September 1983 Follow-up Conference
9.	Stockholm January 1984–September 1986 Conference on Confidence- and Security-Building Measures in Europe (CDE)
10.	Athens March 1984 Expert Meeting on the Peaceful Resolution of Conflicts
11.	Venice October 1984 Seminar on Security and Cooperation in the Mediterranean
12.	Ottawa May–June 1985 Expert Meeting on Human Rights
13.	Budapest October–November 1985 Culture Forum
14.	Helsinki August 1985 Anniversary Meeting
15.	Bern April–May 1986 Expert Meeting on Human Contacts
16.	Vienna 1986–1989 Follow-up Conference
17.	Vienna March 1989 Negotiations on Conventional Force Reductions (CFE)
18.	Vienna March 1989 Negotiations on Confidence- and Security-Building Measures in Europe (CDE)
19.	London April–May 1989 Forum on Information and Communication
20.	Paris May–June 1989 Human Rights Conference
21.	Sofia November–December 1989 Environmental Conference
22.	Bonn March–April 1990 Economic Conference
23.	Copenhagen May–June 1990 Human Rights Conference
24.	Palma de Mallorca September–October 1990 Expert Meeting on the Mediterranean and Ecology
25.	Valetta January–February 1991 Expert Meeting on Peaceful Settlement of Conflicts at Sea
26.	Cracow May–June 1991 Symposium on Europe's Cultural Heritage and Its Preservation
27.	Moscow September–October 1991 Conference on Human Rights
28.	Helsinki 1992 Follow-up Conference

Sources: Wilhelm Bruns, "Bilanz und Perspektiven des KSZE-Prozesses," *Aus Politik und Zeitgeschichte*, No. 10, March 4, 1988; Bruns, "Mehr Substanz in den Ost-West-Beziehungen, Zur dritten KSZE-Folgekonferenz in Wien," *Aus Politik und Zeitgeschichte*, No. 12, March 17, 1989; Wilfried Aichinger, "Der Stand des KSZE-Prozesses zu Beginn des Wiener Folgetreffens," *Österreichische Militärische Zeitschrift*, Vol. 24, No. 6, 1986, pp. 505–512.

follow-up resolutions, and oversee the many multilateral projects approved by the various CSCE expert groups.

The principle of one-nation-one-vote among the CSCE's member states has made possible coalitions that cut across the East-West division of NATO and the Warsaw Pact. At the third CSCE follow-up conference in Vienna that ended in January 1989, the outstanding disputes among member states did not result in the traditional postwar bloc-to-bloc voting lineup.[5] Examples here include the Hungarian-Canadian resolution on protecting national minorities that addressed the human rights abuses suffered by the Hungarian minority in

Romania; the conflict between France and the United States on negotiations on conventional forces in Europe; and the dispute between the European Community (EC) and the United States on the planned CSCE conference on economic cooperation.[6] Transbloc coalitions have in fact played a crucial role in the CSCE, especially through the input of the smaller neutral and nonaligned (NN) states, and have contributed to increasing political differentiation within and across the two postwar blocs. The NN states have been instrumental in working out compromise solutions to break deadlocks within CSCE expert commissions, work groups, and plenums.[7]

Bargaining and Issue-Linkage

The effectiveness of the CSCE as an East-West negotiating framework is tied to its bargaining procedures that link different "issue-areas." For example, the traditional demand of communist countries for Western recognition of their political legitimacy and territorial integrity has been paired with the West's interest in influencing Soviet behavior in international conflicts and in promoting greater freedom of movement of people and information in the East.[8] These two sets of interests have become subject in the CSCE to a bartering process in which compromises and concessions have been traded against each other, thus making consensus possible. The CSCE's "process character" as a series of follow-up conferences and meetings, and the instrument of "issue-linkage" have made for an extraordinarily wide-ranging system of carving down East-West conflicts to sizes and shapes that can be more effectively discussed and subjected to a consensus-building process. As one writer on the CSCE has put it:

> What is important in the CSCE process is that the participating states have given priority to their common interests over the differences which divide them. The CSCE provisions do not eliminate the sources of differences and controversies but instead create instruments to resolve conflicts through peaceful means, through negotiations, political consultation and cooperation.[9]

Although the CSCE has no machinery to enforce its resolutions, the follow-up conferences monitor violations by member states. Members can cite alleged violations by other states or defend their own implementation policies. Despite the absence of enforceable sanctions, there is a majority consensus to abide by the letter and spirit of CSCE decisions. This includes, for example, the striving of each member to improve its respective human rights record in accordance with the principles of the Final Act and subsequent CSCE resolutions. Because of the traditional differences between East and West concerning the definition of human rights, the process-character of the CSCE has been more important than the short-term elimination of all human rights abuses.[10] The advantages of this approach have been confirmed in the dramatic improvement of human rights policies in most East European nations and the Soviet Union.[11]

Baskets 1 and 3 and the Legitimation of Political Opposition

The CSCE process has put into question East-West competition as a zero-sum game by having introduced a more complex and flexible form of interaction in which member states can adjust benefits and disadvantages of prospective agreements against one another.[12] Protagonist states are willing to accept obligations and to make concessions because the sum total of benefits is perceived to outweigh their respective costs.[13] An important example here is the acceptance in principle by Eastern countries of Western demands on human and civil rights.[14] As discussed in preceding chapters, measures to guarantee greater political and individual freedom, including rights to protest official policies in the East, are recognized today by Eastern states and the Soviet Union as indispensable in the process of modernization and international integration.[15] This awareness is linked to the current reform movement throughout the communist world, but it is also the result of the evolution of the human rights debate and its linkage to East-West cooperation in other areas within the CSCE.

In this context, the seventh principle of the Helsinki Final Act—the guarantee of "respect for human rights and fundamental freedoms, including the freedom of thought, conscience, religion or belief"[16]—had the effect of politically rousing social groups and minorities in Eastern Europe and the Soviet Union. They used the wide circulation of the Final Act by their respective governments to promote their own political demands for basic rights by calling for its domestic implementation.[17] The CSCE thus helped create an East-West dynamic that promoted political and human rights liberalization. The Final Act and subsequent CSCE resolutions on human rights have continued to function as a pan-European set of nonobligatory but nevertheless powerfully influential norms and standards protecting and legitimizing the rights of minorities, as well ecological and other types of opposition groups, political refugees, and separated families seeking to be reunited across East-West and East-East boundaries.

The preamble to Basket 3 of the Helsinki Final Act states that "increased cultural and educational exchanges, broader dissemination of information, contacts between people and the solution of humanitarian problems" foster security and cooperation in Europe.[18] Although the general principles of Basket 3 have been differently interpreted in East and West, particularly in their implementation, they have set a historical precedent by creating for the first time a catalogue of standards jointly recognized for the further development of relations between individuals, groups, and societies across Europe's East-West division.[19]

Like the seventh principle, Basket 3's preamble has been used since 1975 by political groups and minorities in the East to justify their demands regarding emigration rights, political liberalization, and other political and social issues. Similarly, the many East-West agreements that developed in the second half of the 1970s between youth organizations, sports clubs, scientific associations, towns, churches, trade unions, and cultural groups, as well as the general increase in East-West tourism, are linked to the principles of Basket 3 and their implementation.[20]

The CSCE also has provided a measure of protection for opposition groups against violent state repression, particularly from Eastern regimes wanting greater recognition and cooperation from the West. Incidents of official violence to quell opposition are still frequent in Romania, the GDR, Hungary, Czechoslovakia, and the Soviet Union.[21] Nevertheless, with the exception of Romania, such action tends to be reported more openly in the international media because of the greater access afforded journalists. Official violence is in many cases of a milder sort than would have been the case only four or five years ago. This development is linked to the CSCE's achievements in the areas of human rights, rights of journalists, and multilateral political and economic cooperation.[22] International publicity and internal reform have reinforced each other: Foreign media coverage has helped to generate international support and pressure, which has created more favorable conditions for both bureaucratic and popular reform movements. These movements have in turn been able to expand domestic support by pointing to both the easing of East-West tension and to the reaction of international public opinion.

Transnational Contacts and Communication as an Instrument and Form of Détente

The extension of interpersonal relations across system and national boundaries is both a product of and a driving force for détente. A group of West German authors has commented on the relationship of détente and East-West political and societal interaction:

> Without the pressure exerted by the groups of people affected by the easing in human contacts, without the mobilizing forces of mass tourism, without the universalist tendencies of the mass media, of culture, science and education, and without the economic incentives to supranational co-operation, the incentives to make the "Iron Curtain" more permeable would probably have been much weaker.[23]

Political Liberalization and Economic Structural Reform

The CSCE's role as a catalyst and East-West clearinghouse of political liberalization is also linked to the economic benefits for the East resulting from internal economic decentralization, expanded East-West trade, joint ventures, scientific exchange, and technology transfer, as discussed in the preceding two chapters.[24] These activities presuppose the expansion of political freedom to facilitate free-market economic activity and to assure the minimum flow of commercial information and goods necessary to achieve a macroeconomic impact. By promoting political liberalization, the CSCE has functioned as a crucial, dynamic force in the ongoing restructuring of the economies of Eastern Europe and the Soviet Union.

The Soviet reform process, as discussed in Chapter 9, is characterized by its linking of the internal restructuring and external market integration of the Soviet economy with disarmament initiatives and a far-reaching democratization of Soviet society. Realizing these goals is inseparable from the progressive dismantling of East-West iron curtains. An example of such complex linkage is Gorbachev's proposals at Murmansk for domestic development projects in Northern Europe and the Arctic that combine East-West disarmament initiatives for demilitarizing this region with ecological protection.[25] As an approach to transforming East-West relations, Gorbachev's style of combining disarmament with nonmilitary forms of East-West cooperation follows the pattern pioneered by the CSCE.[26]

Similarly, many of the initiatives and statements about common security discussed in Western and Eastern Europe have been influenced by the CSCE. These include proposals for nuclear-free zones, large-scale reductions of troops and weapons by NATO and the Warsaw Pact, radical changes in military doctrine and force postures, and greater cooperation in general between East and West—all of which would be hard to imagine without the historical precedent and learning experience of the CSCE.

The CSCE as a System of
Conflict Management and Resolution

During the period of deterioration in U.S.-Soviet relations from 1979 to 1986, often referred to as "Cold War II,"[27] the CSCE process functioned as a politically steadying influence. Without the sustained political force of détente emanating from the CSCE, cold war pressures during the early 1980s could have triggered a return to more authoritarian forms of domestic political control and repression in Eastern Europe.[28] The fact that the Soviet Union did not invade Poland in 1981 is linked to the European structures and pressures of détente. West European states, though critical of the Polish government's actions, did not place the Polish government under additional pressure; they in effect refused to throw overboard the achievements of détente and thereby risk further raising international tension and triggering political and economic instability throughout Europe.

The CSCE's increasing political and normative influence to manage conflict has been described as follows:

The collection of rules of conduct, declarations of intent and practical recommendations on every conceivable area of relations, which has been developed in the course of the CSCE process, is gradually creating *a pan-European system of conflict management and promotion of co-operation.* The longer this body of rules is in force, and the more it is actually called upon to solve problems in East-West relations, the harder it becomes for the participating countries to extricate themselves from it.[29]

Criticism of U.S. CSCE Policy

In its CSCE policy, the United States has tended to emphasize human rights violations of the Soviet Union and East European CSCE members. According to West European critics, this narrow approach has often neglected cooperative instruments that are regarded by the majority of CSCE members as forming the core of the CSCE process.

The U.S. approach derives in part from early pre-Helsinki history of the CSCE. In the 1970s Henry Kissinger, echoing U.S. official opinion, was convinced that the CSCE would be a short-lived experiment and upbraided West Europeans for making so much of the Helsinki Final Act.[30] Congress, having adopted the narrow view that the CSCE would be little more than a forum for the Soviet Union to gain propaganda points against the West, transformed this preconception into a long-term policy track by legislating the Commission on Security and Cooperation in Europe as the main organ of monitoring and reporting on the work of the CSCE in the United States. G. Jonathan Greenwald has described the limitations of the U.S. approach in his discussion of the commission and the events that led up to the 1986–1989 CSCE meeting on human rights in Vienna:

> The commission concentrates on individual human rights cases, systemic criticism of the Soviet Union, and legalistic accounting of the implementation record. It shows little sympathy with the broader policy interests of European governments, is skeptical of new agreements and largely unconcerned about how the meetings affect East-West atmospherics. That this appeals to the few Americans who follow the CSCE suggests political pressures push Americans and Europeans in different directions at Vienna.[31]

Although U.S. concentration on Soviet and East European human rights violations has contributed in crucial ways to the civil rights movements and political reform in the East, some West European observers say it has led the United States to shortchange itself on the potential benefits that could be derived from the CSCE. The strident U.S. emphasis on human rights has also been viewed as an abusive reading of the Final Act, which explicitly stresses in the seventh principle the functional link between respect for human rights and the preservation of peace and détente: "The participating nations recognize the universal significance of human rights and fundamental freedoms, the respect for which is an essential factor for *the peace, justice and well-being necessary to ensure the development of friendly relations and cooperation among themselves as among all States.*"[32]

Van Staden points out that in the past, the United States has often used the seventh principle as an anticommunist propaganda tool, thereby risking isolation from Western, Eastern, and nonaligned members of the CSCE. He points out that this was the case, for example, at the Berne Expert Meeting on Human Contacts in 1986. A difficult debate produced a hard-won draft consensus on the concluding report, but the United States at the last moment withdrew its earlier approval.[33] The ensuing rift among the Western CSCE members was unprecedented and marked a new level of conflict between U.S. CSCE policy and the understanding of détente of most West European partners.

A major weakness in the U.S. approach in the eyes of critics has continued to be the U.S tendency to remove the seventh principle from the larger CSCE negotiation context and bargaining game and to use it one-sidedly. West German Foreign Minister Genscher implicitly took issue with the United States when he commented in a Bundestag speech that "a human rights policy that wants to retain the assertiveness of a moral right must forgo . . . any instrumental intention. It must not atrophy into an ideological weapon."[34] Similarly, according to another West German view, while the unspoken aim of the seventh principle is "gradually bringing the conduct of socialist countries towards their citizens into line with western conceptions of basic civil and political freedoms," it has frequently become in the hands of the United States "a fundamental, unnegotiable obligation in regard to the immediate implementation of human rights."[35]

The lack of consensus within the Western Alliance concerning the interpretation and implementation of Basket 1 issues on human rights is related to the similar pattern of differences concerning East-West contacts; travel and emigration policies; flows of information; East-West media infrastructures; and educational, cultural, and scientific exchange issues.

The difference in the U.S. and West European positions on Basket 3 is whether the CSCE process should serve primarily as a means of gradually extending the modus vivendi already achieved or as merely a forum for denouncing the other side for alleged violations of resolutions.[36] This divergence as it manifested itself during the Carter and Reagan administrations has been described as follows:

> The US governments under Carter and Reagan stressed the necessity
> of publicly denouncing violations by the Soviet Union and its allies
> of human rights agreements and the regulations contained in Basket

III, but the majority of . . . [Western CSCE members] wanted to use such an appraisal to negotiate concrete improvements in those areas where the other side's scope for compromise offered the opportunity to do so. They were, in any case, interested in maintaining the CSCE process in order to secure further advances towards greater freedom of movement, even though such advances might only be very gradual.[37]

U.S. and West European CSCE policies have also diverged on the question of economic and scientific cooperation with Eastern Europe and the Soviet Union. A basic motive of Eastern economies in accepting Basket 2 resolutions was to increase their foreign trade with the West, to obtain Most-Favored-Nation (MFN) status from the United States, and thereby to improve their access to Western markets and goods. However, a major stumbling block to greater East-West economic and scientific cooperation has been U.S. policy,[38] including the Western security export restrictions of COCOM, past U.S. economic embargoes, and the Jackson-Vanik Amendment to the Trade Act of 1974, which, critics maintain, has not had its intended effect of forcing change in Soviet emigration and human rights policies.[39]

Since the first wave of détente, the U.S. punishment-and-reward approach to East-West trade has been met with increasing reserve and mounting West European criticism. West European governments generally reject the punitive linkage of human rights with economic cooperation and the use of economic sanctions as an instrument of foreign policy.[40] This rejection is partly a result of the experience of European détente based on the Final Act and the positive effects of economic cooperation directly or indirectly linked to the CSCE. The majority of West European countries tend to see such cooperation as an instrument that can facilitate greater stabilization of East-West relations and thereby create a climate favorable to domestic political and economic liberalization in the East, including human rights reforms.[41]

The United States has also laid more stress than its partners on the need to prevent the Soviet Union from acquiring Western military and dual-use technology in the belief that such acquisition allows the Soviets to upgrade their military technology, modernize their armed forces, and thereby reduce Western security.[42] This rationale also underlies the U.S. policy of withholding scientific data from the East and can be linked to past U.S. reluctance in the CSCE to support greater technological and scientific cooperation.

The Shift in the East-West Debate on Human Rights

Notwithstanding the European criticism of U.S. CSCE policy, it should be kept in mind that there are basic theoretical differences in the Eastern and Western conception of human rights. The CSCE has provided a forum for the emergence of an East-West political culture of controversial debate on defining and implementing human rights policy. Historically, the Western understanding of human rights is based on the notion of inalienable rights and basic freedom of thought and expression derived from the eighteenth-century Enlightenment and the French and American revolutions. The Eastern notion of human rights owes much of its origin to the "second European revolution," whose historical goals as theorized by Marx and Engels included the liberation of the working class and human society from material misery and exploitation.[43] The early stages of European industrialization formed the historical setting of the Marxian ideal.

Despite the differences in the Eastern and Western conceptions, however, basic rights and freedoms are recognized as general principles and as political ideals in the constitutions of communist states.[44] Similarly, there is an underlying connection between the economic and cultural human rights emphasized in the East and the basic freedoms of expression, press, and conscience more readily associated with Western tradition.[45] Götz von Groll, in his attempt to show how these two traditions interact, has written the following:

> Naturally, the artist cannot make much use of freedom of expression and freedom of the press, no matter how complete it may be, if he is starving. This is understood in both East and West. But freedom to express one's views and freedom of conscience are the precondition of every creative process. The principle of tolerance by the state, especially in regard to critical voices, flows from the classical notions of human rights and basic liberties. Important writers are in fact always critical. What is the point of suppressing or denying talent, which then goes on to express itself in exile? In this situation "Glasnost" can help. The word comes from the south slavic, in which "glas" means voice. "Glasnost" thus contains the call to courageously speak out the truth. The often radical critique of our own society by "creative travelers between East and West" demonstrates the necessity of a European order, in which every citizen can develop his creative powers. In the final analysis these also benefit the society as a whole.[46]

This statement reflects not only several important themes of the flourishing international debate on human rights but also the qualitatively greater mutual empathy that became evident on both sides of the East-West European divide in the late 1980s. Although there have remained fundamental differences in the application of general notions of human rights in Eastern and Western societies, the CSCE process has provided an international regime in which East and West appear to be succeeding in cooperatively removing this division. This dialogue has generated sum-positive results particularly in the field of human rights. At the CSCE Ottowa meeting in May 1985, a breakthrough occurred when the Soviet

Union and other states of Eastern Europe began to discuss seriously the question of individual human rights. At the 1986–1989 Vienna CSCE follow-up conference, the Eastern members initially responded to Western criticism of their human rights record by refusing to discuss civil and political rights until the West was willing to discuss the abolition of unemployment and guarantees of other economic and social human rights.[47] This standoff declined in the course of the meeting, however, as both sides began to make innovative, mutual concessions. The Eastern side adopted the position that although the significance of economic, social, and cultural human rights should be reinforced, all human rights are to be viewed as interconnected. Therefore, it was further argued, the concrete realization of human rights is incompatible with a one-sided emphasis on one category of human rights at the expense of another.[48] At the same time, Western delegates, who hitherto had stressed only the importance of individual fundamental freedoms in Eastern Europe, adopted the position that the individual can only fully develop and preserve his or her human dignity when, together with civil and political human rights, economic, social, and cultural human rights are also realized.[49] The 1989 concluding document of the Vienna meeting and their detailed subsections reinforce the Helsinki Final Act's integration of human rights issues into international relations and East-West cooperation. Paragraph 11 stresses fundamental freedoms:

> 11. [The member states of the CSCE] confirm that they will respect human rights and fundamental freedoms, including the freedom of thought, conscience, religion or belief, for all without distinction as to race, sex, language or religion. They also confirm the universal significance of human rights and fundamental freedoms, respect for which is an essential factor for the peace, justice and security necessary to ensure the development of friendly relations and co-operation among themselves, as among all States.[50]

The importance of economic and other "material rights" are emphasized in paragraph 12 and are again similarly formulated in paragraph 14:

> 14. The participating States recognize that the promotion of economic, social, cultural rights as well as of civil and political rights is of paramount importance for human dignity and the attainment of the legitimate aspirations of every individual. They will therefore continue their efforts with a view to achieving progressively the full realization of economic, social and cultural rights by all appropriate means, including in particular by the adoption of legislative measures.
>
>   In this context they will pay special attention to problems in the areas of employment, housing, social security, health, education

and culture. They will promote constant progress in the realization of all rights and freedoms with their countries, as well as in the development of their relations among themselves and with other States, so that everyone will actually enjoy to the full his economic, social and cultural rights as well as his civil and political rights.[51]

The historic, conceptual rapprochement between East and West in Vienna is also reflected in and directly linked to the revolution in Soviet policy on human rights. In August 1988 the U.S. CSCE Ambassador Warren Zimmermann described the progress in the Soviet implementation of its new commitment to human rights as follows:

The people of the Soviet Union are living through an exciting and critical historical period. There have been important advances in political and civil rights; and more have been promised. In November 1986, when our meeting began, there were over 700 prisoners of conscience in the Soviet Union; today that number has been reduced by more than half. In November 1986, 36 Helsinki monitors were imprisoned in the Soviet Union; today the number is down to nine. During the entire year of 1986, fewer than a thousand Jews were permitted to exercise their right to leave their country; the total for last month alone was nearly twice that. In November 1986 there were nearly 200 outstanding bilateral cases—divided families, separated spouses, blocked marriages, dual nationals—between the United States and the Soviet Union; the number is now well under 100.[52]

The changing positions in East and West on human rights are the product of the evolution of the CSCE process since its pre-Helsinki beginnings in the early 1970s. This forms the historical background of the recent advances in the implementation of CSCE Basket 3 resolutions that have opened up a new era in East-West relations. The following examples are only a small sample of significant improvements in human rights and related humanitarian issues covered in Baskets 1 and 3.

The Unification of Families and Easing of Travel Restrictions

The Soviet Union, the German Democratic Republic, Hungary, and Poland have liberalized their policies on emigration, foreign travel, visits to relatives in other countries, and reunification of families separated by national or system boundaries. In 1987 more ethnic Germans were permitted to emigrate from the Soviet Union in one month than had been possible previously over an entire year.[53] Approximately 200,000 ethnic Germans are now expected to return to West Germany as a result of Soviet and East European reform. As previously noted, the Soviets have also eased restrictions on Jewish emigration in what must be regarded as an ongoing and comprehensive reform of earlier policy. By December 1988 the number of émigrés increased to such an extent that the United States began rejecting applications from some Soviet Jews who did not qualify in the eyes of U.S. officials as "political refugees."[54] The number of visitors from the FRG to the GDR has exponentially increased in recent years and topped the 7-million mark in 1987. In the same year, 5 million East Germans visited the FRG, also a record.[55] Poland and Hungary have radically reduced their restrictions on travel to the West.

City-to-City Partnerships and Youth Festivals

There are 350 counties, cities, and villages in the Federal Republic that have expressed interest in establishing partnerships with their counterparts in East Germany. Today there are about 40 such partnerships.[56] In the Soviet Union and West Germany, 20 cities have established city-to-city relations. Youth festivals and sporting events across national and system divisions have traditionally occupied a special place in Europe predating Helsinki and were therefore incorporated as an important part of Basket 3. In recent years, such meetings have become generally uncontroversial and are steadily increasing.

Exchange and Free Flow of Information

The decision of the Soviet Union in late November 1988 to stop jamming Russian-language broadcasts by the U.S.-financed Radio Liberty and two other foreign radio stations must be viewed as a milestone in the history of the CSCE and in East-West relations in general. The move cleared Soviet airwaves of deliberate interference in foreign broadcasts for the first time since the early 1950s.[57] This was preceded shortly before by the cessation of jamming of the West German Deutsche Welle and the clearing of programs of the British Broadcasting Corporation (BBC) and Israeli Radio in January 1987 and the Voice of America in May 1987.[58] Similarly, jamming had also been halted in recent years in all East European countries with the exception of Czechoslovakia and Bulgaria. Ambassador Zimmermann, the chief U.S. delegate at the Vienna meeting, conceded that the clearing of the airwaves was "a very positive move and one unprecedented in the Soviet Union in the postwar period."[59]

The Soviet cessation of jamming also eliminated in the same breath one of the major hurdles blocking the commencement of the Negotiations on Conventional Armed Forces in Europe (CFE). The United States had taken the position that the Soviet Union must improve its human rights record as well as end the jamming of Western broadcasts as a precondition to opening negotiations on conventional reductions. This linkage between security and human rights continued to be emphasized in U.S. statements on the CFE talks.[60]

Cultural Exchange and Cooperation

The Helsinki Final Act committed CSCE members to promote a high degree of cooperation and exchange in all areas of art and culture, including bilateral and multilateral agreements for exchange programs, conferences, seminars, exhibitions, and collaboration in the arts and sciences. The "culture basket" of the CSCE became in the late 1980s a cornucopia of expanding cooperation in all areas of culture understood in the widest sense of the term. With Eastern policies of perestroika and glasnost, as well as the lack of respect shown by information technologies and media for political boundaries, East-West communication and cooperation in all artistic fields began to experience an unprecedented boom.

A consequence of this phenomenon was the greater exposure of policies in the relatively more restrictive East European states such as Romania, Czechoslovakia, Bulgaria, and Albania to Western influence and criticism. These are regimes in which glasnost has either been rejected or has not yet really been launched. In reform-oriented Eastern European societies such as Hungary and Poland, the greater openness to Western cooperation and influence has brought with it an expanding pressure for greater and more expeditious reform. In contrast, greater cooperation has produced increased tension in the GDR because it has rejected perestroika and glasnost yet has greater exposure to the West as a result of its link with the Federal Republic. Nevertheless, the government's actions against the proliferating peace, civil rights, and ecology groups have been designed less to stop the reform process than to control its tempo and limit its goals.[61]

In the field of "cultural diplomacy," bilateral arrangements between Western and Eastern countries to open cultural institutes on each other's territories also markedly increased in the late 1980s. This interaction became a particularly welcome form of East-West cooperation because of the various channels of international communication and empathy it tended to generate and the fact that it directly benefits broad sections of society. The opening of the Goethe Institute in Budapest during a West German culture festival in 1988 is an example.[62] The West German–Hungarian cultural agreement, besides clearing the way for a Hungarian institute in the Federal Republic, also set up a wide variety of programs. The Federal Republic was particularly active in pursuing long-term cultural exchange programs with East European nations and the Soviet Union.

An important example of cultural détente was the Budapest Culture Forum. Organized as a CSCE meeting, it brought together 900 writers, directors, publishers, designers, architects, representatives of other cultural fields, and politicians and diplomats from East and West.[63] Divided into different work groups, they discussed the present and future role of art and culture in European society and concluded with 250 proposals for improving East-West cultural exchange and cooperation. The conference, though unable to reach agreement on certain key issues, nevertheless reflects the potential of this dimension of the CSCE.

The CSCE and Western Security Policy

The Stockholm Agreement and the CDE Negotiations

The Conference on Confidence- and Security-Building Measures and Disarmament in Europe—usually referred to more simply as the Conference on Disarmament in Europe (CDE)—was created within the CSCE framework with the aim of reducing the dangers of armed conflict, misunderstanding, and miscalculation in military activities in Europe. In September 1986, the CDE concluded the historic Stockholm Agreement between NATO and the Warsaw Pact. The most important measures enshrined in the agreement were the commitment of both sides to give a 42-day prior notification of military activities above a threshold of 13,000 troops or 300 tanks; to exchange annual forecasts of notifiable activities; to prohibit military exercises involving more than 75,000 troops, unless scheduled two years in advance; to allow mandatory observation by the other side of exercises with more than 17,000 troops; and to permit on-site inspection, on the ground and from the air, for the purpose of verification.[64]

In contrast to the earlier 1977 CDE accord, compliance with which was not obligatory, the Stockholm Agreement is binding for all signatories. Also, all military activities in the European portion of the Soviet Union extending to the Ural mountains fall under the agreement's jurisdiction. The Stockholm Agreement is the first East-West accord in which the Soviet Union agreed to inspection of military activities on its territory.[65] The implementation of the agreement has been successful, according to the U.S. State Department, and has exceeded "what many observers would have believed possible a decade ago."[66]

The follow-up CDE conference opened March 9, 1989. NATO called for deepening the Stockholm Agreement through more detailed data exchanges regarding the notification of military exercises; further improvements in the arrangements for observing military activities; and measures to strengthen compliance and verification. More comprehensive annual exchanges of information concerning military organization, major weapon deployments, manpower, and equipment in the Atlantic-to-the-Urals area were requested.[67] According to the State Department, NATO also will "propose an organized exchange of views on military doctrine tied to actual forces structures, capabilities, and dispositions in Europe."[68]

The Negotiations on the Conventional Armed Forces in Europe (CFE) also opened in Vienna in March 1989. The official goals of the CFE are to create a stable and more secure equilibrium at lower levels of conventional force structures, weapon systems, and equipment. This is to be accomplished by eliminating imbalances and making both sides unable to launch a surprise offensive attack.[69]

The CFE talks mark a new beginning in negotiations following the unsuccessful Mutual and Balanced Force Reduction talks (MBFR) on troop reductions in Europe, which ended without an agreement after a fifteen-year stalemate. The shutting down of the MBFR framework and its replacement by the CFE followed a debate in the United States about whether such a move would set a precedent not in U.S. interests.[70] At issue was the prospect that the United States might henceforth be obliged to negotiate security issues before a pan-European body of 34 other nations. Washington accepted the CSCE framework for the talks but with the proviso that participation be restricted to the 22 NATO and Warsaw Pact nations, plus France.[71] Although the other CSCE states will not have a veto over CFE proposals, the negotiating "group of 23" is formally obliged to confer with all CSCE members on the progress of the talks, to consider the views of the CSCE's NN states, and also to confer with each of them bilaterally.[72]

The MBFR negotiations covered a relatively restricted area in central Europe consisting of East Germany, Poland, and Czechoslovakia on the eastern side and West Germany, the Netherlands, Belgium, and Luxembourg on the western side. Potential reductions were limited to that region. The current CFE talks, in contrast, cover the area from the Atlantic Ocean to the Urals.[73] Nuclear weapons, sea-based forces, and chemical weapons are not included in the negotiations.[74] Conventional weapons that are dual-capable—able to deliver conventional or nuclear weapons—were initially excluded, but will be included as soon as both sides can agree on which categories and types (such as fighter aircraft, artillery, and missiles) they wish to include.

The opening proposals of NATO at the CFE talks were the following:[75]

- The number of weapons on each side should be reduced to 20,000 battle tanks, 16,500 artillery pieces, and 28,000 armored troop carriers. According to NATO figures, these ceilings would amount to 50-percent reductions of Warsaw Pact forces in these categories.
- Any one country would be prohibited from deploying on its territory more than 30 percent of its overall forces.
- Weapons of any one nation outside its national boundaries would be

limited to 3,200 tanks, 1,700 artillery pieces, and 6,000 armored troop carriers.

The main Soviet opening positions were as follows:[76]

- Forces should be reduced 10–15 percent below present NATO levels. This would leave approximately 14,000 battle tanks, 12,300 artillery pieces, and 3,600 armored infantry fighting vehicles, but would exclude from the reductions all other armored personnel carriers.
- A militarily thinned-out corridor free of tactical nuclear weapons would be established along the border of the alliances.
- After these reductions, follow-up cuts of conventional forces of 25 percent would be carried out.
- Remaining forces would be reorganized to meet the criteria of a strictly defensive force structure based on the structural inability to attack.[77]

On the opening day of the CFE talks, Ambassador Stephen Ledogar, head of the U.S. delegation, emphasized to the press the areas of potential convergence of NATO and the Warsaw Pact: reduction of military advantages and asymmetries, limitation of offensively oriented deployments, and mandatory verification.[78] Soviet officials also emphasized the closeness of the Eastern and Western positions. In this context, the Warsaw Pact's willingness to accept on-site inspections, which, according to Foreign Minister Shevardnadze, would be "without right of refusal," was considered by Western officials as a breakthrough and was important in creating an atmosphere of cautious optimism.[79]

Nevertheless, areas of serious difference were cited by commentators as potential stumbling blocks to reaching an agreement.[80] These included NATO's initial rejection of the Warsaw Pact's proposal to include in the negotiating menu the withdrawal of tactical weapons, such as fighter aircraft and combat helicopters. NATO also resisted the call for parallel negotiations on the withdrawal of short-range nuclear weapons. Although both sides agreed that naval forces were to be excluded from the talks, the Soviet Union held that they must be considered at some point. There were also differences in each side's assessment of existing forces: According to Western numbers, the Warsaw Pact enjoys a superiority of about 4,000 fighter aircraft over the West; Eastern numbers say the West has a superiority of about 1,400 aircraft. Similarly, Warsaw Pact figures for antitank weapons show a NATO superiority of about 6,500 systems (18,020 versus 11,650), while NATO asserts a Warsaw Pact superiority of almost 26,000 (44,200 versus 18,240).[81] Finally, views also differed about the geographical area the talks should cover.

NATO wanted the coverage area divided into three zones: northern Europe (made up of Norway and a section of the Soviet Union); southern Europe (made up of most of Turkey and part of the Soviet Union); and central Europe.[82] The Warsaw Pact wanted a further geographical differentiation in central Europe for its proposed zone along the border of the two alliances.

The Political Outlook for the Success of the CFE

Although the opening of the CFE talks were accompanied by relatively optimistic and visionary statements of foreign ministers of East and West, assessments of the potential results of the talks were mixed.[83] The public statements of both sides pointed toward a desire to reach an early agreement, but the negotiations could stretch over years because of the differences in NATO and Warsaw Pact positions as well as intra-NATO disagreements on the long-term aims of the negotiations and the fear in some Western circles that far-reaching outcomes could endanger Western security and/or the future of NATO. Internal discord was particularly evident in official British statements, which emphasized the importance of nuclear deterrence and of retaining nuclear weapons for the defense of Western Europe, regardless of Warsaw Pact proposals and concessions.[84]

The lack of unity within NATO was particularly evident in the debate on the question of replacing the short-range Lance nuclear missile with a longer-range, more advanced missile. The United States and Britain led one side, the Federal Republic and Belgium the other, and NATO members remained polarized on whether and when the Lance should be replaced after it is withdrawn.[85] At the NATO summit in late May 1989, a compromise was reached, according to which there would be no separate negotiations with the Soviet Union on short-range missile systems until an agreement would be reached at the CFE. Differences also concerned the pace of the talks. West Germany pressed for early and far-reaching progress, while Britain took a more cautious position. Similarly, the Warsaw Pact proposal for a militarily thinned-out zone between the two Germanies free of tactical nuclear weapons was strongly supported in West Germany but rejected by the United States and Britain. These differences gave rise to the predictions of some experts that the talks would not produce an agreement for at least four or five years.[86]

Other observers found reasons for more optimistic prognoses regarding possible results from the talks. The Warsaw Pact repeatedly demonstrated its political will to reach an early agreement, and its submission of data to the CFE—the first time that it publicly released such information—was recognized in NATO circles as an important advance and a confidence-building measure. The Warsaw Pact had made other unprecedented concessions as well, including the unilateral measures outlined by Gorbachev before the United Nations in December 1988 for reductions in troops, tanks, artillery, and fighter aircraft over two years.[87] He also reiterated the Soviet intention to reorganize Warsaw Pact forces in order to make them structurally incapable of attacking Western Europe by removing offensive combat units and forward-based assault equipment.[88] Other Warsaw Pact nations have also embarked on programs of reducing defense spending: Hungary announced a 17 percent cut in military spending, Czechoslovakia a 15 percent reduction by 1991, and the GDR a 10 percent cut by 1990.

Furthermore, the historic Brussels NATO summit of May 29–30, 1989, formally approved the Bush administration's new proposals for the CFE talks, which superceded NATO's opening position by calling for reductions by NATO and the Warsaw Pact of combat helicopters and land-based combat aircraft in the Atlantic-to-the-Urals zone to ceilings at levels 15 percent below current holdings, with all withdrawn equipment to be destroyed. The U.S. president also advocated a 20-percent cut of combat manpower in U.S. forces and a ceiling of about 275,000 U.S. and Soviet ground and air force personnel in Europe. The administration made clear it wanted to achieve an agreement within six months to a year and implement any agreed reductions by 1992 or 1993. The Brussels statement also called for overcoming the division of Europe; significantly increasing East-West cooperation in trade, culture, science, and technology; and taking East-West collective action to solve global problems such as the environmental crisis, arms proliferation, and drug trafficking.[89]

The U.S. input into the NATO summit document represented an unexpectedly positive response of the Bush administration to West German demands within NATO for a Western comprehensive and long-term plan. Besides bringing the Western negotiating position closer to that of the Warsaw Pact, the summit statement set a new tone by emphasizing that the Atlantic Alliance for the first time would "move beyond the post-war period" and replace the military antagonism between East and West "with cooperation, trust and peaceful competition."[90] The Brussels declaration also affirmed NATO's newfound determination "to reduce the excessive weight of the military factor in the East-West relationships" and "to exploit fully the potential of arms control as an agent of change."[91] The summit declaration thus set a historic new agenda for the Atlantic Alliance by committing the United States and NATO as a whole to the larger nonmilitary and demilitarizing aims of the CSCE. In this sense, it can be compared in importance with the Harmel Report of 1967, which marked a turning point in NATO policy by emphasizing the role of détente in addition to military strength for maintaining Western security.

To understand the significance of the Brussels summit declaration, it should be seen in connection with the successful conclusion of the 1986–1989 Vienna conference of the CSCE discussed earlier in this chapter. The concluding document of the Vienna conference laid the basis for qualitatively new forms of East-West interaction by bridging the Western political concept of fundamental individual freedoms with the Marxist-humanist tradition, which focuses on the collective economic, social, and cultural context of individual rights and their link to the organization and development of the means of production. The Vienna statement commits CSCE member states to promoting the realization of both types of human rights through political reforms and by improving housing, education, working conditions, health, education, culture, and other essential spheres of individual and social life. These goals, now enshrined in a common East-West definition of universal human rights, imply a new era of interstate and intersocietal cooperation.

This approach to human rights legitimates a joining of hands of the two universal political-philosophical traditions. Both these heritages have been distorted and robbed of much of their rich potential for improving the human condition by having been straitjacketed and ideologically polarized through the postwar era's preoccupation with bloc-against-bloc confrontation. The significance of the Vienna document lies in its liberation of these two perspectives on human rights from their postwar anticommunist and anticapitalist fetters, thus making possible their rediscovery and their being productively teamed in the CSCE framework.

The Vienna document and the statement of the Brussels NATO summit form the basic foundation for the actual work of constructing a pan-European order, which will begin in earnest in the CSCE meetings from 1989 to 1992 and beyond.[92] Although these two declarations by no means eliminate the dangers of the status quo arms race between NATO and the Warsaw Pact, they bestow to the disarmament process a qualitatively more powerful legitimation that in turn delegitimates East-West military-technological competition as a lasting condition. The NATO modernization programs thereby lose their justification except as part of a policy to be carefully dismantled through disarmament agreements and replaced by the progressive deepening of political and economic partnership. Both the Vienna document and the Brussels summit statement should make it much easier for NATO and the Warsaw Pact to come to disarmament agreements that could have far-reaching effects not only on the East-West arms race but also on developing new constraints on its spillover into the Third World in the form of arms exports, arms proliferation, and regional military conflicts.

Conclusions

The decision to end the MBFR talks on troop reductions in Europe and to open the CFE in their stead reflects the West's cautious advance beyond the framework of the postwar order to a progressively more pan-Europeanized framework of cooperation for dealing with security questions. The CFE talks also reflect the changing relationship of the United States to the CSCE. In effect, the United States set a policy precedent by accepting the new framework for negotiating conventional reductions—a legitimation of the CSCE that received even greater impetus with the statement of the NATO summit of May 1989. If and when a CFE agreement materializes, it would not only reduce NATO troops, offensive weapons systems, and equipment in Europe, but would also have the effect of removing barriers that have hindered a broader and more active U.S. participation in the construction of a pan-European order. A CFE accord would also relieve pressure on U.S., West, and East European defense budgets, free scarce financial resources, and promote further steps in East-West détente.

The Stockholm Agreement represents a major step in reducing the risk of a surprise Soviet attack on Western Europe. The capability to launch such an attack is one of the main justifications for the NATO doctrine of the first use of nuclear weapons. The Stockholm accord reflects in this context the movement of European security politics away from unilateral action-reaction arms racing in the direction of a common security approach.[93] Important elements of the agreement include the increase in predictability of the military activities of both sides; the cooperative nature of its verification procedures; and the presence of hundreds of inspectors of both sides in each other's territories.

The dialogue between East and West on human rights and the radical progress made in the human rights policies of the Soviet Union and East European nations reflect the shift of East-West relations away from the postwar model of East-West antagonism and assumptions of the irreconcilability of the two systems to a new pattern of interaction, mutual criticism, and rapprochement. The definition of human rights in the Vienna document of 1989 is an example of a cooperative and mutually critical approach in which the Western and Eastern traditional notions have been combined in a single comprehensive concept, with the nations of both social systems pledging themselves to respect and to implement both types of human rights. The CSCE human rights regime has legitimized universal norms, obligations, standards of behavior, and long-term goals linked to the future social progress of not only Europe but of humanity as a whole. The member states of the CSCE have committed themselves to this comprehensive concept in the awareness that its implementation will require political patience, a spirit of mutual criticism, understanding, and empathy, and tireless, long-term cooperation. The Vienna document, it should also be noted, is likely to be cited not only by governments but also by nongovernmental organizations, reform movements, and interest groups in both East and West. Only if it is so used can it fulfill its potential in the coming decades as a rich and complex agenda for social and economic development in Europe and throughout the rest of the world.

The adoption by the United States of a more active engagement of the

CSCE process could have the effect of restructuring and intensifying U.S. relations to Western and Eastern Europe and the Soviet Union. The result would be the gradual development of a pan-European U.S. foreign policy, in which Europe will no longer be construed as simply Western Europe and NATO but as also including all European nations of the CSCE. If the United States does not take this route, many in Washington will continue to interpret the process of pan-Europeanization as a weakening and not a broadening and enrichment of the Atlantic Alliance. The Brussels summit declaration provides the basis for the United States to accede to a more multilateral view of its own interests based on the post-containment model of security, which would allow the United States to move beyond the dilemmas of the postwar era while at the same time enhancing its security and that of its partners.

The Stockholm Agreement, the INF Treaty, the NATO summit statement of May 1989, the human rights progress of the Soviet Union, and the prospective agreements in the three baskets of the CSCE suggest the possibility of integrating East and West in a mesh of interconnected economic, political, ecological, and humanitarian regimes that will be the basis of a new type of East-West relationship. Their construction will be based on the post-containment model of security. They will not abolish the differences between the two social systems—nor should this be the goal—but if successful, they will create a nonadversarial and more civilized framework for relations, in which both systems can interact, learn from each other, and come closer together.

Notes

1. *Helsinki Final Act,* reprinted in Edmund Jan Osmanczyck, ed., *Encyclopedia of the United Nations and International Agreements* (Philadelphia: Taylor and Francis, 1985), pp. 333–354; U.S. Department of State, ed., *The Conference on Security and Cooperation in Europe: Public Statements and Documents, 1954–1986,* (Washington, D.C.: Government Printing Office, 1986). For an overview of the CSCE, see Mathias Jopp, Berthold Meyer, Norbert Ropers, and Peter Schlotter, *Ten Years of the CSCE Process: Appraisal of, and Prospects for, All-European Detente and Co-operation,* PRIF Research Report (Frankfurt: Peace Research Institute Frankfurt, 1985); Vojtech Mastny, *Helsinki, Human Rights, and European Security* (Durham, N.C.: Duke University Press, 1986). For an official U.S. assessment of the CSCE, see U.S. Congress and the Commission on Security and Cooperation in Europe, *The Helsinki Process and East-West Relations: Process in Perspective* (Washington, D.C.: Government Printing Office, 1985). On the early history of the CSCE see John Maresca, *To Helsinki: The Conference on Security and Cooperation in Europe 1973–1975* (Durham, N.C.: Duke University Press, 1985). For a comprehensive overview of the CSCE, see Hanns-Dieter Jacobsen, Heinrich Machowski, and Dirk Sager, eds., *Perspektiven für Sicherheit und Zusammenarbeit in Europa* (Bonn:

Bundeszentrale für politische Bildung, 1988). The members of the CSCE are Austria, Belgium, Bulgaria, Canada, Cyprus, Czechoslovakia, Denmark, Finland, France, the FRG, the GDR, Greece, the Holy See, Hungary, Iceland, Ireland, Italy, Liechtenstein, Luxembourg, Malta, Monaco, the Netherlands, Norway, Poland, Portugal, Romania, San Marino, the Soviet Union, Spain, Sweden, Switzerland, Turkey, the United Kingdom, the United States, and Yugoslavia.

2. Jopp et al., ibid.; Adam-Daniel Rotfeld, "Developing a Confidence-Building System in East-West Relations: Europe and the CSCE," in Allen Lynch, ed., *Building Security in Europe* (New York: Institute for East-West Security Studies, 1986), pp. 69–127.

3. A major advance in East-West cooperation on ecological problems was the European Convention on Transboundary Air Pollution in 1979. See in this context Jopp et al., ibid., pp. 52–54.

4. Jopp et al., ibid., pp. 64–78. On political evolution of Basket 3 from the perspective of the former Polish CSCE representative Marian Dobrosielski, see "Der 'Dritte Korb' im KSZE-Prozess," in Jacobsen et al., pp. 441–455; see also in the same volume Barthold C. Witte, "Neue Perspektiven systemübergreifender kultureller Zusammenarbeit," pp. 462–469.

5. Wilhelm Bruns, "Mehr Substanz in den Ost-West-beziehungen, Zur dritten KSZE-Folgekonferenz in Wien," *Aus Politik und Zeitgeschichte*, No. 12, March 17, 1989.

6. See also in this context Gwyn Edwards, "Minderheiten in Europa im Prozess der europäischen Zusammenarbeit," in Jacobsen et al., op. cit., pp. 481–490; in the same volume see János Hajdu, "Die Bedeutung der kleineren Staaten Europas für das Ost-West Verhältnis," pp. 123–131.

7. Bruns, op. cit., see also Hanspeter Neuhold, ed., *CSCE: N+N Perspectives* (Vienna: Wilhelm Braumüller, 1987).

8. Jopp et al., op. cit., pp. 8f.

9. Rotfeld, op. cit. In this context the CSCE can be viewed as an example of a "regime" as defined in the U.S. scholarly literature on international regimes—a "regime-generating regime" because creating regimes is in fact one of the CSCE's principal ongoing activities. It is surprising how little attention the CSCE has received from U.S. regime theorists. On regimes, see Stephen D. Krasner, ed., *International Regimes* (Ithaca, N.Y.: Cornell University Press, 1983).

10. Jopp et al., op. cit., pp. 9f.

11. See the remarks of U.S. Ambassador Zimmermann at the CSCE plenary, August 5, 1988, in "Zimmermann Says End to CSCE Vienna Meeting in Sight," *U.S. Policy Information and Texts*, August 8, 1988.

12. Jopp et al., op. cit., pp. 8f; Rotfeld, op. cit.

13. Ibid.

14. See Jean-Bernard Raimond and Hans-Dietrich Genscher, "Sicherheit hat nicht nur eine militärische Dimension," *Süddeutsche Zeitung*, November 4, 1986.

15. See in this context Götz von Groll, "Die Bedeutung der humanitären Fragen für die Beziehungen zwischen Ost and West," in Jacobsen et al., pp. 431–440.

16. *Final Act* (Basket 1, Section 7), in Osmanczyck, op. cit.

17. A good example is the letter of Prague poet and member of the Charta 77 movement in Czechoslovakia, Vaclav Havel, to the CSCE. For a reprint of the text, see Vaclav Havel, "Krieg gegen geistige Identität," *Frankfurter Rundschau*, December 5, 1987.

18. *Final Act*, in Osmanczyck, op. cit.

19. Jopp et al., op. cit., Chapter 7. See also Gerhard Henze, "Neue Aufgaben der Entspannungspolitik, Freizügigkeit und verbesserte Informationsmöglichkeit als Ziele der KSZE," in Hermann Volle and Wolfgang Wagner, eds., *KSZE: Konferenz über Sicherheit und Zusammenheit in Europa in Beiträgen und Dokumenten aus dem Europa-Archiv* (Bonn: Verlag für Internationale Politik, 1976); von Groll, op. cit.

20. Jopp et al., pp. 63ff.; Norbert Ropers, *Tourismus zwischen West and Ost: Ein Beitrag zum Frieden?* (Frankfurt: Campus, 1986); Dobrosielski, op. cit.; von Groll, ibid.

21. "East Bloc Countries Fall Short of CSCE Commitments," *U.S. Policy Information and Texts*, December 7, 1988.

22. On the role and problems of journalists in East-West relations, see the following in Jacobsen et al., op. cit.: Gerd Ruge, "Die Rolle der Journalisten im Ost-West-Dialog," pp. 491–497; Wolfgang Nette, "Die Probleme der Berichterstattung über das Ost-West-Verhältnis," pp. 498–504; and Dirk Sager, "Die Rolle der Medien für das Ost-West-Verhältnis," pp. 505–510.

23. Jopp et al., op. cit., p. 71.

24. On recent developments of the CSCE in economic cooperation, see Ekkehard Eichhoff, "Das Dritte KSZE-Folgetreffen in Wien, Implementierung der Wirtschaftsbestimmungen," *Europa-Archiv*, Vol. 42, No. 2, 1987, pp. 59–66. On East-West economic relations, see also Hans-Dieter Jacobsen, Heinrich Machowski, and Klaus Schröder, "Perspectiven der Ost-West Wirtschafts-beziehungen," in Jacobsen et al., pp. 320–333; Mathias Schmitt, *Das Ostgeschäft von morgen* (Baden-Baden: Nomos Verlagsgesellschaft, 1988).

25. Mikhail Gorbachev, "Speech at a Formal Meeting in Murmansk on October 1, 1987," in *Reprints from the Soviet Press*, Vol. 45, No. 9, November 15, 1987, pp. 5–35.

26. Ibid.

27. Fred Halliday, *The Making of the Second Cold War* (London: Verso, 1983).

28. See in this context Mieczyslaw Tomala, "Das Verhältnis zwischen Polen und der Bundesrepublik Deutschland und seine Bedeutung für die Ost-West Beziehungen," pp. 141–147; and Georg W. Strobel, "Das Verhältnis zwischen der Bundesrepublik Deutschland und Polen und seine Bedeutung für die Ost-West Beziehungen," in Jacobsen et al., op. cit., pp. 148–160.

29. Jopp et al., op. cit., p. 9.

30. G. Jonathan Greenwald, "Vienna—A Challenge for the Western Alliance," *Aussenpolitik*, Vol. 38, No. 2, October 1987, pp. 155–167.

31. Ibid.

32. *Helsinki Final Act* cited in Bernd van Staden, "From Madrid to Vienna: The CSCE Process," *Aussenpolitik*, Vol. 37, No. 4, 1986, pp. 350–364 (emphasis from van Staden).

33. Ibid.

34. *Bulletin des Presse-und Informationsamtes der Bundesregierung*, No. 77 of July 1, 1985, p. 674, quoted in ibid. Criticism of the U.S. CSCE policy is not restricted to Europeans. In 1980 the U.S. delegate to Geneva described the approach of the U.S. delegation (headed by Arthur Goldberg) to the CSCE meeting in Madrid:

> Goldberg's one thought was to protect Carter's credibility on human rights. . . . As he self-righteously hammered away at the cause of

Soviet dissidents, reaping encomiums from emigré groups and the president, he progressively alienated friend and foe alike . . . The confrontation strategy adopted unilaterally by the United States—was viewed—as a threat to the CSCE process and to the health of political détente in Europe. The confrontation policy has proved to be a sterile approach.

Albert W. Sherer, Jr., "Goldberg's Variation," *Foreign Policy*, No. 39, 1980, pp. 154–159. The passage is quoted in Dobrosielski, op. cit., in Jacobsen et al., op. cit., p. 453.

35. Jopp et al., p. 19.
36. Ibid., p. 74.
37. Ibid., p. 75.
38. See Chapter 8.
39. See the excerpts of the testimony of Dr. Karen Dawisha at the hearings of the U.S. Commission on Security and Cooperation in Europe (March 15, 1988) in "Perestroika and Eastern Europe," *CSCE Digest*, March 15, 1988; Maresca, op. cit., pp. 77–79, 179.
40. On security policy and export controls, see Chapter 8.
41. Ibid.
42. Ibid.
43. Von Groll, op. cit.
44. Ibid.
45. Ibid.
46. Ibid.
47. Ibid.
48. Ibid.
49. Ibid.
50. *Concluding Document of the Vienna Meeting 1986* (hereafter *Concluding Document*), reprinted in *CSCE: A Framework for Europe's Future*, U.S. Information Agency, Washington, D.C., 1989.
51. Ibid.
52. Zimmermann, August 8, op. cit.
53. Warren Zimmermann, Introduction to *Concluding Document*, op. cit. See also von Groll, op. cit. For a more detailed discussion of advances and areas in which progress on human rights are still to be made, see the twenty-fifth semiannual U.S. CSCE Report, excerpts from which can be found in "East Bloc Countries Fall Short," op. cit.
54. Robert Pear, "U.S. Bars Some Soviet Jews as Refugees," *International Herald Tribune*, December 5, 1988.
55. Zimmermann, Introduction, op. cit.; von Groll, op. cit.
56. Von Groll, ibid.
57. Serge Schmemann, "Soviet Union Ends Years of Jamming of Radio Liberty," *New York Times*, December 1, 1988.
58. Ibid.
59. Ibid.
60. "Confidence- and Security-Building Measures Negotiation" (State Department "Gist" article), *U.S. Policy Information and Texts*, March 8, 1989 (hereafter "Gist").
61. See in this context Helga Hirsch, Marlies Menge, Joachim Nowrocki, and Gerhard Spörl, "Mit Glasnost gegen die alte Garde," *Die Zeit*, Vol. 43, No. 6, February 5, 1988.

62. Witte, op. cit.

63. Auswärtiges Amt der Bundesrepublik Deutschland, *Das KSZE-Kulturforum in Budapest* (Bonn: Auswärtiges Amt, 1986).

64. *Conference on Security and Cooperation in Europe, Document of the Stockholm Conference,* September 1986 (Stockholm: CSCE, 1986); John Borawski, Stan Weeks, and Charlotte Thompson, "The Stockholm Agreement of September 1986," *Orbis,* Vol. 30, No. 4, Winter 1987, pp. 643–662.

65. Stanley Sloan, "Conventional Arms Control in Europe," *SAIS Review,* Vol. 7, No. 2, Summer/Fall 1987, pp. 381–390.

66. "Gist," op. cit.

67. Ibid. The concept laid down by the concluding document of the Madrid CSCE Meeting of September 6, 1984, contains four criteria for confidence- and security-building measures. They must be (1) militarily significant, (2) politically obligatory, (3) linked to appropriate forms of verification, and (4) applicable to the entire European region. It should be mentioned that all 35 member states of the CSCE participate in the CDE negotiations and that in principle every member may introduce proposals for confidence- and security-building measures. See Bruns 1989, op. cit. Bruns points out that besides military confidence- and security-building measures, there are also many types of nonmilitary confidence-building measures, such as dismantling images of enemies, particularly in school textbooks and the mass media.

68. "Gist," ibid.

69. Ibid.

70. Sloan, op. cit.; Reinhard Mutz, "Konventionelle Stabilität auf niedrigem Kräfteniveau: Von MBFR zu KRK," in Jacobsen et al., pp. 290–305.

71. The "group of 23" consists of Belgium, Bulgaria, Canada, Czechoslovakia, Denmark, France, the FRG, the GDR, Greece, Hungary, Iceland, Italy, Luxembourg, the Netherlands, Norway, Poland, Portugal, Romania, the Soviet Union, Spain, Turkey, the United Kingdom, and the United States.

72. Joseph Fitchett, "Allies Nearly Ready to Begin Talks on Conventional Arms," *International Herald Tribune,* November 24, 1988.

73. Sloan, op. cit. This area includes the entire territory of the participating states. In the case of the Soviet Union, it will cover all territory west of the Ural River and the Caspian Sea, the European section of the Soviet Union.

74. "Gist," op. cit.

75. Christoph Bertram, "Hoffnung auf ein neues Zeitalter," *Die Zeit,* Vol. 44, No. 11, March 10, 1989; Jill Smolowe, "Let's Count Down," *Time,* March 20, 1989.

76. Bertram, ibid.

77. On structural nonoffensive defense, see Dieter Lutz, "Frieden schaffen mit ganz anderen Waffen," *Tageszeitung,* November 23, 1987; Lutz, "On the Theory of Structural Inability to Launch an Attack," *Hamburger Beiträge zur Friedensforschung und Sicherheit,* Heft 25, January 1988.

78. "East-West Conventional Arms Talks Off to a Good Start" (Transcript of Ledogar press conference March 9), *U.S. Policy Information and Texts,* March 17, 1989.

79. Smolowe, op. cit.

80. Ibid.; Bertram, op. cit.

81. Bertram, ibid.

82. Ibid.

83. Ibid.

84. Smolowe, op. cit.; Robert Mauthner and Judy Dempsey, "Moscow Plan on Nuclear Arms Opposed," *Financial Times*, March 3, 1989.

85. Thomas Meyer, "Entscheidung über Modernisierung der Kurzstreckenraketen vor Mitte 1989?" *Kölner Stadtanzeiger*, November 22, 1988; Philippe Lemaitre, "La Belgique n'a pas caché son hostilité à la modernisation des armes tactiques américaines en Europe," *Le Monde*, October 31, 1988.

86. Smolowe, op. cit.

87. "Gorbachows dramatischer Abrüstungsbeschluβ," and "Wir werden euch des Feindes berauben," *Der Spiegel*, Vol. 42, No. 50, December 12, 1988.

88. Ibid.

89. North Atlantic Council Declaration, May 30, 1989, reprinted in *U.S. Policy Information and Texts*, May 31, 1989.

90. Ibid.

91. Ibid.

92. This point was suggested to the author in interviews with West German CSCE experts and government advisers.

93. On the concept of common security, see the essays in Egon Bahr and Dieter S. Lutz, eds., *Gemeinsame Sicherheit, Idee und Konzept* (Baden-Baden: Nomos, 1986).

CHAPTER 12

The United States and Forging a Post-Containment Policy

The preceding chapters demonstrated that postwar security arrangements in East and West have been eroded and a new paradigm of security is unevenly developing. This shift was explored at length and linked to the signing of the INF Treaty, Soviet and East European reform efforts, economic pressures in East and West to significantly reduce military spending, and massive popular rejection of status quo defense policies.

Disarmament has ceased to be an empty ideological slogan of the cold war and has emerged as a decisive dimension of East-West relations and an indispensable fulcrum of reform in the East. The pro-détente elite and mass constituencies that emerged on the world political stage in the 1980s have been concerned not only with security policy in its literal sense but also with its implications for economic, political, ecological, and cultural change. The mounting contradictions and inconsistencies between the status quo and the new horizon of changing conditions have set in motion a powerful—albeit difficult—policy adjustment process that is now evident throughout the international system.

Throughout this book, I have emphasized the structural links and dynamic interaction between security and nonmilitary areas of policy, pointing out that the three dimensions of the post-containment model of security—disarmament, common security, and deepening economic-political détente—form a complex conceptual unity and a policymaking framework that are helping East and West move unevenly beyond the postwar order. Nevertheless, the discussion concedes that despite the momentous character of present policy reform efforts, their short- and middle-term outcome remains ambiguous: As shown in Parts 1 and 2, the current interregnum between the postwar and a post-containment security order is witnessing a continuation of the East-West arms race and a wave of research and development of new weapons systems and military technologies—a gray area of potential arms racing that could become a disruptive and hindering factor in the current transition. A regression can only be avoided if all classes of weapons and activities that contribute to the East-West arms race (including chemical weapons, weapons based on new technologies, and military R&D) become subject to the disarmament process.

Several broad conclusions about the imperative of East-West cooperation flow from the analysis in foregoing chapters.

1. Policy adjustment and the creation of a new East-West economic-political order of cooperation and disarmament have become necessary for both the Soviet Union and the United States. Neither country can avoid such adjustment without courting serious crisis. Economic and many of the traditional defense-related barriers to normalizing cooperation must be removed in order to maintain international stability in the coming decades.

2. The economic difficulties in Eastern Europe and the Soviet Union today are symptomatic of the potentially implosive dead end of the postwar organization of international relations. This destabilizing potential in the East is not merely a problem there—it has obviously profound regional and global implications. Continued Eastern economic deterioration, especially if made worse by political instability, would have severe ecological, technological, cultural, and human rights consequences for the future of Europe as a whole. Policies that could function as safety nets in this context are hardly conceivable or practicable, however, under the present conditions of East-West technological-military competition.

3. A corollary of the preceding point is that the Soviet policy of opening to the West and of economic perestroika must be viewed as part of a larger international process of economic restructuring and a greater opening of all major economies to one another. Political and economic adjustment in the West, although differing in character from that in the East, is nevertheless as dependent on simultaneous Eastern adjustment as successful restructuring in individual Eastern countries is dependent on the cooperation and opening of Western economies. For this reason, Western nations can ill afford complacency or ideological self-congratulaton over the crisis in the East. The largely unavoidable process through which the two social systems will have to learn to relate to each other in the post-containment era is a common project—and one that confronts countries in both systems with daunting economic, cultural, military-political, and ideological obstacles.

4. As interdependence between East and West grows in the post-containment era, the economies of both systems will necessarily become qualitatively more vulnerable to their common international environment. Resisting interdependence or failing to utilize its potential sum-positive relationships will tend to become increasingly costly and politically untenable as a long-term policy. Thus there is a need for a new ethics of interstate and intersocietal behavior and responsibility that cannot be based on

traditional nationalism or realpolitik inherited from the nineteenth century and its corollary of competitive arms racing.

In the contradictory watershed of change discussed in this book, the postwar verities that sustained U.S. leadership have been challenged as never before. Yet the United States has been conspiciously slower to respond, even appearing deliberately to lag behind both Western Europe as well as the Soviet Union in adjusting its policy. The following discussion, based on the results of the analysis in preceding chapters makes a number of recommendations for a redirection of U.S. policy.

NATO and the United States

The Brussels NATO summit of late May 1989 reflected the uneven and ambiguous transition of the United States to a post-containment approach to European security. On the one hand, the United States proclaimed in the summit declaration the goal of overcoming the postwar division of East and West through reconciliation and far-reaching economic, scientific, and ecological cooperation with Eastern Europe and the Soviet Union that would represent a historic breakthrough and implies profound changes in U.S. economic, defense, and foreign policy. On the other hand, notwithstanding this new position (and the Stockholm Agreement and INF Treaty), it remains to be seen whether the United States will be able to carry out the official commitment to adjustment at the pace and with the urgency necessary to deal effectively with its economic and defense-related problems. Given the trends analyzed in preceding chapters, it is likely that U.S. economic and foreign policy adjustment will continue to lag behind that of Western Europe, a result likely to generate new crises in NATO as U.S. allies deepen their economic and political rapprochement with Eastern Europe and the Soviet Union through a progressively more unified Common Market, the CSCE, and bilateral agreements of individual states.

Despite the signs that official U.S. views are beginning to change under the pressure of European, particularly West German, "new thinking" on security and the desire to preserve the unity of the Atlantic Alliance, security continues to be defined in U.S. official circles in terms of military balance, military strength, and the postwar status of the United States in managing East-West relations. In this and other respects, the United States has failed to recognize the full breadth and scope of policy change necessary to place it on the same track of adjustment vis-à-vis the East that its more forward-thinking West European partners have adopted. Important in this context are the differences in U.S. and West German thinking on security. Washington still clings to developing and deploying a replacement for the Lance missile, but there is a majority elite and popular consensus in West Germany that the Soviet military threat in Europe is being dismantled and therefore should no longer be the basis for planning future West European defense policy. In this view, more (or more advanced) NATO nuclear or conventional weapons cannot be justified.

The Brussels summit did not overcome existing differences in the alliance on the Lance system, but only provided a breathing space until the next round of internal crises erupts. New disputes are likely to occur after the 1990 West German elections and a CFE agreement, when the fate of the Lance and other systems planned for development and possible deployment on West German soil must be decided. The crux of the problem that was underlined by the Lance debate is the larger approach of the United States to the future of East-West security. Is the Bush administration ready to formulate in detail a long-term, systematic strategy for disarmament and cooperation on the basis of the comprehensive plan of the Brussels summit? Is it prepared to enter actively into a step-by-step process to move beyond the policy of military, political, and economic containment of Eastern Europe and the Soviet Union? As long as these questions are not satisfactorily answered, the status quo U.S. and NATO policies of achieving military advantage through FOFA, SDI, and the doctrine of competitive strategies will remain a major obstacle to building a new Western consensus on future NATO military doctrine, deployments of new weapons systems, burden sharing, the second wave of détente, and the role that arms control and demilitarization should play in shaping the future of Europe.

It is not sufficient for NATO, under U.S. and British insistence, to continue to demand more Soviet troop and weapons cuts in order merely to achieve a better military balance. The removal of the numerical superiority of the Warsaw Pact in Europe can only bring genuine stability if NATO

1. Removes its own destabilizing offensive weapons systems in coordination with the Soviet Union and cancels programs being planned in conjunction with NATO modernization
2. Shifts to a posture of nonoffensive defense based on the structural inability to launch a large-scale or surprise attack, coordinating this shift with the planned restructuring of Soviet forces
3. Moves from the position of seeking to achieve a better military balance at lower levels to that of genuine disarmament based on a process of replacing military with nonmilitary forms of security in bilateral and multilateral cooperation with the Soviet Union and East European countries

Implications of the Post-Containment Model of Security

Moving more rapidly to post-containment security arrangements and overcoming the military division of Europe have become of vital interest to the Federal Republic and other central European nations. Their aim is to create cooperative structures of stability that are not based on military threats and that could facilitate a viable reform transition of Eastern Europe and the Soviet Union.

West-West unity. In contrast to the requirements of military stability and East-West division in the postwar era, the basis of cohesion of the West now depends on helping East European countries in their efforts to democratize, to implement the comprehensive CSCE concept of human rights, to accelerate economic and political adjustment, and to stabilize new socialist market structures that can attract reliable partners throughout the world economy. If the United States is to play an active role in forging a new basis for Western unity, it must formulate a long-term strategy aimed at achieving extensive West-West cooperation capable of providing appropriate forms of aid and stimuli to help catalyze self-reproducing economic activity in Eastern Europe and the Soviet Union. Here the problems of providing the precise kind of aid that can prime productive potential—instead of merely providing short-lived, consumptive relief and, in the process, buttressing obsolete economic and political structures—will remain a complex and difficult challenge for the United States and other Western countries well into the 1990s. The probabilities of unpredictable and negative outcomes in the agonizing transition of Eastern Europe and the Soviet Union dare not be underestimated—nor, for that matter, the effort that must be made in the West to develop appropriate aid to accelerate Eastern adjustment while sustaining European stability. Here the principle of the complex interdependence of the different instruments of cooperation should be firmly kept in mind. Economic, ecological, cultural, and technological-scientific cooperative efforts can rebound positively off each other. Given a conducive international political environment, they can generate synergies of East-West political liberalization, economic development, and disarmament. Western policy consensus could be based on harnessing these dynamic factors.

West European populations, particularly those of central Europe, have become highly sensitized to the consequences of a failure of reform in Eastern Europe for the economic, ecological, and cultural future of all of Europe. This awareness explains why construction of the "common European house"—with wings for the United States, Canada, and the Soviet Union— expresses a profoundly common East-West interest and a deeply felt political-moral imperative.

Although the logic of European East-West cooperation is equally valid for global East-West relations, it is not perceived by the United States with the same urgency and concern as it is by West and East European nations. The cooperation of the Soviet Union and Eastern Europe is indispensable for the United States to create a new security environment that would allow it to reduce its defense budget and work cooperatively with other nations to solve common global problems. Similarly, the Soviet Union and

Eastern Europe need the cooperation of the United States for largely the same reasons.

Military doctrine and export controls. East-West discussion of radically reforming military doctrine is of particular importance not only because it could open up a new dimension of the East-West disarmament process but also because of its economic implications. Changes in military doctrine in the direction of nonoffensive defense and common security arrangements could pave the way for greater technological cooperation between East and West. As discussed in Chapter 8, U.S. technology export controls are linked to the U.S. military doctrine of competitive strategies and East-West military-technological competition. These restrictions have become a prickly source of West-West irritation that is likely to worsen if the United States fails to reduce the COCOM list and put into question the cold war assumptions of its entire export control policy. Conditions must be created in West and East to eliminate the need for high-tech restrictions on West-West and West-East trade. Failure to create a regime to combine disarmament and verification of the nonmilitary use of advanced technology will make it increasingly difficult for the United States and Western Europe to achieve a durable policy consensus on a variety of security and economic issues. A U.S. policy of overcoming the division of Europe and "integrating the Soviet Union into the community of nations"[1] cannot be practically implemented if the technological division of Europe and between the Soviet Union and the West continues to worsen as a result of security export barriers.

U.S.-Soviet relations. A shift of U.S. policy toward the Soviet Union based on the principles of the post-containment paradigm of security would entail accepting the assumption that the U.S. policy of placing Gorbachev under pressure through a policy of arms racing and competitive strategies is self-defeating. A united Western policy of radically accelerating the disarmament process could provide Gorbachev with the necessary safety net of Western trust and support to push ahead with reshaping the Warsaw Pact along the lines of structural nonoffensive defense and demilitarizing Soviet relations with Eastern Europe. Western policy reform would thereby give East European countries greater room for policy choice vis-à-vis both the Soviet Union and the West; for example, Poland and Hungary could establish an appropriate combination of Eastern and Western integration that would help promote a successful reform process in both East and West.

Disarmament as an instrument of domestic economic reform. Policy reform toward the Soviet Union and Eastern Europe can also promote U.S. domestic economic adjustment. The United States, like the Soviet Union, has little choice in the coming years but to redesign its economic policy beginning with significant reductions in military spending. The levels of cuts necessary for a major reordering of priorities would entail economic and social dislocation, given the role of defense in the U.S. economy, and would therefore require a form of U.S. economic perestroika that could map a step-by-step economic-political strategy leading beyond the postwar Military Keynesian approach to macroeconomic management. A problem here, however, is that the United States, unlike the Soviet Union and other COMECON economies, has not yet experienced the degree of economic crisis sufficient to catalyze major economic restructuring, despite the ample signs of continuing economic deterioration discussed in Chapter 6.

A second problem in this context is U.S. reluctance to view the structural adjustment of the U.S. economy in connection with developing a new East-West and West-West security relationship. The triad of disarmament, common security, and deepened economic-political détente would be indispensable for this two-sided military-economic process. Economic reform linked to a strong disarmament and demilitarizing thrust could contribute to lowering the U.S. federal and external trade deficits, to overcoming the U.S. economic-security dilemma, and to reversing the decline in manufacturing performance. The alternative to moving in this direction is to remain on a road that is leading to serious domestic and international economic crisis and instability.

U.S.-Polish relations and the CSCE. The role of the United States in the historic Polish reforms of April 1989 illustrates U.S. ability to pursue a policy of cooperation toward the East that (1) contributes to political-economic reform and demilitarization; (2) corresponds in a sum-positive manner to Eastern and Western economic interests; and (3) contributes to peacefully overcoming the division of Europe.

The U.S. policy of "active reengagement" in Poland vividly contrasts with the one-sided U.S. emphasis on human rights in the CSCE. With the new possibilities of East-West cooperation opened up by the reform process in Eastern Europe and the Soviet Union, the United States could greatly benefit from radically broadening its activities in the CSCE and using it as a framework for adjusting U.S. policy to a more pluralistic and a progressively demilitarizing management of West-West and East-West affairs. The United States cannot avoid such adjustment if it is to play a vital role in international politics in the future.

Pan-Europe and U.S. domestic policy. The market unification process, the normalization of economic relations with COMECON countries, and the CSCE framework are laying the basis for a pan-European order. This development should be viewed by the United States not as a threat but as a historic opportunity for organizing its own domestic and foreign policy reform. If the United States is to implement its declared goal of "going beyond containment"[2] and overcoming the division of Europe, these goals must be made into national priorities, which would facilitate the dovetailing of demilitarizing forms of East-West cooperation with the dismantling of domestic institutions that have underpinned nearly a half century of U.S. containment policy. Foreign policy reform could then be used to justify and politically drive U.S. domestic policy reform and vice versa. The official presentation of foreign policy goals thus could be brought into harmony with the task of mobilizing popular constituencies and policymaking elites in the United States to support the historic project of moving beyond the postwar era.

Notes

1. George Bush, "World Is Witnessing Eclipse of Communism, Rise of Democracy" (Speech at the Coast Guard Academy May 25, 1989), *U.S. Policy Information and Texts*, May 26, 1989.
2. Ibid.; "Bush Says NATO Aim Is to Overcome Division of Europe" (News Conference May 30, 1989), *U.S. Policy Information and Texts*, May 31, 1989.

Index

Advanced visible infrared sensor
   technology, 122–123
AEC. *See* Arms Export Control Act
Aerospatiale, 118
Albania, 237
Armed forces. *See* Military
Arms control, 15, 33, 38, 77, 123–
   124, 242; CFE, 240–242
Arms Export Control Act (AEC), 147
Arms market, 94, 118–119
Arms race, 1, 3, 34, 41, 159, 180,
   220, 243, 251–252, 253; new
   technology, 121–122; reduction,
   19–21
Artificial intelligence, 123
Atlantic Alliance. *See* North Atlantic
   Treaty Organization
Atlanticism, 17, 76, 77, 79–80(n2),
   82(n3); defense, 64–66

Balanced Technology Initiative, 51
Balkans, 30–31(n46)
BAP. *See* Biotechnology Action
   Program
Barre, Raymond, 12
Baumel, Jacques, 12
BBC. *See* British Broadcasting
   Corporation
Belgium, 61, 134, 239, 241
Benelux countries, 20, 57. *See also*
   Belgium; Luxembourg;
   Netherlands, the
Berne Expert Meeting on Human
   Contacts, 231
Biotechnology, 99, 100
Biotechnology Action Program
   (BAP), 130
"Bold Sparrow," 69
BRITE, 130
British Broadcasting Corporation

(BBC), 236
Brzezinski, Zbigniew, 68
Budapest Culture Forum, 237–238
Bulgaria, 30–31(n46), 237
Bush administration, 242, 254

Canada, 225
CAP. *See* Forecasting and Analysis
   Center
Carlucci, Frank, 36–37, 59, 151, 154
Carter administration, 231–232
CCL. *See* Commodity Control List
CDE. *See* Conference on Confidence-
   and Security-Building Measures
   and Disarmament in Europe, 238
CDU. *See* Christian Democratic Union
CFE. *See* Negotiations on the
   Conventional Armed Forces in
   Europe
Chevènement, Jean-Pierre, 18,
   27(n14)
China Team Center, 150
Christian Democratic Union (CDU),
   10, 11, 73
Christian Socialist Union (CSU), 10,
   11, 15, 35, 73
COCOM. *See* Coordinating
   Committee on Multilateral
   Export Controls
COMECON. *See* Council for Mutual
   Economic Assistance
COMETT, 130
Commission on Security and
   Cooperation in Europe, 230
Commodity Control List (CCL), 147
Communications. *See*
   Telecommunications
"Complex Program for Scientific and
   Technological Progress to the
   Year 2000," 215